SOUTH AFRICA
AND THE WORLD

*"The Union of South Africa stands
alone today in the whole world.
They may be a brave people,
they may decide to stand firm, but
they stand alone, isolated in a
kind of moral wilderness, against
the whole-hearted opposition of the
whole world."*
Sir Claude Corea (Ceylon),
Meeting of the United Nations
Security Council, April 1, 1960

*"It is nothing short of a tragedy
that the word apartheid has
become one of the ugliest swear
words in the world."*
DIE BURGER (Cape Town),
April 21, 1961

*"The race policies of the
Government are like an octopus
and its tentacles stretch into
every corner of our life, and one
cannot discuss any subject for very
long without touching one of
those tentacles. The plain fact is
that, whether we like it or not,
apartheid (or any other name
you like to use) as practised by
this Government is anathema to the
rest of the world."*
Hon. S. F. Waterson,
House of Assembly,
South African Parliament,
February 2, 1965

SOUTH AFRICA and the WORLD

The Foreign Policy of Apartheid

Amry
Vandenbosch

THE
UNIVERSITY
PRESS
OF KENTUCKY

Standard Book Number
8131–1223–0
Library of Congress Catalog
Card Number 76–111516

Copyright © 1970 by The
University Press of Kentucky

A statewide cooperative scholarly
publishing agency serving Berea
College, Centre College of
Kentucky, Eastern Kentucky
University, Kentucky State College,
Morehead State University,
Murray State University, University of Kentucky, University
of Louisville, and Western
Kentucky University.

Editorial and Sales Offices:
Lexington, Kentucky 40506

Preface

Among the very large number of books that have been written on South Africa during the last two decades, there has not yet appeared a serious and systematic study of South Africa's foreign relations. Judging by the preoccupation of the United Nations with South African issues, one might conclude that the Republic of South Africa is the world's foremost problem. And in a sense that is true since the conflict revolves around two of the chief issues of the mid-twentieth-century world—race relations and colonialism. While I share the views of many critics of apartheid, I am not unaware of the difficult situation in which the South African whites find themselves.

I gratefully acknowledge indebtedness to the Social Science Research Council and the University of Kentucky's Research Fund for grants which enabled me to spend some time in London and to visit South Africa and neighboring countries, and to my wife, for generous and indispensable help.

Contents

Background
1652–1910

1

From Tavern of the Seas
to British Dominion

South Africa may be situated in an outlying corner of the world but it
has been an important factor in world politics for more than three
centuries. The antecedents of the Republic of South Africa go back to
the planting of a colony by the Dutch East India Company on Table
Bay at the Cape of Good Hope in 1652. Long before the establishment
of Cape Town, Dutch and English ships had stopped with increasing
regularity at the Cape to break the long voyage to and from the East
and to take on a supply of fresh water. Agents of the English East India
Company made a move to take possession of Table Bay in 1620, but the
act was repudiated by King James. The directors of the Dutch East
India Company became convinced that the establishment of a post at the
Cape was highly desirable for economic and strategic reasons. Ships
engaged in the Eastern trade could break their long voyage there, and
take on water, vegetables, and fresh meat, while a small fort at this
strategic point would afford Dutch ships that were engaged in the
Eastern trade protection against the Portuguese and Spanish enemies.
In the closing months of 1651 an expedition composed of three ships
was sent to the Cape to establish a post. Thus were laid the foundations
of the present Republic of South Africa.

The composition of the colony reflected something of the political situation in Europe at the time. In 1688–1689 some two hundred Huguenot exiles joined the colony. Though they constituted at the time only about a sixth of the total population, they were important to the community. Socially and economically they were more advanced than the Dutch settlers. Since they were refugees and could not return to their native land they undoubtedly contributed to the development of an independent, nationalist spirit of the colonists. They were of the same religious faith as the Dutch, so they were easily assimilated. There was also a sprinkling of Germans among the colonists.

The European colony at the Cape was important not only as a halfway house to the East; it was by far the best point—practically the only feasible one—from which the temperate inland plateau could be reached. Better harbors on the west coast lacked fresh water, while the very good harbor of Delagoa Bay was swampy and malarial and infested with the deadly tsetse fly. As a leading historian of South Africa puts it, "the Cape was the best training-ground for South African colonization."[1] Cape Town was surrounded by fertile valleys; the natives were so few and weak as to offer no great resistance. The colonists were irresistibly attracted inland, just as the European colonists in North America were drawn westward.

This popular movement to the interior largely determined the history of southern Africa for nearly two centuries. As they advanced eastward and northward, the *Boer trekkers* (*boer* is simply the Dutch word for farmer, but it came to be applied especially to the Dutch settlers in South Africa; *trekker* is the Dutch word for migrant or pioneer) met the Bantus moving southward under pressure from tribes farther north. The Bantu were so numerous that the Boers could not drive them back nor destroy them. Moreover, the Bantu were useful in operating the huge farms of the *trekkers*. Thus the white minority reduced the blacks to slaves and servants and introduced a rigid social and political segregation.

At first an attempt was made to maintain a frontier between the Europeans and the Bantu, but this proved impossible. In 1779 there broke out the first of the Kaffir or Frontier Wars, a series of hostilities lasting about a century. They were essentially a continuous struggle

[1] C. W. De Kiewit, *A History of South Africa: Social and Economic* (London, 1951), p. 1.

between two streams of colonists for possession of land. The less numerous but more highly developed whites won and became masters.

Since Cape Town was not intended to be a settlement colony but a refreshing station, there were few accessions from Europe after the early years. Not until after the British took over Cape Colony was any effort made to induce Europeans to settle in the country. Thus to great geographical isolation was added cultural isolation, especially for those large numbers who pressed farther and farther inland. The Boers acquired characteristics of the frontiersman, both the good and the bad. About the only cultural influence was the church, which continued to play a dominant role in their lives. Their environment, however, colored their interpretation of the Bible. They saw themselves in a role like that of the Israelites; they felt themselves called of God to open the northern regions for civilization and the propagation of the Christian gospel among the inferior heathen.

Britain occupied Cape Colony from 1795 to 1803, reoccupied it in 1806, and acquired sovereignty over it by treaty with the Netherlands in 1814. Britain wanted to make the Netherlands a strong buffer against France or any other continental power which might arise in Western or Central Europe. This was done by uniting Belgium to Holland and by restoring most of the Dutch colonies which England could have considered hers by right of conquest. The Gold Coast, Cape Colony, and Ceylon were not returned because they were strategic points on the road to India and were considered necessary for the security of the British Empire in the East. Moreover, since the Netherlands was dependent on the British navy for the security of its colonies, the cession to Britain of the two strong naval points of the Cape and Ceylon was in the interests of the Dutch as well as the British.

With British rule there came English immigrants, a considerable number of missionaries, and more liberal political and social ideas. By a policy of assisted immigration the British government was able to settle about 5,000 English in Cape Colony in the 1820s. It was not, however, until after the discovery of diamonds and gold in the 1860s that Europeans went to South Africa in any numbers. The missionaries clashed frequently with the Boer frontiersmen over their treatment of the Bantu. The *trekkers* disliked the restraints of any government, as is evident from their difficulty in setting up governments in new settlements. They complained that the British government did not protect the frontier regions against Bantu raids; they were profoundly dissatisfied with the liberal British policy which culminated in the emancipation of the slaves in 1834. This was probably the chief cause of the Great Trek during the years 1836–1854.[2] The *Voortrekkers*, as these pioneers came to be known, resolved to move beyond British jurisdiction, establish their own governments, and deal with the Bantu according to their own ideas.[3]

As a result of the Great Trek two Boer states finally emerged: the Orange Free State and the South African Republic (generally called the Transvaal). Britain annexed the latter in 1877, but restored internal self-government in 1881 after a rebellion which broke out in 1880. The brief war, known among the English as the First Anglo-Boer War but among Afrikaners[4] as the First War for Freedom, fanned the slowly developing Boer spirit of nationalism even among the Afrikaners in the Cape. Under a new agreement, the Convention of 1884, Great Britain gave up the right to conduct the foreign relations of the republic but reserved a veto on its treatymaking powers.

British policy was often contradictory. The judgment of James Anthony Froude, the historian, was harsh but not far from the truth. The British statesmen had, he said, certain ideas not always consistent: "At one time we have insisted that South Africans shall act as we please. Then we told them to do as they pleased and to trouble us with their affairs no further. The story of our rule at the Cape is a story of vacillation varied with tyranny, which can be paralleled only in the history of our rule in Ireland."[5]

With the discovery of diamonds and gold in the territories of the two Boer republics around 1870 the whole situation in South Africa became

---

[2] In a passionate attack on British policy in *Eene Eeuw van Onrecht* (A Century of Wrong) published anonymously in Pretoria in 1899, the British government was accused of offending the Afrikaner people at the most sensitive point "by taking in countless ways the side of the natives above that of the Afrikaner." The tract was written by Jan C. Smuts, at the time state attorney of the South African Republic.

[3] "Rebellion against so strong a power as that of Britain was evidently foredoomed to failure. But to the north and east a great wild country lay open before them, where they could lead that half-nomadic life which they loved, preserve their old customs, and deal with the natives as they pleased, unvexed by the meddlesome English" (James Bryce, *Impressions of South Africa*, 3d ed. [New York, 1900], p. 116).

[4] Afrikaners are the descendants of the early Dutch colonists.

[5] *Two Lectures on South Africa* (London, 1900), p. 7. Delivered at Edinburgh, 6 and 9 Jan. 1880.

transformed. The mining industry developed rapidly in the Transvaal. Foreign capital flowed in; railways were built. As the producer of over half of the world's supply of diamonds and about a quarter of its gold, South Africa gained a place in the world economy. The influx of large numbers of aliens (*uitlanders,* the Boers called them) deeply disturbed the economic structure and life of the republics. The Boers were determined to keep their countries under Boer control. The struggle among the Europeans for African territories was at the same time reaching a climax. Britain was determined to establish her supremacy over all South Africa. The conflict over the rights of the *uitlanders* culminated in the Second Anglo-Boer War or simply the Boer War, but which the Afrikaners prefer to call the Second War for Freedom.

Some Englishmen justified the war as an inevitable conflict between the English and the Afrikaners for supremacy in the country and some even believed in the existence of a countrywide Afrikaner conspiracy to oust the British from control. Until the Jameson Raid[6] the Cape Afrikaners were loyal to the Empire, and continued so even after the shock of that event. In 1898 the Cape Assembly, in which there was an Afrikaner majority, unanimously voted a large annual contribution for the support of the British navy. Jan Hofmeyr, the political leader of the Afrikaner party, made every effort to induce the Transvaal to make concessions in order to avert war. The Orange Free State was on good terms with the British government and likewise used its influence for peace.[7]

The war, which lasted from 1899 to 1902, ended in the annexation of the two republics. The heroic struggle of the small farmer states in holding a world empire at bay for three years amazed the world and evoked almost universal admiration and sympathy. The bitter struggle intensified Boer nationalism.

Self-government in South Africa had a varied history. In Cape

[6] On 29 Dec. 1895, L. S. Jameson, friend and agent of Cecil Rhodes, invaded the Transvaal with an armed force. The German emperor, Wilhelm II, sought to make political capital out of the raid by sending President Kruger a cablegram congratulating him on having repelled "the armed hordes which had burst as disturbers into his country." See Amry Vandenbosch, *Dutch Foreign Policy since 1815* (The Hague, 1959), ch. 6, "The Boer War," for repercussions of the raid and the Boer War in the Netherlands and on how it complicated its foreign policy.

[7] For an interesting collection of essays and excerpts from books on the causes of the war see Theodore C. Caldwell, ed., *The Anglo-Boer War: Why Was It Fought? Who Was Responsible?* (Boston, 1965).

Colony it enjoyed a slow but steady growth almost from the time the colony came under British rule until a grant of responsible government in 1872. Natal, which was annexed by Britain in 1843 and was made a separate colony in 1856, was granted responsible government in 1893. The republics, which had been reduced to colonial status, were accorded responsible government in 1906. With the formation of the Union in 1910 the colonies lost the right of self-government, but the new, larger political entity began with a popularly elected paraliament and a ministry responsible to it.

FORMATION OF THE UNION

Federation was not a new idea in South Africa. In the 1850s the Orange Free State was interested in federating with the Cape. Its imports came by way of Cape Town; federation would force the Cape to share customs receipts with it. The Orange Free State was weak and some Free Staters doubted whether it could stand alone. Sir George Grey, British high commissioner at the time, advanced a scheme for joining the colonies and the republics in a federation under the crown, but he failed to win for it the approval of London. Lord Carnarvon, when he was colonial secretary from 1874 to 1878, vainly sought to form a South African federation on the Canadian model.[8]

There was much to be said for union in South Africa. The Transvaal and the Orange Free State were landlocked. The natural ports for the Transvaal were Lourenço Marques in Portuguese Mozambique and Durban in British Natal, almost equally distant from the Rand. This enabled the Transvaal to play one against the other, but it made for tension. In addition to a war of railway rates and customs there were the problems of controlling the plagues of nature and the questions of labor and native policy. Of all these problems, the desirability of uniform native policy was not the least important as was clearly seen by Lord Selborne, who succeeded Lord (Alfred) Milner as British high commissioner. No reasoning man, wrote Selborne, "can live in this land and doubt that the existence here of a white community, must from first to last, depend upon their success or failure in finding a right solution

[8] Carnarvon sent Froude, the historian, on two missions to promote his scheme. See James Anthony Froude, *Two Lectures on South Africa*.

of the coloured and native questions, or in other words, upon the wisdom they can show in determining the relative places which the white, coloured and native populations can fill."[9]

The Transvaal and the Orange Free State were prepared to enter a federation but only on their own terms. The situation was succinctly put by a historian of the Union Convention, Sir Edgar Walton: "There were ideals in the North which were incompatible with union, ideals which found a leader and a vigorous protagonist in Paul Kruger. To many the establishment of a great Dutch Afrikaner Republic was an aspiration which moved them profoundly. It was the dominating passion of their lives and it could not be reconciled with the idea of a Union of British South Africa including the Transvaal."[10]

Political unification was furthered by the British conquest of the Boer republics, but British South Africa was still a multiplicity of authorities. There were the Orange River and Transvaal colonies, the self-governing colonies of the Cape and Natal, three protectorates under the high commissioner, and Southern Rhodesia administered by the British South Africa Company. There were four railway systems, four customs administrations, and a variety of legal systems, united only by the distant imperial authority in London.

Lord Milner moved at once after the Boer capitulation to bring about some unification. He called the Inter-Colonial Conferences in 1903 which resulted in a customs union and created the Inter-Colonial Council which established joint control over South African railways. These agreements were for only two years and might not be renewed, as both Natal and the Transvaal were dissatisfied with them. Unless a federation could be achieved the outlook was for perpetual strife which might lead to war. Milner wanted to delay federation until the British would be numerous enough (through the encouragement of immigration) to write the constitution, but his successor, Lord Selborne, saw no possibility of this in the foreseeable future. He therefore promoted the movement for an early union. On the Afrikaner side, Prime Minister Louis Botha and his able colleague, General Jan Christiaan Smuts, strongly

[9] Great Britain, Parliamentary Papers, *The Selborne Memorandum: A Review of the Mutual Relations of the British South African Colonies in 1907*, Cmd. 3564 (London, 1925), p. 113.

[10] Sir Edgar Walton, *The Inner History of the Convention of South Africa* (Cape Town, 1912), pp. 8–9.

supported the movement. Smuts believed that matters had reached a critical point: either a united South Africa or an isolated Transvaal.[11]

Economic considerations were important in the union movement, but the native question was a no less weighty factor, and it was a difficult subject on which to get agreement. Merriman wrote to Smuts that one of the chief objects of union was to get rid of "the pernicious and ill-informed interference that has worked so much mischief in the past."[12] There was general agreement that there must be one native policy throughout the country and that the natives everywhere must be subject to the same law. Leading Britishers had let it be known that South Africans would be given a free hand in drafting the constitution with the exception of two questions, namely, the native franchise and control of the Protectorates. The imperial government regarded itself as the guardian and trustee of the natives. The Cape had granted the franchise to the natives and coloreds, and the leading men there were "pledged as far as the most solemn assurances can go to maintain the rights conferred by our franchise."[13]

The native franchise posed a troublesome question for the convention. General J. B. M. Hertzog, a political leader from the Orange River Colony, expressed great anxiety about the granting of the franchise to the natives, however restricted. There would be constant pressure to lower the qualifications and it would not be long before the Europeans would be swamped.[14] The native problem in all its forms baffled Smuts. He wrote to Merriman that on the question of the native franchise his mind was full of "Cimmerian darkness,"[15] but he was certain a provision in the constitution conferring on the natives the right to vote would make union impossible for the people to accept.[16] General Botha told the

[11] W. K. Hancock and Jean van der Poel, eds., *Selections from the Smuts Papers*, 4 vols. (Cambridge, Eng., 1966), 2:405 and 407. Letter to M. T. Steyn, former president of the Orange Free State, and in the same vein to John X. Merriman, prime minister of Cape Colony, 17 and 18 Feb. 1908.

[12] Ibid., 2:446–47, 19 July 1908, Merriman letter to Smuts.

[13] Ibid. W. P. Schreiner wrote very emphatically to Smuts about his commitment to the franchise for the natives. Ibid., 2:450.

[14] Walton, *Inner Hist. of the Convention of So. Africa*, p. 133. The population of the colonies at the time was as follows: Transvaal—420,000 whites, 1,250,000 blacks, and a few thousand Indians and coloreds; Orange River—175,000 whites, 325,000 blacks; Cape Colony—600,000 whites, 450,000 coloreds, 1,500,000 blacks; Natal—90,000 whites, 133,000 Indians, and nearly 1,000,000 blacks.

[15] Hancock and van der Poel, eds., *Smuts Papers*, 2:526.

[16] Ibid., 2:440–42, 13 July 1908, letter to J. A. Hobson.

convention bluntly that he and his supporters faced great difficulties in persuading the Transvaal electorate to accept union, and that if he had to tell them that they had to accept the principle of the native franchise his position would become impossible.[17]

A compromise was the only solution. Nonwhites were not granted the right to vote, the Cape gave up the right of coloreds to sit in the Cape Parliament—a right which had never been exercised—but obtained the right for Cape coloreds to vote for (white) members of the Union Parliament, and this latter right was safeguarded by the requirement of a two-thirds vote to modify this provision. The question of federation or union presented no real problem for the convention; in fact this question was settled in favor of union before the delegates convened. Hertzog and other Afrikaners, concerned about the language question, insisted upon a guarantee of absolute equality for Dutch with English. It was agreed to make both official languages of the Union. The Protectorates were not incorporated in the Union but provision was made for the possibility of transferring them later, subject to certain conditions (Art. 151). A similar provision was included for Southern Rhodesia.

The British ministry and Parliament were confronted with the same dilemma that confronted the South African convention.[18] They believed that South Africa would reject union if the British Parliament insisted upon a provision granting the natives the right to vote. However, W. P. Schreiner, former premier of Cape Colony, went to England with a deputation to argue before Parliament that the incentives toward union were so strong that none of the parties to the convention would reject union merely on that basis. The members of the British Parliament did not believe that Schreiner represented the views of the majority of South Africans and apparently were not willing to risk the failure of union.[19]

[17] Walton, *Inner Hist. of the Convention of So. Africa*, p. 137.

[18] The British faced a similar problem at Vereeniging in 1902 when the peace agreement ending the Boer War was signed. Instead of incorporating a provision for native suffrage in the terms of surrender it stipulated that "The question of granting the franchise to natives will not be decided until after the introduction of self-government" (Great Britain, Parliamentary Papers, *Correspondence respecting Terms of Surrender of the Boer Forces in the Field*, Cd. 1096 [London, 1902]). When the British granted self-government to the Transvaal and the Orange River Colony in 1906 and 1907 respectively, it granted them a franchise which excluded non-Europeans from the vote and from sitting in Parliament.

[19] See L. M. Thompson, *The Unification of South Africa, 1902–1910* (Oxford, 1960), pp. 402–32.

The undersecretary of state for colonies, Col. J. E. B. Seeley, declared that if the franchise provisions were changed the Union would be destroyed and the natives, whom they wished to protect, would suffer. The fact that four to five million natives were to be governed by whites made it essential that a single government with strength, power, and sympathy should pursue one common policy with regard to all native races.[20] The constitution was approved by Parliament in August 1909 as the South Africa Act.

The failure of the British Parliament to insist upon the incorporation of a provision guaranteeing suffrage for the nonwhites had profound and long-range consequences. It probably set the stage for the ultimate complete triumph of Afrikaner nationalism. James Anthony Froude's comments made in 1880 were prophetic: "We speak of South Africa as an English colony. It is not a colony. It is a conquered country, of which we took possession for our own purposes against the wishes of its proper owners. English colonists have settled there, but South Africa is Dutch. . . . It is their country. . . . They look upon us as intruders. They hope to have it again one day for themselves, and the Dutch are a tough, stubborn independent people, as the Spaniards found to their cost when they tried to master them in Europe."[21] A similar prophecy was made some twenty-five years later by Lord (Alfred) Milner, the British high commissioner for South Africa.[22]

[20] Great Britain, *Parliamentary Debates* (Commons), 5th ser., 9 (1909): 953, 959.

[21] Froude, *Two Lectures on South Africa*, pp. 9–10.

[22] In 1905 Milner wrote to Lord Selborne, his successor: "I need not tell you what their dream and ideal is—that of a separate Afrikaner nation and State, comprising, no doubt, men of other races, who are ready to be 'Afrikanerized,' but essentially autochthonous, isolated and non-British, though some of them are prepared to see their object realized, for a time at least, under the British flag" (Cecil Headlam, ed., *The Milner Papers, South Africa* [London, 1931], Vol. 2, 1899–1905, p. 552). Smuts concluded his tract *A Century of Wrong* with: "Then shall it be from Zambesi to Simons Bay: Africa for the Afrikaners."

2

Social Structure
and Foreign Policy

The foreign policy of South Africa has become almost totally a defense of its racial policy against the hostile pressure of nearly the whole world. Occasionally its prime ministers talk as if South Africa had found the solution to the racial problem and had an obligation to carry this glorious news to all those parts of the world which have to struggle with it. But few people in South Africa take this seriously. They know that their racial policy is not for export. They will be happy enough if their country can escape serious outside intervention and ultimately obtain some relief from the present external pressure. However, in few countries is there so close a relation between economic and social structure and domestic policy on the one hand and foreign policy on the other.

The Republic of South Africa has an area of 472,359 square miles and a population in 1970 of about 20,000,000.[1] South West Africa, which is administered virtually as a part of South Africa, has an area of 319,099 square miles and a population of about 600,000.[2] The racial composition of South Africa's population has varied little in over half a century, but the changes that have occurred have been unfavorable to the whites, whose percentage of the total dropped from 21.6 in 1904 to 19.3 in 1960. Each of the other three racial groups gained slightly, the

Bantu increasing their percentage from 67.5 to 68.2; the coloreds from 8.6 to 9.4; and the Asians from 2.4 to 3.0. The racial composition varies greatly from province to province. Three-fourths of the Indians are found in Natal, while the Cape has nearly nine-tenths of the coloreds. The Free State has practically no Indians and few coloreds. The percentage of whites in the total population in 1960 was highest in the Transvaal with over 23 percent and lowest in Natal where the figure was less than 12 percent.[3] Twenty-seven percent of the Bantu live in urban areas, 35 percent in white rural areas, and the remaining 38 percent in Bantu reserves.

Until recently when South African whites spoke of the racial problem they were not referring to relations between the European and non-European sections of the population but between Afrikaner and English-speaking whites. This did not mean that the Europeans were not conscious of the problem created by the fact that they constituted only a fifth of the population and yet practically monopolized political power. Rather the non-Europeans did not present an immediate threat to the position of the Europeans and the struggle between Empire and Afrikaner republicanism had been so long and bitter that conciliation between the two white groups was difficult. In 1960 the home language of 58 percent of the Republic's white population was Afrikaans and of 37.3 percent it was English, while 1.4 percent used both languages in everyday life. Between 1951 and 1960 the percentage of Afrikaans-speaking persons increased from 57 to 58 percent, while that of the English-speaking decreased from 39.3 to 37.4.[4]

In his challenging speech to the Parliament of South Africa on

[1] At the time of the 1960 census the population was 15,982,664, divided among the races as follows: whites, 3,088,492; Bantu, 10,907,789; coloreds, 1,509,258; Asians 477,125. (*State of South Africa: Economic, Financial and Statistical Year-Book for the Republic of South Africa, 1963* [Johannesburg, 1963]); hereafter cited as *State of South Africa*. The South African Department of Statistics gave the total population as of mid-1969 as 19,618,000, of whom 13,340,000 were African; 3,728,000, white; 1,959,000, colored; and 591,000, Asian (*The Star* [Johannesburg], Weekly Air Edition, 13 Dec. 1969).

[2] The population in 1960 was 525,000 divided racially as follows: whites, 73,154; Bantu, 427,980; coloreds, 23,900.

[3] For Cape Province and Orange Free State the percentages were 19.8 and 20 respectively. These figures have remained almost constant over the years. For a convenient and useful source of statistics see *State of South Africa* published annually.

[4] Due chiefly to a higher Afrikaner birth rate.

February 3, 1960, British Prime Minister Harold Macmillan declared, "here in Africa you have yourselves created a full nation—a new nation . . . the first of the African nationalisms." Presumably he meant the Afrikaner nation. Although a white South African nation is in the process of formation, it could not be said that such a nation existed in 1960. As late as 1968, H. B. Thom, rector of the University of Stellenbosch, expressed the opinion that the Afrikaner and English-speaking peoples were not becoming a united nation and he saw no likelihood of it in the foreseeable future.[5] The Afrikaner differs in spirit and thought from the other peoples of South Africa because of his entirely different historical background. That the Afrikaners as a people possess most of the earmarks generally associated with nationalism must be acknowledged: a separate language, a distinct culture, a unity reinforced by strong religious and ecclesiastical ties, and a history of struggle for the preservation of their culture and for political independence.

A number of factors played a part in the making of the Afrikaner nation. Geographic and cultural isolation made for a separate and distinct development. When the Netherlands ceded Cape Colony to Britain, political ties with the motherland were severed and cultural relations weakened still further. The long struggle with the Bantu and then with the British strengthened their group consciousness. For a while it seemed as if fusion of Afrikaners and English would take place, but when the former began to suspect the British of trying to anglicize them, they became aroused. Many Afrikaners decided to move out of British territory and set up their own governments. Continued British imperial pressure on the Boer republics, culminating in the Boer War of 1899–1902, intensified their national spirit. Many Britishers, closely involved in the struggle between Afrikaner and Briton, saw it as a contest between Kruger republicanism and British imperialism for the whole of South Africa.[6] Toward the end of the Boer War, Lord Milner wrote: "There is no doubt whatever in my mind that the Dutch will try,

---

[5] *The Star*, Weekly Air Edition, 29 June 1968.

[6] In 1896, J. P. Fitzpatrick wrote of President Kruger: "By the force of his own strong convictions and prejudices, and of his indomitable will, he has made the Boers a people whom he regards as the germ of the Africander nation; a people chastened, selected, welded, and strong enough to attract and assimilate all their kindred in South Africa, and then to realize the dream of a Dutch Republic from the Zambesi to Cape Town" (*The Transvaal from Within* [London, 1899], p. 1. The book was written in 1896, privately circulated, and then published in 1899).

for a time at least, to recover by politics what they have lost by arms."[7] Milner was prophetic but only half-right. The Afrikaners not only tried but ultimately achieved far more by politics than they lost by arms.

Social and economic factors were influential in the development of Afrikaner nationalism. The Boers were agrarian and many of them were impoverished. The so-called poor whites constituted about 20 percent of the white population and most of them were Afrikaners. The rural population had to contend with rinderpest, locusts, and severe droughts.[8] The British controlled finance, commerce, industry, and government. Since the Afrikaners held a secondary position in nearly every phase of life, they easily developed an anti-British, anticapitalist, anti-imperialist spirit. It was therefore not strange that many Afrikaners were attracted by national socialism in the 1930s and during World War II.[9] After the formation of the Union, the Afrikaner's numerical superiority gave him the political power not only to obtain a status of equality for his culture but also to improve his economic and social position.[10]

The English-speaking community has shown no inclination toward separate nationhood. The position of the British was quite different from that of the Afrikaners. They were a minority, even of the whites, and they had no long history in South Africa. Their problem was to

[7] Cecil Headlam, ed., *The Milner Papers, South Africa*, 2 vols. (London, 1931 and 1933), 2:407.

[8] Carnegie Commission Report, *The Poor White Problem in South Africa*, 5 vols. (Stellenbosch, 1932).

[9] Oswald Pirow, General J. B. M. Hertzog's biographer, states that Hertzog, after his defeat by Smuts on the war issue in 1939, was completely converted to national socialism based on the Portuguese model. Pirow himself had founded the *New Order* based on the socialism of Salazar (*James Barry Munnik Hertzog* [London, 1958], p. 259). Pirow was minister of defense under Hertzog. See also C. M. van den Heever, *General J. B. M. Hertzog*, Afrikaans ed. (Johannesburg, 1943), pp. 749ff.

[10] While the economic position of the Afrikaners has improved greatly during the past few decades they have not yet caught up with the English-speaking section of the population. Only 1.5 percent of the Afrikaans population are university graduates compared with 3 percent of the English-speaking population, and the percentage of English-speaking matriculants is still twice as high as that of the Afrikaans-speaking (*The Star*, Weekly Air Edition, 6 July 1968). On the development of Afrikaner nationalism see F. A. van Jaarsveld, *The Awakening of Afrikaner Nationalism, 1868–1881* (Cape Town, 1961); D. F. Malan, *Afrikaner Volkseenheid en my Ervarings op die Pad Daarheen* [Afrikaner National Unity and My Experiences on the Path Thereto] (Cape Town, 1959); Edwin S. Munger, *Afrikaner and African Nationalism* (London, 1967).

prevent subjection or absorption, and for this they needed the support of Britain. For them it was important to remain a part of the British world-nation and to keep South Africa in some fashion a part of the British Empire or Commonwealth. The political weakness of the English after Union strengthened their feeling of identity with Britain, but this exposed them to the Afrikaner charge of being more loyal to Britain than South Africa, or at best, of having a divided loyalty. Afrikaners regarded themselves as the only genuine South Africans.[11] A Nationalist member of Parliament, P. Koornhoff, declared in 1966, "We desire no integration between Afrikaner and English-speakers because it will lead to the downfall of Afrikanerdom and White civilization in South Africa."[12]

Until recently South African politics has been dominated by the struggle between the British imperial and the Afrikaner National ideals for supremacy. "Between these two millstones all other considerations have been ground to paste," said an Afrikaner journalist.[13] In this great struggle immigration policy became a bone of contention. There are two compelling reasons for encouraging white immigration. South Africa desperately needs skilled workers to realize its potentialities for industrial development. Moreover, white immigrants are needed to strengthen the position of the Europeans relative to the non-Europeans, or at least not to allow it to weaken. But until recently the Nationalists were opposed to the encouragement of immigration. In 1921, Daniel F. Malan, in a bitter attack on the immigration policy of the Smuts government, which he characterized as political immigration, stated that if it were continued South Africa would become a second Ireland. The Nationalists were convinced that the immigration policy of the United party was motivated in large part by the purpose of "ploughing under" Afrikanerdom.[14] C. P. Mulder, who became minister of immigration in

---

[11] On the relations of the white communities see G. H. Calpin, *There Are No South Africans* (London, 1941) ; G. H. Calpin, ed., *The South African Way of Life* (New York, 1953) ; Leo Marquard, *The Peoples and Policies of South Africa* (London, 1952, 1960).

[12] Quoted in article by Marius Steyn, *The Star*, Weekly Air Edition, 17 May 1969.

[13] W. van Heerden, "Africa in South African Politics," in *South Africa in the African Continent* (Stellenbosch, 1959).

[14] "The United Party's policy was to allow anyone to enter, no matter in what numbers, even with the aim of ploughing under National Afrikanerdom" (South African *Parliamentary Debates*, House of Assembly, vol. 99, col. 55, 27 Jan. 1959) ; hereafter cited as *Hansard*. This charge was made frequently by Nationalists.

1968, charged the United party with having misused immigration for their own party purposes.[15] During the period 1924 to 1961, 377,000 white immigrants entered South Africa, but 247,000 emigrants left. During World War II the Union suffered a net loss of 5,500. In the postwar years 1946 to 1961 immigrants numbered 268,000 and emigrants 177,000.[16] In 1961, probably because of the disturbances at Sharpeville and Langa during March 1960 and in Pondoland in 1960 and 1961, emigrants exceeded immigrants by 2,824. Since 1962 there has been a sharp increase of immigrants over emigrants for an annual surplus of about 30,000.[17]

What worries the Afrikaner Nationalists is that so large a percentage of the immigrants are British and southern Europeans, nearly all of whom are absorbed by the English-speaking community.[18] The Federal Council of Liaison Committees (of Afrikaner cultural associations) calculates that the Afrikaans section of the population was increasing at the rate of 33,200 a year (32,000 by natural increase and 1,200 by immigration), whereas the increase of the English-speaking people was 50,000 (12,000 natural and 38,800 by immigration). At this rate the Afrikaner's numercial superiority could be wiped out in twenty-five years.[19] Afrikaners also assert that the religious composition of the white population is being changed because so large a percentage of the immigrants are Roman Catholics.[20] Afrikaners have wanted a large number of immigrants from the Netherlands, but Dutch immigration has been disappointing. Of all the immigrant nationalities, the Dutch

[15] *Hansard*, vol. 7, col. 7234, 4 June 1963.

[16] Ibid., vol. 18, col. 2897, 26 Sept. 1966.

[17] The number of immigrants rose from 9,789 in 1960 to 48,048 in 1966, but dropped to 38,937 the following year. Of significance is that many have come from Kenya, the Rhodesias, Malawi, and Tanzania. In 1963 nearly half of the white immigrants came from these countries.

[18] The origin of immigrants in the 1960s was about as follows: United Kingdom, 30 percent; Germany and the Netherlands, 15 percent; Mediterranean countries, 15 percent; and African countries, 15 percent.

[19] *The Star*, Weekly Air Edition, 7 Jan. 1967.

[20] The religious composition of the whites, according to the 1951 census, was as follows: Reformed, 53.2 percent; Anglican, 15.8 percent; Methodist, 8.3; Roman Catholic, 5.3; Presbyterian, 3.8; and Jewish, 4.1 percent (*State of South Africa, 1959–1960*, p. 76). Dr. C. P. Mulder, minister of immigration, told a National party congress that between 1960 and 1967 the proportion of Roman Catholics in the white population had increased from a meager 6.2 percent to 6.4 percent (*The Star*, Weekly Air Edition, 21 Sept. 1968).

have been the least likely to stay. More than half return home. Moreover, nearly half of them are Roman Catholics.

The Afrikaners are in a dilemma on immigration. For its security South Africa must be strong militarily, but this in turn requires a healthy and flourishing economy, and the maintenance of a sound economic growth requires about 30,000 skilled immigrants annually. If Protestants were to be sought as immigrants, South Africa would be largely restricted to Britain for recruitment—distasteful to the Afrikaners. Some Afrikaners have thus advocated a higher birthrate among Afrikaners rather than immigration to supply the needed population growth. The discontent among Afrikaners about immigration policy is causing the government considerable concern. The former minister of immigration, Senator A. E. Trollip, and his successor, C. P. Mulder, have sought to assure the Afrikaners that immigration was not disturbing the religious or ethnic balance of the population and they promised that the government would administer the policy so as to avoid such disturbance.

The Afrikaner Nationalists need the support of the English against the non-Europeans yet they want to keep them neutralized politically as much as possible. In spite of all their successes during the past two decades Afrikaner Nationalists still suffer from an inferiority complex. They fear that their language and culture may be lost, that the Afrikaner will be absorbed or assimilated by the English community. The more militant among them urge teachers to fight Afrikaans-English integration. This is an uphill struggle, since English is a world language. The Afrikaner seems to resent this advantage of the English-speaking community. In an address to teachers in March 1967, D. P. Goosen, director of the *Suid Afrikaans Akademie vir Wetenskap en Kuns*, stated that the Afrikaners were still "hewers of wood and bearers of water in [their] own fatherland." In 1967 the Afrikaners' share in trade was 28 percent, in industry 10 percent, in finance 14 percent, and in mining 10 percent. Integration was taking place; almost 200,000 Afrikaners had become completely anglicized. The immigration stream was strengthening the English community in all modes of life. Afrikaners were being fed with English newspapers, magazines, books, textbooks, and entertainment—all carriers of liberal thought.[21]

21 *The Star*, Weekly Air Edition, 18 Mar. 1967.

While on the one hand the Afrikaner fears assimilation with the English-speaking community, on the other hand he is disturbed about the low birth rate among the English, which, he feels, is imperiling the future of the whites in South Africa, and the English are urged to have more children.[22] The Afrikaner Nationalist finds himself in a strange dilemma. He feels that he must resist integration with the English or he will lose his identity, but that he also must cooperate closely with them or the white, European civilization will disappear.

Prime Minister Hendrik F. Verwoerd tried to win the support of the English-speaking for his policies. In the protracted national crisis which South Africa faced, unity of the whites was not only desirable but necessary for survival. He appointed two English-speaking South Africans to his cabinet in 1961. Prime Minister Balthazar J. Vorster has also stressed the need for Afrikaner-English unity. But Albert Hertzog in April 1969, in a speech in Parliament, declared that the English-speaking South Africans could not be entrusted with political power, that "only Calvinist nationalist Afrikaners should rule South Africa."[23] This return to the old Nationalist line was very disturbing to Vorster and other party leaders.

POLITICAL DEVELOPMENT

Alan Paton has said that history lies like a sword between the two white races. There was too much history and it was too well remembered. It is sometimes said that up to the end of World War II South African politics was a quarrel among Afrikaners about the attitude they should take toward Britain and the English and since then it has been a debate among the whites about what to do with the non-Europeans.[24]

The Politics of Conciliation: Botha-Smuts Period, 1910–1924. General Louis Botha, commandant-general of the Transvaal forces in the Boer War, became the Union's first prime minister. He followed a conciliatory policy toward Britain and the English in South Africa. His

[22] Address by Professor S. Pauw of the University of South Africa at a meeting sponsored by the South African Bureau on Racial Affairs (*The Star*, Weekly Air Edition, 29 Oct. 1966).

[23] *New York Times*, 22 April 1969.

[24] Some pessimists foresee a third phase when South African politics will be a debate among the blacks about what to do with the whites.

cabinet was about equally divided between Afrikaners and English. He and Smuts, his righthand man, were desirous of promoting cooperation between the two peoples in order to further their fusion into a single nation. Smuts spoke frequently of the British treatment of the former Boer republics as a "miracle of trust and magnanimity." Botha and Smuts felt that the only honorable as well as wise response to such magnanimity was loyalty and cooperation. They won the trust and support of most English-speaking persons but became alienated from many Afrikaners.

Even before World War I broke out this policy of conciliation ran into difficulty. Statements by Leander S. Jameson (of Jameson's Raid), leader of the ardently pro-British Union party, evoked distrust and extremism from Afrikaner Nationalists.[25] Botha had taken into his cabinet another wartime comrade, General J. B. M. Hertzog, who was highly unpopular with the English. Hertzog feared Botha's conciliatory policy would ultimately mean the disappearance of the Afrikaans language and culture. When Hertzog, in several speeches in 1911 and 1912, advocated a "two streams of life" and "South Africa first" policy, Botha reorganized his cabinet and left Hertzog out. In January 1914 the latter organized the National party whose program of principles formulated at the time cast a long shadow ahead.[26]

General Smuts, who succeeded General Botha as prime minister upon the latter's death on August 27, 1919, had to deal with a grave postwar economic situation and serious labor unrest. Violence broke out in March 1922, and martial law was declared on the Rand. Order was restored only after the destruction of much property and the loss of over two hundred lives. Smuts, who had taken command of the police action in person, lost prestige and followers.

The drawing together of Nationalism and Labor was of great political significance. Afrikaner Nationalism and English trade unionism were divided on a number of matters, but they were united on racial policy. Both were determined to keep the Africans out of skilled employment and to reserve it for the whites. In view of the situation it was not

[25] Unionist party of South Africa, *Programme* (Johannesburg, 1910). See D. W. Kruger, ed., *South African Parties and Policies* (London, 1960), p. 45.

[26] The program called for fostering a strong sense of national, political, and cultural autonomy, the supremacy of the European population and "utterly rejecting every attempt to mix the races" (Kurger, ed., *South African Parties and Policies*, pp. 69ff.).

surprising that General Hertzog and Colonel F. H. P. Cresswell in 1923 announced the formation of a Nationalist-Labor election pact whereby the two parties agreed to avoid three-way election contests by allocating districts to each other. In the election precipitated by Smuts in 1924, the National party won sixty-three and Labor seventeen parliamentary seats to only fifty-four for the South African party. Smuts had lost Afrikaner votes because he was pro-British and lost labor votes, mostly English, because he was pro-capitalist.

The Nationalist-Labor Pact Ministry, 1924–1933. Smuts branded the pact an "unholy alliance," yet it was not without logic and a meeting of interests. The chief difficulties were the republicanism of the Nationalists and the socialist ideals of Labor, but the slogan of a "civilized labor policy," which was essentially a demand for a racial labor policy with job reservation for the whites, drew them together. The Nationalist party agreed not to take steps, during the next parliament, in the direction of establishing a republic but individual members remained free to make propaganda for it while Labor agreed to scale down its socialist aims. Hertzog gave Labor two and later three cabinet posts in fulfillment of the bargain he had made. Color was the dominant issue for the first time in the election campaign of 1929. The campaign centered on Hertzog's native bills and on the Pan-African speech by Smuts which his opponents interpreted as a proposal to make South Africa a part of a confederation in which the whites would be completely submerged by blacks. The government parties issued a "Black Manifesto" which was very effective. It is certain Smuts had no intention of submerging the whites of South Africa, but the black peril issue came near drowning Smuts politically.

Fusion, World War II, and Its Aftermath, 1933–1948. The world depression hit South Africa with great force. At the same time the country was hit with one of its worst droughts. The opposition, the mining interests and farmers, supported by the press, clamored for leaving the gold standard. Prime Minister Hertzog and his able minister of finance, Nicolaas C. Havenga, held out as long as they could, but in December 1932 the government was forced to abandon the gold standard. This put the Nationalist party in an extremely weak position; on March 30, 1933, Hertzog and Smuts announced they had formed a coalition. A year later their two parties fused to form the United party.

D. F. Malan and his followers refused to join the new party and formed the Purified Nationalist party.

Hertzog and Smuts were never wholly agreed on foreign policy. This became clearer as the crisis in Europe deepened. When World War II broke out, Hertzog proposed that South Africa follow a policy of neutrality. This was impossible for Smuts. He introduced a declaration of war resolution in Parliament and won by a narrow margin. Hertzog rejoined the Nationalists. The majority of the United party in Parliament was small, especially for the purpose of carrying on a war, but fortunately for Smuts, the Nationalists were badly divided. Hertzog was not fully accepted by them; he was much too moderate. In December 1940 Hertzog and Havenga retired from politics and left Malan alone in the field to fight a number of organizations, half-political, semimilitary, and committed in various degrees to national socialism.

Malan was an astute political leader. While waging a determined battle for leadership of Afrikanerdom he was preparing the ground for an ultimate National victory. He steadily pressed the issues of white supremacy, republicanism, South Africa first, and anticommunism. Smuts, the great internationalist, was defeated because of the pressure of world opinion on South Africa. The white electorate wanted certainty and positive action in what it regarded as a crisis. Although seeking to avoid extremes, Smuts stood for white supremacy. Indeed, in a speech in London on May 27, 1917, in which he outlined South Africa's traditional racial policy he foreshadowed the Nationalists' apartheid policy of three decades later.[27] It was the uncertain quality of Smuts's commitment to white supremacy which contributed to his defeat.[28]

The Triumph of Nationalism, 1948–. Apartheid defeated Smuts and his party.[29] For the first time in its history the Union had an exclusively

[27] Jan C. Smuts, *Plans for a Better World* (London, 1942), pp. 15ff. In a speech in Parliament on 21 Sept. 1948, Smuts declared that the policy of his party had been "European paramountcy" and that it never had "any truck with equal rights. It is an abstraction forced upon us by our opponents. We stand and have always stood for European supremacy in this country. . . . We have always stood and we stand for social and residential separation in this country, and for the avoidance of all racial mixture" (*Hansard*, vol. 65).

[28] In Parliament, Malan said, "Under his policy there has always prevailed the greatest confusion" (*Hansard*, vol. 76, col. 120, 26 Jan. 1949).

[29] In terms of popular votes the National party did not win. See Chapter 9. In 1958 the National party received 642,069 popular votes to only 503,639 for the United party, which shows a decline in support for the United party.

Afrikaner cabinet. As world pressure mounted, so did the domestic support for the National party. Apartheid was gradually transformed from a vague slogan to a comprehensive and drastic program of racial legislation. This was especially marked under the premiership of Hendrik F. Verwoerd, an able and determined political leader. As a result, Verwoerd and his party came to be regarded more and more as the champions of white and not merely Afrikaner interests. As an appeal to the English-speaking voters for their support he appointed two of their number to membership in his cabinet. But this move was not made until all the aims of Afrikanerdom had been achieved. The right of appeal to the Privy Council in London was abolished in 1950; in 1957 the Afrikaans *Stem van Suid Afrika* was made the sole national anthem; and in 1961 the Union was declared a republic and withdrew from the Commonwealth. Many laws were enacted to enforce a rigid separation of the races, including as a capstone of their policy territorial separation.

APARTHEID

This Afrikaans word *apartheid* used to designate the racial policy of South Africa means apartness or separateness. The policy has for its object the complete separation of the races. It has two aspects—"little" (or "petty") and "big" apartheid. By the former is meant social segregation and the denial of the ordinary civil and political rights to non-Europeans. "Big" apartheid goes beyond this to territorial segregation of the races. Its end ideal is the division of South Africa into a strong white state and a number of small black states which may ultimately become independent if their peoples desire it and prove themselves capable of self-government. It is a development of the pattern of race relations which began almost at once after the planting of Cape Colony. Two trends with respect to native policy can be detected in the first years of the Union. The South African party in its program of principles advocated the "encouragement of desirable European immigration and the prevention of Asiatic immigration" and stated that "all questions affecting Native policy should be approached by the White people of South Africa, in a broad spirit of cooperation between parties, and in the endeavor to secure for Native races their natural and distinct development, and to ensure that in the building up of South

Africa all grounds for future discord between White and Black shall be avoided."[30] There is considerable agreement between this statement of principles and that of the National party. One speaks of "natural and distinct development" of the natives and the other of development according to their "natural talent and aptitude"; the South African party principles assume white supremacy and the National party definitely states that its "fundamental principle is the supremacy of the European population"; the first speaks of ensuring that "all grounds for future discord" between whites and blacks would be avoided, while the latter speaks of carrying out its native policy in a spirit of "Christian trusteeship" but "utterly rejecting every attempt to mix the races." The differences in the racial policy advocated by the two parties were not great. The South African party's attitude was somewhat pragmatic; that of the National party was more dogmatic.

As the South African whites see it, any policy other than segregation would lead to their political and ultimate biogenetic extinction, either by force or assimilation. Since South Africa is their only home the Afrikaners feel this more keenly than other white groups. Because they believe that continued cultural contacts result in social and eventually in biological assimilation they are convinced that their policy of segregation must be drastic and complete. For this reason they apply the principle of separation to cultural and social contacts as well as prohibit miscegenation.[31]

Basic in the development of racial policy was the Land Act of 1913, which marked the beginning of the territorial separation of the Africans from the whites. It created native locations and reserves in each of the four provinces for a total of more than 22 million acres. More land was added later. The act prohibited the Bantu from buying land from non-natives, and the reverse. Job reservation for whites had already been instituted in 1911 by the Mines and Works Act, which excluded nonwhites from skilled jobs as defined by government regulation. In 1923 the Native Urban Area Act was passed and subsequently frequently amended; this act restricted the number of Africans in urban areas and concentrated them in segregated living quarters. This basic legislation has been expanded to cover every conceivable situation and

[30] Kruger, ed., *South African Parties and Policies*, pp. 59–60.
[31] For a sympathetic and reasoned defense of apartheid see N. J. Rhoodie and H. J. Venter, *Apartheid* (Cape Town, 1959).

relationship and chiefly in a discriminatory manner—prohibition of the sale or supply of liquor to Africans; differential payments in old age pensions; the exclusion of aliens from the Blind Persons Act; the prohibition of issuing firearms to nonwhites; the nonrecognition of African trade unions and the prohibition of strikes by Africans; the requirement of apprenticeship for skilled trades and vocations from which nonwhites are barred; the prohibition of mixed marriages; the registration of all South Africans by race; the restriction of movement of non-Europeans; separate facilities for whites and nonwhites which need not be equal; and so on.[32]

The rise to power of the Nationalists in 1948 did not mark a new departure in racial policy. What it brought was an increased intensity, an unabashed frankness, toughness, and determination in the pursuit of the long-established policy of maintaining white supremacy. Since 1948 there has not been a session of Parliament which has not passed a law differentiating between the rights of whites and nonwhites. The few political rights which the non-Europeans had were taken away from them. But so flagrant a violation of basic human rights required some moral justification. The Nationalist leaders saw that they could not hold the line between the races where they had drawn it. In the face of a hostile opinion, apartheid as it had developed became more and more difficult to defend against world opinion as well as against the forces welling up at home. The march toward independence of the numerous African colonial territories had begun, making the situation urgent. Unwilling to move at all toward a policy which would endanger white supremacy, the Nationalist leadership shifted to a far-reaching policy of territorial separation. South Africa was at the crossroads. Prime Minister Verwoerd stated that the country had to decide "whether it would go in the direction of a multi-racial society with a common political society" or whether it would bring about "total separation in the political sphere." His government had chosen the course by which "the White man alone retained full rights of government in his area" and yet the Bantu would be granted "under our care as their guardians, a full

[32] On apartheid in practice see L. E. Neame, *The History of Apartheid* (London, 1962) ; G. M. Carter, *The Politics of Inequality* (London, 1958) ; K. L. Roskam, *Apartheid and Discrimination* (Leiden, 1960) ; L. Rubin, *This Is Apartheid* (London, 1959) ; UNESCO, *Apartheid: Its Effects on Education, Science, Culture and Information* (Paris, 1967).

opportunity in their own areas to put their feet on the road of development along which they can make progress in accordance with their capabilities." His government desired "to build up a South Africa in which Bantu and Whites can live next to one another like good neighbors and not like people who are continually fighting for domination."[33]

In this speech Verwoerd evaded the question of whether the Bantustans (areas reserved for the Bantu) would be granted independence. Pressed on this point a few months later he said that independence was not excluded but that his government by its statesmanship would try to carry out the policy so as to ensure continued friendship, "but without the White man ever finding himself under any form of Bantu control, whether in a federation or a union."[34] Some Nationalists were unhappy about this proposal to Balkanize the country, but Verwoerd contended that white South Africans had to choose between a smaller state which was white and which controlled its own police and defense forces and would stand as a bulwark for white civilization, or a larger state dominated by the Bantu. There was no other alternative. He assured his worried followers that his government would proceed slowly and cautiously, that the period of training for self-government might be a long one.[35]

With this decision the long drive for South African territorial expansion and integration suddenly went into reverse. Confronted, as they saw it, with the necessity of choosing between black supremacy and territorial fragmentation, they chose the latter as easily the lesser of two great evils.

The goal of separate development is total separation of whites and blacks.[36] In conformity with this basic aim, Africans living in the white areas are regarded as migrants whose true home is in the reserves or future Bantustans. The African, therefore, has no political rights in white South Africa but only in the territory which is his "homeland," even though he may not have been born there or have any real interest in it. The Nationalist leaders freely admit that millions of Africans will

---

[33] *Hansard*, vol. 99, cols. 40ff., 27 Jan. 1959.

[34] Ibid., vol. 101, cols. 6215–18, 20 May 1959.

[35] See also speech in House of Assembly, 25 Jan. 1963, *Hansard*, vol. 5, col. 244.

[36] As stated by a Nationalist member of Parliament: "Year after year at every possible opportunity when the matter arises, we will draw that line of demarcation wider and deeper, industrially, socially and politically" (M. J. Van Den Berg, 18 Jan. 1956, *Hansard*, vol. 90, cols. 64–65).

be needed as laborers in the white area for an indefinite period and that it will be a long time before the total separation is achieved. Nevertheless, they regard their policy as a sufficient moral basis for differential treatment of the races. Unfortunately, their solution solves nothing for the coloreds and the Indians. These two groups, numbering over two and a half million and more advanced than the Bantu, are to be accorded neither independence in separate areas nor political participation at the national level. The colored's case is especially tragic. The more they developed economically, educationally, and socially, the more they lost politically until finally they were deprived even of the token representation they had in Parliament. What makes their case especially poignant is that culturally, and most of them also religiously, they are Afrikaners.

Conciliation
1910–1924

3

World War I:
Development of an
Independent Foreign Policy

It was generally assumed that when Great Britain declared war on Germany on August 4, 1914, South Africa automatically became a belligerent. The Union was part of the British Empire and when the United Kingdom became involved in war, so did the whole Empire. Constitutionally the Union had no choice as to its legal status, but the Union had the right to determine the degree of its actual participation in the war. The Union had been granted self-government, hence to what extent and how it would participate in military activities was for it to determine. It was only twelve years since the Boers had laid down their arms after a bitter war against the Empire—insufficient time to heal the deep wounds of all Afrikaners. The Union was less than five years old and the country was far from unified. Prime Minister Louis Botha and his deputy, General Jan Smuts, faced grave difficulties. With Britain in trouble, some Afrikaners quite naturally saw in the situation the possibility of establishing a republic. Under the circumstances, the government might well have decided to limit its military activities to what was strictly necessary for the defense of the Union's territory.

On the day Great Britain declared war, the Union government sent a message to London that it was prepared to employ its defense force for the performance of duties entrusted to the imperial troops in South Africa. In accepting this offer in a cable of August 7, the British government inquired whether the Union government would undertake "to seize such part of German South-West Africa as will give them command of Swakopmond, Luderitzbucht, and the wireless stations there or in the interior." The Union government, three days later, notified London of its willingness, if Britain would provide the necessary naval support.

The Union government, thinking it wise to seek the approval of Parliament before moving on South West Africa, convened a special session on September 9. Botha stated that the Union was an ally in the British Empire, and the Empire being involved in the war, South Africa was *ipso facto* involved. That proposition seemed clear to him. For a territory in the British Empire there were, as he saw it, only two ways open in case of war: the path of faith, duty, and honor, or the path of dishonor and disloyalty.[1]

The prime minister informed the House that the British troops were leaving South Africa; thus the country to a large extent would have to look after its own defense. He also indicated that his government had agreed to undertake important military operations in South West Africa. Botha emphasized that neither the British government nor the Union government had any desire to acquire more land. They were engaged in a defensive war. Because of South West Africa's situation on the flank of an important sea route, its ports and powerful wireless station could not be left under German control. If South Africa refused to undertake this military mission Great Britain would call upon other members of the Empire—probably India or Australia—which certainly would not be in South Africa's interest.[2]

General James B. M. Hertzog, the leader of the Nationalist party, stated that while it was true that South Africa was in a state of war as a consequence of the war that existed between Britain and Germany, this did not make it South Africa's war. South Africa could decide whether it would take part actively in the war. He questioned whether the expedition against the Germans in South West Africa would contribute anything to the outcome of the war, as this would be determined in Europe. South Africans were in a bad situation. There was a severe

[1] *Hansard*, Extraordinary Session, 1914, col. 58.
[2] Ibid., cols. 58–60.

drought, the people had no arms, and there was danger of a native uprising. General Hertzog warned against the dangers of a military attack on the Germans in South West Africa. If the Allies were defeated and ruined, the Union would be exposed to retaliatory action and South Africa might suffer the fate of Belgium. He expressed great sympathy for the Belgians, especially since they were for the most part a Dutch-speaking people. However, once all the facts were known, the German action might be proved to have been justified. If the Allies won, South West Africa would fall like a ripe fruit into the lap of Great Britain. He warned the government that it might meet with popular resistance at home if it proceeded with the campaign.[3]

Prime Minister Botha had emphasized the defensive character of Britain's involvement in the war, asserting that Germany had forced it into hostilities. General Smuts in his speech charged Germany with militarism and aggression. The issue of the war was whether militarism would triumph or freedom prevail. Germany was guilty of aggression.[4]

In this debate the national interest in acquiring control of this neighboring territory was not mentioned, much less pressed. This was especially strange in view of Afrikaner attitudes. The Afrikaner's record from the earliest years of the Cape settlement to the British conquest of the Boer republics in 1902 was one of expansion. Their attitude was expressed in the old Republican slogan, "Then shall it be, from Simons Bay to Zambesi, Africa for the Afrikaners." The explanation of this attitude probably is that since they viewed the war as waged solely in Britain's interests, they believed that whatever might be won in southern Africa would accrue to Britain, not to the Union. Prime Minister Botha was well aware of the bitter opposition of many Afrikaners, even among members of his own party, to South African participation in the war and in particular to the use of Union troops outside of the country. He made a strong plea for tolerance. It was the duty of the House, he said, to see that the South African people emerged from the war not as a divided but as a united nation.[5]

The military campaign against the Germans in South West Africa was successfully completed within a year, but it was accompanied by events which constituted a great tragedy for Botha and Smuts person-

[3] Ibid., cols. 77–78.
[4] Ibid., cols. 84–85, 89.
[5] Ibid., cols. 62–63.

ally and left a heritage of bitterness. Some Boer War comrades of Botha and Smuts staged a rebellion, which was suppressed without great difficulty, but the fratricidal strife incited many Afrikaners to embittered republicanism. Botha and Smuts were henceforth regarded by many as renegade Afrikaners. The war did not unite the people of South Africa, as Prime Minister Botha had hoped, but divided them more deeply.

The parliamentary election in October 1915 indicated how deeply the country was divided. The Nationalists won 78,186 of the popular votes to 94,317 for the South African party and 49,619 for the Unionists. The Nationalists won 30 percent of the popular votes. Exclusive of Natal, where they received less than 2,000 votes, they won 43 percent of the poll to 49 percent for the South African party. The Botha ministry was a minority government; it remained in power on sufferance of the Unionist party.

After the conquest of South West Africa the Union government undertook to send 20,000 men to East Africa and early in 1916 Smuts accepted the invitation of the British government to take command of the army in that theater—a polyglot force of whites, Indians, and Africans. He faced an army smaller and less well equipped but commanded by an able and resourceful leader, General Paul von Lettow Vorbeck. Smuts did not succeed in catching the German general nor in completely destroying his forces, but he drove him into the wastelands of the south of the territory and across the frontier into Mozambique where he was rendered relatively harmless.

SMUTS: IMPERIAL STATESMAN

In March 1917 Smuts went to London to represent South Africa at an imperial conference. The Union had already rendered the Empire great service; its influence in the imperial councils now rose to remarkable heights, and the personal position of Smuts became such as few men have enjoyed. British statesmen and the public soon acclaimed this former bitter enemy as one of their own and sought his views and advice on the most important matters. They bestowed upon him every honor at their disposal. Smuts had planned to return to South Africa in May but the British political leaders urged him to stay longer. "So deep was the impression that General Smuts made at this time upon his colleagues, nay upon the nation," wrote Prime Minister David Lloyd George later, "that we would not let him leave us when the Conference ended. We insisted on keeping him here to help us at the centre with our war efforts."[6]

In his letters to his wife, General Smuts wrote in glowing terms of his reception, the importance of his work, and of his great influence in England. "I am told," he wrote on June 9, 1917, "that I have made an amazing impression on the public by my activities. . . . My speeches are now being printed in pamphlet form."[7] On August 29 he wrote, "My work here is really very important and I do not see how I can be spared here in the immediate future. . . . I am even asked to Russia."[8] On October 5 he wrote Mrs. Smuts that "there is the greatest demand for my services here."[9]

Smuts remained in London until after the Paris Peace Conference. He was offered and declined the command of the Allied forces in Palestine (May 1917), but he accepted appointment to membership in the War Cabinet.[10] There he rendered valuable services. He helped organize the war effort, formulating plans for the defense of London, playing a leading role in establishing the Royal Air Force, and with Milner arranging for unity of command in France. He participated in making strategic decisions.[11] Much as he was concerned about military organization and strategy, Smuts was even more interested in preparations for the peace settlement. Here is where a student of South African foreign policy meets a problem. To what extent did Smuts's views represent South African opinion? Botha and Smuts were the official spokesmen of the Union, but they represented a minority government. However that may be, Smuts's influence was very great.

[6] *War Memoirs*, 4:1766. Smuts was asked to help with other problems, as, for example, the Irish problem.

[7] W. K. Hancock and Jean van der Poel, eds., *Selections from the Smuts Papers*, 4 vols. (Cambridge, Eng., 1966), 3:350.

[8] Ibid., p. 538.

[9] Ibid., p. 554.

[10] Smuts suggested to Lloyd George that he approach the United States government about putting him (Smuts) in command of the American forces in Europe. He questioned General Pershing's competency and pressed his own "unusual experience and qualifications" (Hancock and van der Poel, eds., *Smuts Papers*, 3:661–62).

[11] In February Smuts, with Leopold S. Amery, was sent by the War Cabinet to the Middle East to study the war situation there. For these aspects of Smuts's war activities in England see Hancock, *Smuts*, 1:432ff.

The views of General Smuts on the conduct of the war and the making of the peace were strongly colored by his peoples' and his own bitter experience as a defeated people. He could feel for the German people. But he was equally mindful of the magnanimity of the British after the Boer War. He emphasized the primacy of the political over the military factors, and while he admitted the need for a substantial military victory he disliked the idea of unconditional surrender. If possible, he favored a negotiated peace rather than a dictated peace, but for this idea Smuts received no support from either the Germans or the Americans. The collapse of Russia made the Germans arrogant. While the United States was neutral, President Woodrow Wilson talked about a peace without victory, but after entrance into the war he demanded total destruction of German militarism. Probably because of his background and views the War Cabinet sent Smuts to Switzerland in December 1917 to discuss the prospects of peace with Count Mensdorff, the representative of the Austrian Foreign Minister Count Czernin. The two men held similar views on basic postwar policies and organization, but Mensdorff wanted to discuss the terms of a general peace, and Smuts, in accordance with his instructions, sought to detach Austria from Germany by inducing it to sign a separate peace. Austria was unwilling to desert Germany, but Smuts was convinced that it would exert influence on Germany to enter into general peace negotiations, as Austria had about reached the limits of its endurance.[12]

As a preliminary step to active participation in determining foreign policy Smuts had to fight a skirmish on the constitutional structure of the Commonwealth. Imperial federation, as some influential figures desired, would have left little if any room for an independent external or defense policy on the part of the Dominions. Such a plan was put forward at the 1911 Imperial Conference by Sir Joseph Ward, prime minister of New Zealand, inspired by Lionel Curtis. Botha, at that conference, joined forces with Sir Wilfrid Laurier, prime minister of Canada, to defeat the Ward-Curtis plan. Smuts continued this fight at the Imperial War Conference in 1917. He succeeded in winning the adoption of a resolution which fairly well settled that issue. The resolution stated that the question should form the subject of a special imperial conference to be convened as soon as possible after the war, but the 1917 conference placed on record its view that any readjustment

[12] Ibid., 1:466–68.

of imperial constitutional relations, "while thoroughly preserving all existing powers of self-government and complete control of domestic affairs, should be based upon a full recognition of the Dominions as autonomous nations of an Imperial Commonwealth, . . . should recognize the right of the Dominions and India to an adequate voice in foreign policy and in foreign relations, and should provide effective arrangements for continuous consultation in all important matters of common Imperial concern, and for such necessary concerted action, founded on consultation, as the several governments may determine."[13] The resolution purposely left some legal points vague, if not ambiguous, but it did set the constitutional development of the Empire, here called the Commonwealth, directly on the road to the Statute of Westminster of 1931.[14]

Smuts was also successful in getting an early commitment from the War Cabinet for the support of a world organization for peace. He became convinced that a world organization modeled after the British Commonwealth was necessary if the risk of future wars was to be reduced. The War Cabinet affirmed "in principle that some form of conference or conciliation among the Powers should be established to deal with international disputes not susceptible to arbitration or judicial procedure." The Cabinet felt that the details of the scheme should be discussed with the British allies and especially the United States before the end of the war, and that the scheme to promote future peace should, "if possible, be embodied in the peace treaty itself."[15]

General Smuts submitted his ideas on the organization and functions of the League of Nations to the Imperial War Cabinet on December 16, 1918.[16] To combat the impression that the League of Nations was not really a matter of practical politics, he had drawn in rough outline what appeared to him a practical, workable scheme. Apparently his idea of the place and functions of the League had grown over the months. If the League was to be a success it would have to occupy a much greater

[13] Imperial War Conference, 1917, *Extracts from Minutes of Proceedings and Papers Laid before the Conference*, Cd., 8566 (London, 1917), p. 45.

[14] A year later the Imperial War Conference recommended official communications between the British and Dominion governments be direct instead of through the secretary of state and the governor general (Hancock, *Smuts*, 1:469).

[15] Hancock and van der Poel, eds., *Smuts Papers*, 3:477, 21 April 1917.

[16] This paper was published under the title *The League of Nations: A Practical Suggestion* (London, 1918), pp. vi, 71.

position and perform many other functions than those ordinarily assigned to it. "Peace and War are the resultants of many complex
forces," he stated, "and those forces will have to be gripped at an earlier
stage of their growth if peace is to be effectively maintained." The
League would have to occupy the great position which had been rendered vacant by the destruction of the old European empires and the
passing of the old European order, and it should be put "into the very
forefront of the programme of the Peace Conference, and be made the
point of departure for the solution of many of the grave problems with
which it will be confronted."

Smuts was deeply concerned about the political implications of military action and developments. He was especially concerned with bringing the United States into the war as a permanent ally of Britain and the
Dominions. He emphasized the moral value even more than the political
value of the United States' entry into the war. There would grow up "on
the battlefields of France not only new armies but a new spirit of
comradeship between the English-speaking peoples."[17]

With these views, Smuts was naturally very eager to get the backing
of President Wilson for the League, so as to insure continued United
States involvement in world affairs. He was pleased that their views
were similar in important respects.[18] Smuts had several long talks with
Wilson about the conception of a world organization. After spending all
evening discussing the League of Nations with Wilson and Lord Robert
Cecil he wrote that Wilson's ideas seemed "mostly taken from my
pamphlet. Even my mistakes are appropriated."[19] When the draft of the
Covenant was completed and published, Smuts was pleased with it. "It
is almost entirely my original conception and I am naturally pleased at
the acceptance of my ideas," he wrote a friend.[20]

It is remarkable how many of Smuts's points or suggestions were
incorporated in the Covenant of the League of Nations. Within brief
compass he discussed most of the basic problems of international
organization. But the League was not given the position in international

[17] Hancock and van der Poel, eds., *Smuts Papers*, 3:639ff.

[18] He wrote on 12 Nov. 1918 that Wilson in a recent address had anticipated
much that he planned to say in a speech on the following night (Letter to M. C.
Gillette, ibid., 4:5–6).

[19] To M. C. Gillett on 20 Jan. 1919, ibid., pp. 49–50.

[20] Letter to A. Clark, ibid., p. 71.

society which Smuts said in his early pages was necessary if the League was to last; it had to be "a great organ of the ordinary peaceful life of civilization."

Smuts was an idealist, but also a practical politician and statesman. He sought as much as possible to safeguard the three chief interests of South Africa—security, status, and virtual territorial expansion—in his scheme for world organization. A main organ of the world body was to be a general conference composed of all the members of the League and each with an equal vote. The British Dominions were to be separately members of this body. He laid down the principle of no annexation of enemy territories by the victorious powers, but he outlined a system of mandate administration which in the case of South West Africa would make the Union the administrator with practically sovereign powers.[21]

The war ended sooner and differently than General Smuts had expected. He thought that the war would continue for many more months, if not years, and he hoped that it would end before Germany collapsed as Russia had. Only in this case was a reasonable peace likely; a total victory was almost certain to lead to a vindictive peace provocative of future wars. As the peace terms were being hammered out and the situation in Europe deteriorated, he became increasingly pessimistic about the future and pinned his hopes more and more on the League of Nations. Immediately after the armistice he was quite optimistic. "The inert mass is visibly heaving and the leaven is working," he wrote to Gilbert Murray on November 12, 1918. "The immediate future is very fateful. The old, immobile world is once more fluid, and the creator can once more mould it to better ends."[22] In a letter to another friend he had written January 2, 1918, "May the peace be, not a German peace or an English peace, but God's peace enveloping all the erring nations as with arms of an Everlasting Mercy."[23] But to Lord Lansdowne he wrote a month later, "There is so much confusion and uncertainty in the international situation today that the peace means to me little more than

---

[21] That this was his object would seem to be clear from a passage in a letter to his friend Leopold S. Amery on 21 Mar. 1919: "While deploring your cynicism on the League of Nations, I agree with you that in cases B and C, the German territory should be vested in the mandatory state, and the draft mandates I prepared before leaving Paris have this in view" (ibid., pp. 78–79).

[22] Ibid., pp. 4–5.

[23] Ibid., 3:585.

the creation of something like the League of Nations that will really work."[24] By June he saw the League as the only alternative to a complete breakdown, but he had lost some of his earlier optimism.[25] To a friend he wrote, "The League of Nations is the only bright spot in a situation of unrelieved gloom."[26]

South Africa was allotted two representatives at the Paris Peace Conference, which was the same as for the small independent states such as Belgium and Serbia. Smuts contrasted his position with that at Vereeniging seventeen years earlier. "There we had to drink the cup to the bitter lees; here South Africa is a victor among the great nations." He was thankful that he had been given a role to play.[27] Moreover, South Africa was given membership and representation in the League of Nations separately from Britain and as an independent state.

Smuts became increasingly concerned about the terms of the peace treaty. He was critical of the clauses dealing with the military occupation, the Saar Basin, reparations, Germany's eastern frontier, punishment, military and air restrictions, and international rivers and railways.[28] He feared that the treaty would have dire consequences. The terms either would not be accepted, or if accepted would not be carried out. They would "leave a trail of anarchy, ruin and bitterness in their wake for another generation . . . [and] outrage the sense of fairness of decent people." He was in a quandary as to what he should do. He did not want to attack his own side during the negotiations, but if he waited it might be too late.[29] On May 20 he wrote to his wife that he might not sign the treaty, which was "not a peace treaty but a war treaty." Germany was being treated "as we would not treat a Kaffir nation." To a friend he wrote that the treaty meant "a new cycle of wars and woes for the world."[30] He did not mince words with Lloyd George about the treaty which, he said, breathed "a poisonous spirit of revenge."[31] The point he stressed was that the treaty was a breach of faith; it was not

[24] Ibid., 4:351.
[25] To A. Clark, 6 June 1919, ibid., pp. 231–32.
[26] To M. C. Gillett, 16 June 1919, ibid., p. 233.
[27] To Mrs. Smuts, 15 Jan. 1919, ibid., 4:43–46.
[28] Memo to Lloyd George, 22 May 1919, ibid., 4:183ff.
[29] To M. C. Gillett, ibid., 4:141. To Alice Clark he wrote, 2 May 1919, that the world might "lapse into complete chaos" (ibid., 4:140).
[30] To M. C. Gillett, 20 May 1919, ibid., p. 179.
[31] Ibid., pp. 219–21.

the kind of treaty that had been promised the people and the Germans. "The breach of this solemn agreement will end the war (as it began) with a scrap of paper."[32] On March 26, Smuts in a memo to Lloyd George voiced his alarm. To him it seemed clear and elementary that to destroy Germany was to destroy Europe and that Europe could not be saved without the cooperation of Germany.[33]

Prime Minister Lloyd George did not fail to make a thrust on Smuts's weak side—that of being generous at the expense of others. The Germans had asked repeatedly for the return of their colonies; was Smuts prepared to restore German South West and East Africa as a concession to induce Germany to sign the treaty? The Germans were complaining about the treatment of their businesses in South Africa; was Smuts prepared to make similar concessions here?[34] Smuts's reply was not direct. In this great business South West Africa was as dust in the balance compared to the burdens which were hanging over the civilized world, he wrote. The repercussion of the treaty in South Africa would be tremendous. It might make the position of men like General Botha and himself very difficult, if not impossible.[35] These high-minded sentiments, however, were not accompanied by an offer to give up the Union's demand for control of South West Africa. Smuts was prophetic about what the peace treaty might do to his position among his fellow Afrikaners. This was to come to a head twenty years later when World War II broke out.

Smuts received little more consideration from President Wilson with respect to his indictment of many of the terms of peace. Wilson agreed with Smuts that the treaty was severe, but not on the whole unjust, much as he would have liked the alteration of certain features. His thoughts inevitably went back "to the very great offence against civilization which the German state committed, and the necessity for making it evident once for all that such things can lead only to the most severe punishment."[36]

Botha and Smuts steadily pressed for the right of the Union to maintain an independent position on foreign policy. Botha wrote to

---

[32] To M. C. Gillett, 1 June 1919, ibid., p. 211.
[33] Ibid., pp. 83ff.
[34] Ibid., p. 218.
[35] Ibid., pp. 219–20.
[36] Letter from Wilson to Smuts, 16 May 1919, ibid., pp. 160–61.

Lloyd George on May 6, 1919, urging that the British Empire should not agree to go to France's assistance in case of an unprovoked German attack unless the Senate of the United States ratified the treaty. "If your undertaking is to bind the Dominions also I trust you will give us another opportunity to discuss the matter," wrote Botha.[37]

As late as June 23 Smuts said he would not sign the treaty. General Botha felt that he had to sign the treaty, for if he did not the Union would not be a member of the League of Nations. Smuts disliked the consequences which would result from his refusal to sign and act in agreement with Botha. Afrikaners would conclude that real differences had arisen between the two leaders. The English-speaking section of the South African population would not like nor understand Smuts's action, nor soon forgive him. It would also mean, so Smuts thought, that he could not succeed Botha as prime minister.[38] On June 24 he announced that he would sign after all as "any other course would make the position of General Botha (who must sign) indefensible and impossible."[39] In a statement to the press on June 28, he explained that he had signed the peace treaty not because he considered it a satisfactory document, but because it was necessary to end the war. The world needed peace above all.[40]

In a farewell statement on leaving England for home he summarized what he thought the war and peace treaty had meant for the Empire: "The Dominions have been well launched on their great career; their status of complete nationhood has now received international recognition, and as members of the Britannic League, they will henceforth go forward on terms of equal brotherhood with the other nations on the great paths of the world. The successful launching of her former colonies among the nations of the world while they remain members of an inner Britannic circle will ever rank as one of the outstanding achievements of British political genius."[41]

[37] Ibid., p. 150.

[38] To M. C. Gillett, ibid., pp. 244–45.

[39] Ibid., p. 247.

[40] Ibid., pp. 256–59. On the margin of his agenda paper Botha wrote, "This day I think back to May 31, 1902" [the date of the signing of the Peace of Vereeniging] F. V. Engelenburg, *Generaal Louis Botha*, Afrikaans ed., [Johannesburg, 1928], p. 298).

[41] Hancock and van der Poel, eds., *Smuts Papers*, 4:268–75.

General Hertzog, as the leader of the National party, carried on a campaign for independence during the war. Though he represented a minority of the total population, indeed only a minority of a minority section, he pressed his demands in universal terms—the inherent, inalienable right of nations to independence. Apparently he thought that the Afrikaners constituted the only authentic nation in South Africa. He and his followers were also stimulated by the slogans of President Wilson and Prime Minister Lloyd George about self-determination and the rights of small nations. At the National party congress held in January 1919, Hertzog took Lloyd George and Wilson at their word. Convinced that Afrikaner convictions and sentiments could best be brought to the knowledge of the British government by their own delegation, the congress decided to send a delegation to London and the Paris Peace Conference to demand "in conformity with the right of self-determination, the full and complete independence of a completely sovereign state."[42]

The delegation of nine, headed by General Hertzog and including another future prime minister, D. F. Malan, arrived in New York on April 1 and proceeded to London on the nineteenth and thence to Paris. The delegation had sent Wilson a cablegram, but he refused to receive them. They had a meeting with Lloyd George, and General Hertzog made a plea for the restoration of independence to the two former Boer republics. Lloyd George interjected questions occasionally. He asked whether there was a single instance of the imposition of regulation or law by the British government or Parliament. Hertzog admitted there was none, but because of the subordination of South Africa to Britain the Union ministers took positions and carried out policies which they would not have made their own but for the British connection.

Lloyd George gave his formal reply to the delegation several weeks later. He contended that the delegation did not represent all the people of South Africa but only a political party drawn from the Afrikaans-

[42] For a sympathetic account of this mission see C. M. van den Heever, *Generaal J. B. M. Hertzog*, Afrikaans ed. (Johannesburg, 1944), Hoofstuk [Chapter] 9. See also the interesting account of the mission by D. F. Malan, *Afrikaner Volkseenheid en my Ervarings op die Pad Daarheen* [Afrikaner National Unity and My Experiences on the Path Thereto] (Cape Town, 1959), pp. 56–64. The Nationalist delegation made a report in 1919—*Verslag Onafhankelykheidsdeputaise* [Independence delegation report].

speaking people. Moreover, the natives did not want independence but wished to remain in the Empire. The whole matter was an internal question and it was the policy of the British government not to interfere in such matters in self-governing parts of the Empire. The Union had been created as the result of a general desire on the part of South Africans. The delegation seemed to desire a return to a Balkanized South Africa as indicated by their demand for independence for the Transvaal and the Free State. This was no longer possible. South Africa was one of the Dominions of the British confederation which determined its own national future in the fullest sense. South Africa participated in imperial conferences on a basis of absolute equality. In conclusion, Lloyd George stated that he addressed them not only as the British prime minister but also as a tested friend and as one who wished the best for the Dutch people, and he himself was a member of one of the small nations of the British Empire.[43]

The sending of the National delegation to London and Paris naturally produced sharp reactions in South Africa. Government leaders and supporters asserted that the delegation, by appealing for outside intervention, had set a dangerous precedent. How would the Nationalists react if Indians and Bantu called on Downing Street for intervention? Great Britain had not the least right to declare the Transvaal and the Free State independent, for they belonged to the Union. What right did the delegation have to expect President Wilson to help the minority against the majority?[44]

The Nationalists were not altogether unhappy about the results of the mission. The highest British political authority had stated that the Union possessed the right of self-determination in the fullest sense of the word, including the right of secession. The constitutional right to carry on a campaign for a republic had been recognized.[45]

---

[43] It is evident from Hertzog's reactions and those of his biographer, van den Heever, that the Nationalists felt themselves at a psychological disadvantage in their rivalry with the English-speaking part of South Africa because the latter belonged to the dominant people of the Empire.

[44] South African Party, *Beweging tot Ontbanding van de Unie en Verbreking van de Konnektie tussen Suid Afrika en Groot Britanje* [Movement toward Dissolution of the Union and Severance of the Connection between South Africa and Great Britain] (Cape Town, 1919).

[45] Malan, *Afrikaner Volkseenheid*, pp. 62–63.

THE LEAGUE OF NATIONS

Smuts as prime minister gave the League of Nations his ardent support. In an unusual move, he appointed Lord Robert Cecil, one of the architects of the League and one of its most loyal champions, as South Africa's representative at the League's 1920 Assembly. This appointment was noteworthy not only because Lord Robert was a non-South African but also because he was not in favor with the British government of the day. Smuts feared that the League was getting off to a bad start because the great powers were using it to advance their own interests. He instructed Cecil to press for the admission to the League of the ex-enemy powers and Russia.[46]

At the Paris Peace Conference Smuts had opposed giving the League of Nations real power to apply military sanctions. He opposed the Geneva Protocol and all attempts to extend the military commitments of League members. The League was to maintain peace by conference and not by coercion.[47]

If Smuts had really believed that South Africa's "C" Mandate to administer South West Africa was practically the equivalent of annexation he was soon to discover otherwise. In 1922 when the administrator of the territory took punitive measures against an unruly tribe, the Bondelzwarts, the action received worldwide publicity, much of it critical.[48] Affairs of this type were common occurrences in Africa and Asia, but because South West Africa was a mandated territory it received more than usual attention.[49]

EMPIRE AND COMMONWEALTH

Smuts's work in obtaining for the Dominions an improved status was a matter of great importance to him. "I cannot and never shall forget we were free republics," he wrote to his wife from London.[50] He wrote her

[46] Hancock, *Smuts*, 2:37.

[47] See Chapter 8.

[48] One hundred and fifteen members of the tribe were killed and two members of the government forces. The Bondelzwarts were of mixed blood; they spoke Afrikaans and were Christians.

[49] See Hancock, *Smuts*, 2:100–110, for an account of the Bondelzwarts affair.

[50] Hancock and van der Poel, eds., *Smuts Papers*, 3:473–74, 5 April 1917.

later that he had told the British government that "we no longer want to remain subordinate parts of the British Empire, but wish to be regarded as equal nations on a level with the English nation."[51] Yet there remained an ambiguity in his views of the Commonwealth, probably because he held two ideals which could not easily be harmonized—the ideals of unity and freedom. When the Hertzog independence delegation returned to Cape Town, Parliament was in session and members of the delegation immediately asked Smuts, then prime minister, whether he agreed with Lloyd George's statement that South Africa possessed the right of self-determination to the fullest degree, he answered with a decisive "No."[52] Apparently Smuts held the view that the Dominions possessed all sovereign rights except that of secession.

The great contribution of Smuts was in loosening the ties of Empire and in obtaining recognition of the autonomy of the Dominions. The freedom of the members having been assured, he became concerned about the unity of the Empire. He had addressed himself to this problem in a cursory way in a speech on May 15, 1917.[53] If there was going to be "all this enormous development towards a more varied and richer life among all its parts," how was this world to be held together? He suggested there were two potent factors which should be relied upon. These were the hereditary kingship, "which is really not very different from a hereditary republic," and the imperial conference system. There should "be called together the most important rulers of the Empire, say, once a year, to discuss matters which concern all parts of the Empire in common, in order that causes of friction and misunderstanding may be prevented or removed," and to lay down a common policy in common matters concerning the Empire as a whole, and to determine the true orientation of our common Imperial policy." In this same speech Smuts said that the Empire was not a state, but "a system of nations." Yet he referred to the Dominions as "almost independent States." Smuts was a lawyer, but this was scarcely legal language. He seems to have envisaged a common foreign policy for all the British Empire, but if the imperial conference had the power to bind all its members, the latter would not be sovereign. The freedom Smuts wanted for the Dominions could be assured only at the expense of unity and the unity for which he yearned

[51] Ibid., p. 495, 5 May 1917.
[52] Malan, *Afrikaner Volkseenheid*, p. 63.
[53] For this speech see *Plans for a Better World* (London, 1942), pp. 31ff.

could be obtained only at the cost of freedom. Neither Smuts nor anyone else could resolve this difficulty. As the Commonwealth expanded by the addition of new states differing widely in geographic environment, culture, development, and interests this unity became more and more rarified and elusive.

The Empire had to be decentralized first and Smuts's role was as a leader in promoting this movement. He strongly asserted dominion freedom, always carefully avoiding the use of the word independence. In a letter that he drafted for Prime Minister Botha to Lloyd George about the treaty of guarantee for France, he suggested that in some future continental war Great Britain might be at war and one or more of the Dominions might stand out and maintain neutrality. "But that result is inevitable, and flows from the status of independent nationhood of the Dominions."[54]

The Imperial Conference, which the Imperial War Cabinet in 1917 resolved would meet as soon as possible after the war to consider the readjustment of the constitutional relations of the Dominions, met in 1921. The opposition in Parliament was attacking both South Africa's involvement in the League of Nations and the dangers of the loss of freedom at the coming conference.

General Hertzog advised Smuts to take as little part as possible in the discussion of the policy of the Empire and not to give advice, for if he did so he would also become morally responsible for the policy. With respect to constitutional development of the Empire he held that South Africa must either separate from the Empire or give up her rights. The one meant breaking up the Empire, the other meant that the Union would become a subject state. The Nationalists advocated separation.

Smuts replied that Hertzog's fear of a new constitution which would bind together parts of the Empire was groundless. The whole trend was toward more "perfect liberty and freedom of each part of the Empire." He could not conceive of this movement being suddenly and artificially reversed by this conference. The Commonwealth was a group of nations working together under one king and pursuing, he hoped, the same peaceful and humanitarian ends. He could conceive of the movement being a great success. "If they failed, the League of Nations must fail also, and failure would be writ large all over the world."[55]

[54] Hancock and van der Poel, eds. *Smuts Papers*, 4:158–59, 15 May 1919.
[55] *Cape Times* (Cape Town), 26 May 1921. Smuts held that the League of

Smuts admitted that the League had not made a very auspicious beginning, but there were reasons for this and he believed the League would establish itself. It represented a great hope for a world beset by troubles. He asserted that the Empire could continue only on the basis of complete freedom and equality. He admitted that certain practices needed to be brought in line with the new situation. Formal correspondence between the Union and British government should be no longer through the Colonial Office; the governor general should represent the king only and not the British government; South Africa should no longer conduct its relations with foreign governments through the British Foreign Office, it should have its own representatives abroad.

Smuts submitted a memorandum to the conference in which all of these ideas were incorporated. His proposals were as sweeping and more specific than the principles promulgated in the Balfour Declaration of 1926, but he encountered the determined opposition of Prime Minister W. H. Hughes of Australia who would have nothing of constitutional change. Hughes opposed loosening of the bonds; he asserted that the need was to concert imperial policies. What was the point in discussing policy problems if no agreement was reached on some of them? Hughes carried the conference with him, at least negatively. Five years later the situation was quite different and Hertzog had no difficulty in getting the conference to adopt the substance of Smuts's proposals.[56]

"BLOCKADE" OF THE NETHERLANDS
AND THE IRISH QUESTION

Smuts's critics at home complained that he neglected South Africa for imperial and world affairs and problems. Had people in England known

---

Nations had added "a new bond of cohesion to the Empire" and that the Commonwealth strengthened the League (Imperial Conference, 1923, *Appendices to the Summary of Proceedings*, Cmd. 1988 [London, 1923], p. 61). His friend Leopold S. Amery, on the other hand, writing at a later date concluded that the League did "no irretrievable damage," but for a time it seriously weakened a sense of common interest and a common responsibility as it offered an easy pretext to shirk real responsibilities. (*My Political Life* [London, 1953], 2:163).

[56] For an account of Smuts's work at the 1921 Imperial Conference see Hancock, *Smuts*, 2:38ff. He stressed the need for peace and an Empire policy for the reduction of armaments and pleaded for a policy of close understanding with the United States (Imperial Conference, 1921, *Summary of Proceedings and Documents*, Cmd. 1474 [London, 1923]).

about the extent of Smuts's influence on imperial and even United Kingdom problems, there might have been protests. London was not intervening in Union affairs and policies, but South Africa through Smuts was profoundly influencing British policy. Two striking examples of this may be cited. The first involved the Dutch neutral convoy. As a result of the British blockade and other actions, commerce between the Netherlands and her colonies virtually had ceased by the early months of 1918. The need to send several cargoes of military supplies and government goods and personnel to the East Indies had become urgent. The Dutch government proposed sending a convoy as a way of meeting the problem. When informed of the Dutch plan the British government objected, stating that it would "exercise the belligerent's right of visit and search" if the proposal were carried out. The British government obviously was prepared for drastic action when it suddenly relented and consented to let the convoy through if certain conditions were met.[57] The reason for the change of attitude may have been an interposition by Smuts in the War Cabinet that "he could not take part in a course of action that might lead to war with Holland."[58]

The second instance was Smuts's intervention in the Irish question. In a letter of May 9, 1918, he urged Lloyd George not to press the Home Rule bill as it was almost certain to fail and its failure would cause the government to fall. "Why start on a journey," he wrote, "which must inevitably lead to ruin. The existence of this country and the British Empire is at stake. . . . My advice in regard to this matter was not followed once before, *viz.* not to touch conscription in Ireland until Home Rule was an accomplished fact. Even so I would again tender you advice."[59]

When Smuts was in London for the 1921 Imperial Conference he was invited to Windsor Castle for lunch. He found King George preoccupied with a serious problem. Prime Minister Lloyd George had requested the king to go to Belfast to open the North Ireland Parliament. King George was reluctant to do so; he feared that his visit would offend South Ireland. He expressed his reluctance to Smuts, who saw that the occasion might be used to enable the government through the king to

[57] See Amry Vandenbosch, *Neutrality of the Netherlands in the World War* (Grand Rapids, Mich., 1927), Chapter 16, "Neutral Convoy."

[58] CAB 23/6. minute 9, 6 June 1918, W. C. 427.

[59] Hancock and van der Poel, eds., *Smuts Papers,* 3:634–36.

announce a new policy of peace. King George was much impressed with Smuts's suggestion and asked him to send a sketch of such a speech to the prime minister. This Smuts did, with a powerful argument for a change of Irish policy. While his guest in Dublin, Smuts urged Eamon De Valera to accept the British invitation to a conference to discuss a settlement along the lines of dominion status. According to Smuts, De Valera was convinced finally and said that if dominion status was offered him he would use his influence to get the Irish people to accept it. The South African statesman had rendered an invaluable service.[60]

THE INDIAN QUESTION

Smuts freely gave advice to peoples and statesmen on situations and problems which he believed threatened the peace and was widely praised for his liberal views on world politics. His protest against the harsh terms of the Treaty of Versailles, his public criticism of France for its occupation of the Ruhr, and his efforts for a settlement of the Irish question led *The Times* (London) and others to acclaim him as a peacemaker. But when India brought the treatment of Indians in the Dominions before the Imperial Conferences of 1921 and 1923, Smuts found himself in the opposite role. The holistic philosopher and world statesman was forced back into the role of a South African politician fighting for his political life. His government was in real danger of losing control of Parliament; a lukewarm fight against the Indian position at the Imperial Conference certainly would have sealed its doom.[61]

The first Indians came to South Africa in 1860 as indentured servants for employment in sugar production in Natal. At the end of the indenture service, which was three years, they had the choice of returning to India at the expense of the government, signing up for another period of indenture, or accepting a piece of crown land in South Africa. The great majority chose freedom and the crown land. Between 1865 and 1874 there was no Indian immigration due to the Indian govern-

[60] Hancock, *Smuts*, 2:50ff.; Harold Nicolson, *King George the Fifth: His Life and Reign* (London, 1952), pp. 355–56.

[61] His waning political support was very probably a motive in Smuts's seeking to induce South Rhodesia to join the Union. The English greatly outnumbered the Afrikaners in this territory and would most likely furnish Smuts and his party much needed support in Parliament.

ment's dissatisfaction with the treatment accorded to Indians, but in 1874 immigration was resumed. Two new provisions were added to the terms of the contract: the period of service was extended to five years and the laborer could not return to India until after he had resided in the country for ten years. These changes were made to ensure laborers, the need for which was very great. Indian traders from Mauritius and India also came in considerable numbers. By 1891 in Natal there were 35,763 Indians to 46,788 Europeans and 455,983 natives. It was generally recognized that Natal's great prosperity was due to cheap Indian labor and Indian traders.[62]

As the number of free Indians increased they became rivals and competitors of the white colonists in business. The sugar planters and industrialists did not want this source of cheap, reliable labor cut off, but the European traders and the public in general wanted Indian immigration stopped or drastically controlled. The Indians were classified as coloreds and since they were British subjects they possessed the right to vote in both municipal and parliamentary elections. The whites began to fear that their presence threatened Western civilization and so began to demand that the Indian laborers return to India at the expiration of their contracts. To exert pressure on them to return home, the government imposed a yearly tax of £3 on each Indian who remained in South Africa after the period of indenture. Furthermore, Natal resorted to a system of licensing traders, which in its administration was so injurious to them that the government of India decided to put a stop to coolie emigration as reprisal. So great a clamor was raised by industrialists that the Natal government urged New Delhi to reconsider its decision. On the assurance that licensing officers would be required to state their reasons for the refusal of licenses and that Indians denied trading licenses would have the right of appeal to the Supreme Court, India agreed to continue the immigrant labor policy. In 1896 Natal abolished the Indians' parliamentary franchise.

Asians were excluded from the Orange Free State[63] and were subject to vexatious restrictions in the Transvaal with respect to residence,

[62] For a survey of the Indian question see G. H. Calpin, *Indians in South Africa* (Pietermaritzburg, 1949); for a presentation of the government's point of view see the pamphlet, Union of South Africa Government Information Office, *The Indian in South Africa* (New York, n.d., [ca. 1947]).

[63] There were only twenty-nine resident in that province at the time of the 1936 census and only seven in 1960.

trade, and property ownership. As soon as the Transvaal was granted self-government, new restrictions were placed on the Indians. Under the leadership of an Indian lawyer who became one of the world's most unusual and greatest leaders, the Indians offered resistance to the enforcement of these laws in ways which often baffled the government. Mohandas K. Gandhi came to South Africa in 1893 to appear for Indian clients in Durban. He remained to practice law, first in Durban and then in Johannesburg. It was in this South African situation that he developed his ideas and tactics of passive resistance. In this struggle he encountered Jan Smuts, who, as a member of the Transvaal government, was assigned the task of dealing with the Indian resistance. The conflict ended in compromise. The objectionable features of the legislation were repealed, but further Asian immigration was prohibited by the Transvaal.

In 1904, the date of the last census before union, there were 122,311 Asians in South Africa, constituting 2.4 percent of the total population.[64] In 1911 India put an end to the recruitment of indentured laborers, but free Indians continued to come to South Africa and they were no longer welcomed by the general public.

With the formation of the Union the regulation of Indian affairs became a function of the central government. In 1912 S. K. Gokhale, a moderate Indian nationalist and a member of the viceroy's Legislative Council, visited South Africa to examine the conditions there as they affected Indians. He believed that Smuts, on behalf of the Union government, had promised him the repeal of the £3 tax on Indians in Natal, but Botha and Smuts denied any such commitment. The Indians were also incensed over a recent Supreme Court decision invalidating Indian marriages. Gandhi organized a demonstration and marched an army of pilgrims from Natal into Transvaal where they were arrested and imprisoned for illegal entry. The awkwardness and expense of imprisoning thousands of men and the general outcry as well as the emphatic protest of the viceroy of India and the personal plea of Emily Hobhouse to Smuts led the Union government to negotiate.[65] In con-

---

[64] By 1951 the Indian population in Natal surpassed that of the whites. The percentage of Indians in the Union population declined from 2.4 in 1904 to 2.3 in 1936 and then increased to 3.0 in 1960.

[65] Hancock, *Smuts*, 2:338. Emily Hobhouse was an English social worker and reformer who was opposed to the Boer War and exposed abuses in the British concentration camps in South Africa.

formity with the settlement which was reached between Gandhi and Smuts, the Union Parliament passed the Indian Relief Act (July 1914), which repealed the £3 tax and affirmed the validity of Indian marriages. An understanding was reached that the vested rights of Indians would be respected.[66]

Gandhi went back to India never to return to South Africa. Smuts hoped that his agreement with Gandhi would settle the Indian question for good; this, however, proved to be anything but the case. In less than a decade he had to fight the battle all over, this time on the difficult imperial stage, and nearly three decades later he had to endure a savage, humiliating attack from the Indians on the world stage. A more restrictive and discriminatory law had been enacted in 1919, but even this did not satisfy many. There were demands in Parliament from members of Smuts's own party for compulsory segregation or the wholesale expulsion of Indians from the country.

India's delegation brought the status and treatment of Indians in the Empire before the Imperial Conferences of 1921 and 1923. At first India moved a resolution claiming for Indians resident in the Dominions the right to acquire full citizenship in their place of residence. Even if he had wanted to, Smuts could not accept this resolution and retain political power in South Africa. He argued that the extension of the franchise to Indians would have disastrous consequences for them. As a small minority in the black mass of the population their protection was in political inequality with the whites, for if equal political rights were granted to the Indians, the same would have to be given the blacks. With the natives politically dominant the plight of the Indians would become worse.[67]

Indian sensitivity had heightened between the 1921 and the 1923

[66] Gandhi was no extremist in his views or demands. He was not without understanding of or sympathy with the white settlers' point of view. (see Hancock, *Smuts*, 1:326, who quotes from M. K. Gandhi, *My Experiments with Truth*, 2d ed. [Ahmedabad, 1940]).

[67] Imperial Conference, 1921, *Summary of Proceedings and Documents*, Cmd. 1474. The 1921 conference reaffirmed the right of the Dominions to regulate immigration from any of the other "communities" but declared that it recognized that there was "an incongruity between the position of India as an equal member of the British Empire and the existence of disabilities upon British Indians lawfully domiciled in some other parts of the Empire" and further declared that "in the interests of the solidarity of the British Commonwealth" it was "desirable that the rights of such Indians to citizenship should be recognized." Also see Hancock, *Smuts*, 2:144ff.

conferences owing to developments in Kenya where a fierce political struggle had developed between the white settlers and the numerous Indians who demanded equal treatment. The chief issues were representation on the Legislative Council and the right to buy land anywhere. So intense was the feeling in India that many voices demanded that the government boycott the conference. This demand went unheeded. Instead, India through its chief spokesman, Sir Tej Bahadur Sapru, made a slashing attack on South Africa. In an appeal for the implementation of the principle of equal political rights of the 1921 resolution, Sapru scathingly reviewed the treatment accorded Indians in the Union. Smuts in reply contended that the Indian claim for equal franchise rights throughout the Empire arose from a misconception of the nature of British citizenship, a misconception the conference would do well to correct. It was based on the wrong assumption "that in an empire where there is a common King there should be a common and equal citizenship, and that all differences and distinctions in citizenship rights are wrong in principle." There was no equality of British citizenship throughout the Empire; there was every imaginable difference. The new conception of the Empire as a partnership of free and equal states meant an even greater departure from the concept of a single or unitary citizenship. The common kingship was the binding link between the various parts of the Empire, but it was not the source of individual rights. The Indian resolution of 1921 ran counter to the new conception of the Empire and was impractical. He wanted the conference to pass a resolution that would affirm the right of each Dominion to regulate both immigration and citizenship as domestic questions.[68]

The Imperial Conferences of 1921 and 1923 revealed in clearest outline the agonizing difficulties of the whites in South Africa and the tragedy of a leader like Jan Smuts. The unity of the Empire-Commonwealth was for him a precious ideal, yet under the pressure of the racial problem in his country he had no choice but to fight for the Empire's decentralization and to appear to champion a narrow racialism. The arguments which Smuts used to justify his position were the same that were used by his successors as prime minister. If the Indians (or the coloreds) were given the franchise, all logic in denying it to the natives

---

[68] Imperial Conference, 1923, *Summary of Proceedings*, Cmd. 1987 (London, 1923) ; *Appendix to Summary of Proceedings*, Cmd. 1988 (London, 1923).

would be swept away, and white civilization in South Africa would be doomed.

There is also a direct line between the Imperial Conferences of 1921 and 1923 and the Commonwealth Conference of 1961 at which occurred South Africa's withdrawal or expulsion, whichever way one cares to view it, from this association of nations. When Smuts declared at the 1921 conference that no South African government which accepted India's resolution for equal rights of citizenship would last very long, the Indian spokesman, Srinivasa Sastri, declared that in that case membership in the Empire could not give India much satisfaction.

4

The Union and
the Borderlands

It was not long after the planting of the colony at Cape Town in 1652 that some of the settlers began to turn their eyes northward and eastward. The dispersion began early and, in spite of attempts by the authorities to check it, the movement gathered momentum reaching its peak in the Great Trek of 1835–1848. As the Boers moved eastward and northward they encountered the Bantu coming southward and for a century the Boers and Bantu fought bitterly for control of the land of southern Africa. Hositilities broke out on the eastern frontier in the late eighteenth century and in 1795 the *trekkers* set up the first Boer republic. Between 1811 and 1878 eight Kaffir wars were fought. Further trekking and the establishment of republics, most of them small and ephemeral, characterized the history of the Boers during these years. Finally, there emerged two Boer republics, the Orange Free State formed in 1854 and the South African Republic (Transvaal) formed in 1856.

The mentality of the South African whites, and especially of the Afrikaners, was strongly influenced by the long struggle with the Bantu tribes for the lands north of Cape Colony. White supremacy became a basic part of their culture. The survival of the white man and his civilization, they were convinced, was dependent upon a rigid adherence to the policy of white domination and strict racial segregation. But the maintenance of this policy within the Union might be defeated by developments in the north; hence there developed among the South African whites an increasing concern about racial policies followed in those lands. But also, as the center of a vigorous Western civilization, there developed in white South Africa a spirit of nationalism and, on the part of some leaders at least, imperialistic sentiments.

Lord Selborne in 1907 drew attention to the problem presented by the bordering territories, pointing to the United States and Canada as examples of the importance of effective occupation of such lands. "South Africans remembering this should look North to the Zambesi, and ask themselves who is to control the settlement of Southern Rhodesia, a great country. . . . Its development may be delayed, but it cannot be prevented, and if there is one warning to be read more plainly than another between the lines of South African history it is that which points to the unwisdom of allowing the political organization of the northern countries to take place in utter independence of the community already established to the South." South Africa's difficult and complex racial problem is ever shadowed by the responsibility of keeping order in the land and of the defense of civilization against any turbulent or unruly element in the uncivilized masses. "No one who realizes the magnitude of the task imposed on this country will doubt that its separation into independent parts is fatal to success from the outset. Such separation means division of national strength in all its forms. It means, what is even more dangerous than this, division in purpose and plan. It means different policies, yielding different results, which sooner or later, must come into contact and conflict with one another . . . [leading to] confusion and miscarriage."[1]

The British victory over the Boer republics had brought a measure of political unification in southern Africa, as all of white southern Africa was brought under the British Crown. With the formation of the Union another step had been taken in the unification of southern Africa, but far short of the anticipation of Cecil Rhodes in 1894 that "five and twenty years hence you might find a gentleman called your Prime

[1] Great Britain, Parliamentary Papers, *The Selborne Memorandum: A Review of the Relations of the British South African Colonies in 1907*, Cmd. 3564 (London, 1925).

Minister sitting in Cape Town, and controlling the whole, not only to the Zambesi, but to Lake Tanganyika."[2]

THE PROTECTORATES

The three High Commission Territories, or Protectorates as they were generally called, were taken under British protection largely to save them from further Boer incursions which threatened to deprive the tribes of their lands. Bechuana, now an independent state under the name of Botswana, is a large semi-arid and desert territory bordering South Africa on the north. Since South West Africa borders it on the west and north, Botswana is virtually surrounded by South Africa.[3] Rhodesia is its neighbor on the northeast. It was declared a Protectorate by Britain in 1885 to protect some of the Bechuana tribes from the incursion of Boers from the Transvaal. Involved also was the pressure of world politics. Lord Hailey states that the declaration was "in effect the British answer to the suspected German-Transvaal conspiracy to establish a hegemony over South Africa."[4] In 1895 the southern part of the territory, some 43,000 square miles, was formally incorporated in Cape Colony.

The Transvaal was very much interested in acquiring control over Swaziland as a possible alternative outlet to the sea in place of Durban and Cape Town in the British colonies. Foreigners, of whom the Transvaalers constituted the largest part, had acquired extensive land, mineral, and other concessions from the chiefs. In conventions of 1881 and 1884 the independence of Swaziland was formally guaranteed, but in 1894 Great Britain gave the Transvaal republic "all rights of protection, legislation, jurisdiction and administration over Swaziland," subject to the condition that it would not be incorporated in the Transvaal.[5] With the outbreak of the Anglo-Boer War in 1899 Britain took over the

[2] Quoted by Jan H. Hofmeyr, *South Africa*, revised by J. P. Cope (New York, 1952), p. 175.

[3] In 1890 Germany acquired from Great Britain the Caprivi Zipfel, a strip of land 300 miles in length and nowhere more than fifty miles in width, separating Botswana from Angola and Zambia.

[4] *South Africa and the High Commission Territories* (London, 1963), p. 8. For a history of these territories see also Jack Halpern, *South Africa's Hostages: Basutoland, Bechuanaland, and Swaziland* (Baltimore, Md., 1965).

[5] Lord Hailey, *South Africa and the High Commission Territories*, p. 13.

administration of the territory. At the end of the war the queen regent as paramount chief requested the British government to annex her country. While acquiring full powers of legislation and administration, the British government did not annex the territory. Britain reluctantly proclaimed Basutoland a Protectorate in 1868, chiefly to save it from annexation by Orange Free State.

Even before the formation of the Union, South African leaders began the drive, which was to continue for fifty years, for the control of the Protectorates. After the Transvaal had been granted self-government Prime Minister Louis Botha did his utmost to get the British to return the administration of Swaziland to Transvaal, but there was strong sentiment in Britain against handing the administration of the Protectorates over to the white South Africans. In reply to a letter[6] from Smuts in which he made a strong plea for the British to commit the government of "the whole of British South Africa" to them, J. A. Hobson declared that he found among many liberals "a quite clear and pronounced objection to handing them [the Protectorates] over to any unified or federal government without explicit guarantees, having particular reference to the alienation of Native lands but extending also to other matters political and economic."[7] Apparently Lord Selborne, who had succeeded Milner as high commissioner for South Africa and governor of the Transvaal and Orange River colonies, gave Botha the impression that the Protectorates would not be turned over "to this or that Colony, but to the future Federation."[8]

The three Territories were placed under the control of the high commissioner in South Africa, whose office was originally attached to that of the governor of Cape Colony, and after 1909 to that of the governor general of South Africa. In 1931 it was separated from the latter office, but the high commissioner to the Union remained responsible for the administration of the three Protectorates, which are more properly designated as the High Commission Territories.[9]

The leaders of the unification movement that led to the formation of

[6] 13 July 1908. W. K. Hancock and Jean van der Poel, eds., *Selections from the Smuts Papers*, 2:442. Smuts observed in conclusion that "such trust is not likely to be misplaced and will most impressively bring home to South Africans their solemn duties in this matter."

[7] Ibid., p. 530, 16 Dec. 1908.

[8] Letter of Smuts to Merriman, 8 Jan. 1908, ibid., pp. 273–74.

[9] See Lord Hailey, *South Africa and the High Commission Territories*, pp. 1–4.

the Union were disappointed that the three High Commission Territories were not incorporated in the Union. The majority of the members of the Constitutional Convention was determined to obtain arrangements which would ensure white control of the Union government. They succeeded, but this made inclusion of the Protectorates in the Union impossible for the British.[10] The South Africa Act contained a provision authorizing the British Cabinet to turn over the administration of the Protectorates to the Union, subject, however, to a number of conditions in the interest of protecting the natives. Moreover, the British government made it clear that it would have to consult the inhabitants before transferring the Territories.

For nearly half a century South African governments beseeched London to transfer the Protectorates, but as time passed, the British became increasingly less inclined to yield to the request. They were disappointed in their hope that South Africans would modify their views on the matter of the franchise for the Bantu. Instead, the dominant whites became more and more determined to keep political control of the country in their own hands and to deny the nonwhites even a limited participation. As this attitude developed and the policy of segregation became more rigidly enforced, the natives in the Protectorates became more strongly opposed to incorporation in the Union. This produced an awkward situation. South Africans saw in the refusal to transfer the Territories a failure to fulfill an implied promise, an implied rebuke for their racial policies, an encouragement to the nonwhites to resist these policies, and an unwillingness on the part of the British to deal with the Union as a sovereign state.[11]

As advocates of the greater political unification of southern Africa, Botha and Smuts were interested in the incorporation of the Protectorates into the Union, but friendly to Britain they were restrained in their attitude. As a member of the Constitutional Convention, General Hertzog was opposed to making any provision for the transfer of the Territories. They were poor and would be a burden to the Union. He

[10] See Chapter 1.

[11] For a general account of the efforts of the Union government to acquire control of the Territories see Lord Hailey, *South Africa and the High Commission Territories;* also British Parliamentary Paper, *Basutoland, the Bechuanaland Protectorate and Swaziland: History of Discussions with the Union,* Cmd. 8707 (London, 1952).

feared that the incorporation of these Territories, inhabited almost exclusively by Africans, would increase the danger of native disturbances and thus increase defense costs.[12] His views changed after he became prime minister.

RHODESIA—SOUTH AFRICAN PROTÉGÉ?

Just as there had been the expectation that the Protectorates would become part of the Union, so it had been thought likely that Southern Rhodesia would join it.[13] Like the Protectorates, Rhodesia was geographically a part of the region of which the Union constituted the core. There was dissatisfaction with the system of government by the British South African Company which administered the territory under the royal charter of 1889 and the white settlers were looking for alternatives. There were three Rhodesian delegates at the Constitutional Convention with the right to speak but not to vote. Botha and Smuts were eager to facilitate the inclusion later of Southern Rhodesia as a member of the Union. They dreamed, as had Rhodes before them, of a large self-governing British dominion embracing all of southern Africa stretching from the Cape to the Zambesi and beyond. Having experienced a Bantu rebellion, the English (who far outnumbered the Afrikaners in Rhodesia) saw the advantages of a common and uniform racial policy in the region, but they were suspicious of the Afrikaner revival. President Paul Kruger had also dreamed of a great southern African empire, but republican and Afrikaner dominated. The English settlers of Rhodesia preferred to wait and see in what direction the Union would move. As a result of these various attitudes, a provision was inserted in the Constitution making fairly easy the admittance into the Union of additional colonies and territories.

The original charter of the company was extended for another ten years in 1914, but as 1924 approached, sentiment in the territory had definitely turned against extending it again. There was much to be said for joining the Union. The white population of Southern Rhodesia at the time was only 33,000, while the Africans numbered 770,000. Rhode-

[12] Thompson, *The Unification of South Africa*, p. 276.
[13] When Northern Rhodesia became independent in 1964, Southern Rhodesia became Rhodesia.

sia was already a member of a customs union with its southern neighbor. Moreover, it was landlocked, depending on its neighbors for access
to the sea. The Smuts government offered Rhodesia generous terms. In
spite of all this, there was no great enthusiasm for union. The general
elections of 1920 in South Africa had indicated that General Smuts's
government was losing favor and that the Afrikaner Nationalists were
in the ascendancy. The Rhodesian settlers feared the attraction which
the growing industry of the south would exert on their African laborers
and they also feared an influx of poor whites from the south. Moreover,
they were asked to accept bilingualism, which was distasteful to the
English Rhodesians. London offered Rhodesia self-government, but
Winston Churchill, as colonial secretary, suggested that Rhodesia appoint delegates to discuss with Smuts arrangements for incorporation in
the Union. In a referendum held in October 1922, Rhodesians were
given the choice of joining the Union or of becoming self-governing.
General Smuts went to Rhodesia to urge its voters to join the Union but
to no avail.[14] Distrust of the Boers would not down and the status of a
separate colony with self-government had a strong appeal. Nor was
everybody in the Union in favor of the merger. The Nationalists under
the leadership of General Hertzog and the Labor party were bitterly
opposed to bringing Rhodesia into the Union, denouncing it as a
maneuver by Smuts to keep himself in power with the aid of Rhodesian
votes.

In spite of his setback in 1922, Smuts continued to entertain ideas of
a special relationship between the two countries. "The Union should be
a radiating centre towards the north," he declared in Parliament in
1926. "I have always taken up the attitude that we should support
Rhodesia as a small sister State on our border, and that she should look
to us as a stronger brother."[15]

[14] The vote was 8,774 to 5,989 to become a separate colony. As General Smuts
sensed it, Rhodesians were "afraid of our bilingualism, our nationalism, my views
of the British Empire." (Letter of 31 July 1922 to M. C. Gillette, quoted by W. K.
Hancock, *Smuts*, 2 vols. [Cambridge, Eng., 1962, 1968], vol. 2: *The Fields of
Force, 1919–1950*, pp. 153–54.)

According to Sir Roy Welensky, Churchill told Smuts that if Southern Rhodesia
chose association with South Africa "Northern Rhodesia would be thrown in as a
gift. Few people had recognized the potential value of the territories' mineral
resources" (*400 Days: The Life and Death of the Federation of Rhodesia and
Nyasaland* [New York, 1964], p. 56).

[15] *Hansard*, vol. 7, col. 2667.

SOUTH WEST AFRICA

Great Britain, which had established control over Walfish Bay, turned over the administration of this small but strategic area to Cape Colony in 1884, about the same time that Germany announced its occupation of South West Africa. Had the government of Cape Colony shown any interest in annexing the territory the British government very probably would have taken over this large territory. In 1908 the German government sought to lease Walfish Bay from Cape Colony as it wished to build a railroad to the port. With respect to this proposal, General Smuts wrote to John X. Merriman, at the time prime minister of the Cape, urging him not to grant the lease. "From the point of view of South Africa's future the German Empire is no desirable neighbor. . . . Now that we are on the eve of closer Union as we all hope, it would be the very worst time to strengthen the German position by making them use Walfish Bay for the development of their territory."[16] The opportunity to get the Germans out of South West Africa came with World War I; Botha and Smuts quickly took advantage of it.

To conquer the Germans in South West Africa was not a difficult task, but to acquire sovereignty over the territory for the Union was another matter. In his Fourteen Points, President Woodrow Wilson had declared opposition to the transfer of territory from the vanquished to the victors. Smuts in a letter from Paris to one of his English friends registers some of the difficulties he encountered at the Peace Conference: "He [Wilson] is entirely opposed to our annexing a little German colony here or there, which pains me deeply. A few days later he wrote: "Yesterday we discussed the Dominion claims to the German colonies. I hope I made a good case to South West Africa, but I don't know. My argument was principally that it was a desert, a part of the Kalihari no good to anybody, least of all to so magnificent a body as the League of Nations!"[17]

Smuts did not succeed in obtaining sovereignty over South West Africa for his country, but he thought he had obtained something nearly as good: the administration of the territory as a mandatory of the League of Nations. In his proposal for an international organization, Smuts had suggested the main outlines of a mandates system for

---

[16] Hancock and van der Poel, eds., *Smuts Papers*, 2:438, 26 June 1908.
[17] To M. C. Gillette, ibid., 4:50, 20 Jan. 1919 and 4:55–56, 25 Jan. 1919.

the administration of the enemy colonies, but he excluded the African territories from his scheme. As the chief draftsman of the mandates articles of the Covenant of the League of Nations (Arts. 22 and 23) he apparently made no effort to exclude the German territories in Africa. However, the section dealing with the "C" mandates clearly was drafted so as to ensure the Union's claim to the mandate over South West Africa and to minimize the supervisory role of the League. "There are territories, such as South West Africa," so ran the article, "which owing to the sparseness of their population or their small size, or their remoteness from the centres of civilization, or their geographical contiguity to the territory of the Mandatory, and other circumstances can be best administered under the laws of the Mandatory as integral portions of its territory." Smuts regarded the "C" mandates as "in effect not far removed from annexation."[18]

South Africa experienced no great difficulties with respect to its administration of South West Africa under the League of Nations, but with World War II new winds began to blow. Of this Smuts became aware at the San Francisco Conference which drafted the Charter of the United Nations. He returned home with forebodings.

PORTUGUESE EAST AFRICA

Mozambique is of great strategic importance to South Africa. This was recognized by Lord Carnavon, the British colonial secretary in the 1870s, when he sought to induce his government to buy Mozambique from Portugal. It was clearly of the greatest strategic interest to the landlocked Transvaal republic. President Thomas F. Burger desired to secure Delagoa Bay, sought to build a railway to it, and thus make his state independent of the British colonies on the southern coast. A railway connecting Johannesburg with Lourenço Marques was opened in 1894, a year before the line with Durban was completed. A large number of Africans from Mozambique found employment in the Transvaal mines. In 1909 the Transvaal, then a colony of Great Britain, concluded an agreement with Portugal by which, in return for facilities to recruit native labor in Mozambique, half of the overseas traffic to the Witwatersrand was to pass through Lourenço Marques. The agreement

---

[18] League of Nations, Permanent Mandates Commission, *Minutes*, 2 (1922): 91.

was revised in 1928 and again subsequently. In the convention of 1938 Mozambique was guaranteed 40 percent of the overseas imports and the number of native labor recruits was reduced from 108,000 to 80,000. With the years South Africa has become less dependent on Mozambique.[19]

The Nationalists always branded Smuts as an imperialist and not without reason. Until Jameson's Raid he had been a loyal supporter of Rhodes and his ideas of a unified southern Africa.[20] He was opposed to making Cape Town the capital of the Union because it was too far from the heart of the Union which "will go up to Congo soon and perhaps embrace [the] whole continent south of that."[21] In 1915 Smuts wrote to Merriman that the British government now practically intimates that in the "future German East Africa will be our destination. If that country were conquered by us, we could probably effect an exchange with Mozambique and so consolidate our territories south of the Zambesi and Kunene."[22] Prime Minister Botha held similar views.[23]

Smuts and South Africa played a leading role in conquering East Africa (Tanganyika, now Tanzania) from the Germans, but the Union acquired no special rights there, and there is no evidence that Botha and Smuts sought to use Britain's obligation to the Union for its large contribution to the conquest of the territory as a bargaining point for gains farther south.

Except for the potential danger of arming the Africans, Smuts was well pleased with the outcome of the war in Africa. With the conquest of the German colonies the British Empire had no threat on the Atlantic or Indian seaboards to essential sea communications, and was also in the good position of having a through land route from Egypt to the Cape.

[19] Imports through Lourenço Marques have declined and fallen below the 40 percent guarantee of the 1938 convention. During the 1965–1966 financial year the South African government paid Mozambique R650,000 ($910,000), which figure rose to R1,311,800 ($1,836,520). The decline is due to the construction of oil refineries in Durban and the construction of an oil pipeline from Durban to Johannesburg and the closing of the Suez Canal. (*The Star* [Johannesburg], Weekly Air Edition, 18 May 1968).

[20] Once D. F. Malan in Parliament, pointing at Smuts, said, "There sits C. J. Rhodes *redivivus*" (*Hansard*, vol. 37, col. 98).

[21] Notes for speech before the National convention (1909), Hancock and van der Poel, eds. *Smuts Papers*, 2:540–42.

[22] Ibid., 3:653–54.

[23] Ibid., pp. 600ff.

LANDS NORTH OF THE ZAMBESI

General Smuts's motives in desiring to annex South West Africa and the High Commission Territories and to bring Southern Rhodesia into the Union were probably mixed. Economic and strategic considerations undoubtedly played a large part in his thinking, but when he thought of the lands farther north his major concern seems to have been chiefly racial policy. With his usual prescience he saw before others that developments in central Africa would be of the greatest importance for his country. He was gravely concerned about these developments because of the influence they might exert on racial problems in South Africa. In a notable speech made in London on May 22, 1917, he expressed his concern about arming Africans.[24] The war had revealed that there was valuable military material in Africa. Powerful armies could be raised in Central Africa, and he hoped that one of the results of the war would be some arrangement or convention among the powers interested in central Africa by which the military training of natives in that area would be prevented, as it was prevented in South Africa.[25]

For Smuts, the Afrikaner, his country's racial problem was never out of mind. What in effect he was urging in 1917 was that the colonial powers in Africa adopt the policies of South Africa in dealing with the race problem. In his views on the race problem Smuts was rarely optimistic. He was never certain that there was a real solution to this difficult problem.

Smuts talked a great deal about pan-Africanism, but without always making clear what he meant by it.[26] Sometimes this talk cost him dearly politically. In a speech at Ermelo in January 1929, he suggested the

[24] "The Future of South and Central Africa," Lieut. Gen. the Rt. Hon. J. C. Smuts, *War-Time Speeches: A Compilation of Public Utterances in Great Britain* (New York, 1917), pp. 71ff.

[25] The views Smuts expressed here were incorporated in the mandate provisions of the Covenant of the League of Nations. Article 22, Clause 5, stipulated that the mandatory in the "B" and "C" mandates must "guarantee . . . the prevention of the establishment of military and naval bases and of military training of the natives for other than police purposes and the defence of the territory."

[26] In a letter to a Rhodesian friend in February 1937 he stated that while the Union Constitution had been an outstanding success as applied to the states at present within the Union, it would not form the basis of a suitable arrangement in regard to territories further north. "For the purposes of close political cooperation with the northern states, a somewhat more elastic arrangement would have to be considered" (P. B. Blankenberg, ed., *The Thoughts of General Smuts* [Cape Town, 1951], pp. 217–18).

formation of a great federation of states composed of South Africa and the territories to the north. He is reported to have said that he hoped "that we would always move northwards, so that the term 'South Africa' will fall away, and a great federation of British states arise."[27] The leaders of the Nationalist party avidly seized on this statement and issued a "Black Manifesto" in which Smuts's suggestion was branded as a threat to drown the white race in a sea of blacks. "Smuts wants a Kaffir State in which we are to be members," declared Tielman Roos, a Nationalist leader, "a black hegemony in which we are all to be on equal footing."[28] Johannes G. Strijdom, who some twenty years later became a Nationalist prime minister, pointed out that if all the British territories in Africa joined such a federation, the total European population of less than 2,000,000 would be increased by 64,000, while the 7,000,000 Africans in the Union would be increased by 13,000,000. "It therefore means that General Smuts is aiming at the establishment of a large native state in which the handful of Europeans will be swallowed up in the quicksands of the native blood."[29] In the "Black Peril" election which followed the Ermelo speech, the Nationalists won an absolute majority in the Assembly.

Smuts may have been the first but he was not the only white leader of South Africa who was concerned about the influence which developments in the lands north might have on South Africa's racial problem. One of the earliest of the many speeches dealing with this question was made by G. Heaton Nicholls in Parliament in 1921. Central Africa, he pointed out, was developing rapidly. Asians and Europeans were exploiting the interior of Africa for their own enrichment and in doing so were engendering forces which might destroy the young nation. He suggested the proclamation of an African Doctrine like the Monroe Doctrine asserting that South Africa had a right to know what was taking place in these territories and had a right to protest "the creation of inimical currents and tendencies" there. He urged the government to seek an early inclusion of Southern Rhodesia in the Union and the purchase of Northern Rhodesia from the Chartered Company.[30]

In his Rhodes Memorial lectures given at Oxford University in 1929, Smuts outlined rather frankly his views on racial policy and expressed

[27] *Volkstem* (Johannesburg), 18 Jan. 1929.
[28] J. C. Smuts, Jr., *Jan Christiaan Smuts* (Cape Town, 1952), p. 296.
[29] *Hansard*, vol. 27, cols. 3138–39, 6 May 1936.
[30] *South Africa in My Time* (London, 1961), p. 279.

his concern about developments in south, central, and east Africa. In the south central highlands where vigorous white settlements had been established the natives had shown "the greatest economic progress, the largest increase, and the greatest advance in education and civilization." By a vigorous policy of settlement in these highlands there would be achieved "a stable and permanent civilization which will give the native peoples of Africa that age-long contact with a higher order of things which the exceptionally slow movement of the native specially calls for. . . . It will be a slow, gradual schooling of peoples who have slumbered and stagnated since the dawn of time."[31]

In view of the essential unity of African problems, he suggested that there be instituted an annual conference, composed of representatives from all the territories from Kenya to South Africa, at which these matters could be discussed. The north should profit from the experience gained by the south which for over a century had labored over the very problems which were now being faced by the communities in the north. By these annual conferences a common policy could be shaped and a more responsible white opinion would be formed to guide the governments in their tasks.[32]

General Smuts seems to have envisaged in the highlands of east central Africa, the potential white areas, an economic, social, and political development like that of South Africa. If this were achieved, white dominion over the vast region from the Cape to Ethiopia would be assured for a long time, probably indefinitely. But the British government had begun moving in the other direction. In 1922 it issued a White Paper in which it declared that the interests of the African natives must be paramount. If these interests and those of the immigrant races should conflict, the former should prevail.[33] The issue was precipitated by the presence of numerous Indians in Kenya. The white settlers in Kenya reacted bitterly to the British declaration and talked of rebellion. They sent a delegation to Pretoria and entertained the idea of a Kenya-South African republic.[34]

[31] "African Settlement," *Africa and Some World Problems* (Oxford, 1930), pp. 59–60.

[32] Ibid., pp. 68–69.

[33] Great Britain, Parliamentary Papers, "Indians in Kenya," Cmd. 1922 (London, 1922), p. 9.

[34] See Nicholas Mansergh, ed., *Survey of British Commonwealth Affairs*, vol. 1: *Problems of Nationality, 1918–1936* (London, 1937), p. 221.

Smuts outlined his views on native policy in a second lecture. He foresaw that the issue of contact of colors and civilizations would become a dominant issue. What was needed in Africa was a "wise, far-sighted native policy." The African was completely absorbed in the present. He had produced no indigenous religion, literature, art, or architecture. The Africans are a unique race, with a mentality and culture quite different from those of Europeans. To de-Africanize them would tend to turn them into either beasts of the field or pseudo-Europeans. Because of these basic differences a different policy should be applied to them. The policy which South Africa had evolved and which he recommended for adoption generally was one of separate, parallel institutions and development for the two races living in their own areas.[35]

From this brief summary of Smuts's ideas it is obvious that he and the Nationalists were not far apart in their views on native policy. Indeed, the latter easily could use Smuts's Rhodes lectures as campaign material for their policy of apartheid. The Nationalists, however, were opposed to Smuts's dream of a greater South Africa and pan-Africanism because any enlargement of the political boundaries of the Union could only weaken the position of the white man relative to the black. But as events unfolded in Africa some Nationalists began to have second thoughts. Italy's attack on Ethiopia jarred white South Africa, and the government strongly supported the League of Nations sanctions against the aggressor. The reasons for their deep concern are revealed by the speeches of the Union delegate, Charles te Water. South Africa regarded a partition of Africa "outside of the covering blanket of the League" as fraught with danger and menace—"danger to the adventuring nations themselves, danger to the black peoples of Africa, and menace to our own white civilization now, after centuries of trial and sacrifice, so firmly, and we believe, beneficently established in Southern Africa." He warned that if Africa was used by Europe for its own designs, it would "in its due and patient time, rise and overthrow, as it has done before in its long and dark history, and revert to that black barbarism which it has been our difficult destiny in the south to penetrate and enlighten."[36]

[35] J. C. Smuts, "Native Policy in Africa," in *Africa and Some World Problems* (Oxford, 1930).

[36] Speech in Assembly, 13 Sept. 1935, League of Nations, *Official Journal*, Sp. Supp. No. 138, pp. 66–67.

National-Labor Coalition
1924–1933

5

Formal Recognition
of Sovereign Status

Whenever in South African history Afrikaners and English-speaking peoples achieved some form of political harmony or cooperation it was at the expense of the nonwhites. Under the terms of the Treaty of Vereeniging the natives were excluded from the franchise in the former Boer republics. With the formation of the Union nonwhites were barred from sitting in Parliament. When the Afrikaner National party of Hertzog formed a pact with the largely English-speaking Labor party the color bar was extended to industrial employment. The fusion of the South African and the National parties in 1934 was followed by the removal from the common roll of African voters of Cape Province. The reconciliation policy of Verwoerd after 1961 and continued by Balthazar Vorster since 1966 is obviously inspired by the desire to unite the whites behind the policy of apartheid against attacks from the outside as well as against resistance from the nonwhites in the country.

While the two parties which formed the Pact government in 1924 agreed on a policy of safeguarding white interests and the privileged position of white labor, there was limited agreement with respect to external policy. The Labor members of the cabinet (at first two in number and later three) were all English-speaking and although they could go along with a policy of achieving a greater and more precise status as a nation, they were opposed to secession from the Empire and Commonwealth. Within this framework, Hertzog did much to clarify the Union's international status and to acquire more of the customary symbols and accoutrements which go with modern statehood.

COMMONWEALTH RELATIONS:
BALFOUR DECLARATION

Smuts insisted that Botha and he had achieved a higher status for South Africa. The Union had participated in the peace conference on the same level as the small independent belligerents such as Belgium; Botha and he had signed the peace treaty for South Africa as a political unit separate from Great Britain; and they had won for the Union membership and representation in the League of Nations as an independent state. But Hertzog and his lieutenants in the National party denied the validity of Smuts's claims. D. F. Malan stated that Great Britain had agreed to consult the Dominions, which was all very well, but it also meant placing responsibilities and burdens on them. Only if the Dominions had the right to separate from England, just as England had the right to divest herself of the colonies, could they call themselves sister states on a footing of equality. Hertzog asked the prime minister to give a clear reply to the question whether South Africa had the right to decide its own destiny just as England had.[1]

In reply Prime Minister Smuts stated that South Africa had exactly the same rights and voice as England in the League of Nations except that England had a permanent seat on the Council. Constitutionally, the Union Parliament was the seat of legislative power for the Union; in fact the British Parliament could no longer, without the consent of the Union Parliament, pass any law binding on South Africa. Smuts interpreted Lloyd George's reply to the Nationalist peace deputation headed by General Hertzog as precluding the right of secession. He pointed to the United States as evidence that secession was an evil thing. "The path of secession is a path which must lead to a broken South Africa, a discredited South Africa, with the Native population outnumbering the White population."[2]

[1] *Cape Times* (Cape Town), 9–11 Sept. 1919.
[2] Ibid.

Hertzog went to the 1926 Imperial Conference determined to secure a declaration of equality of the Commonwealth members. He could not use the threat of secession to obtain such a declaration in view of the terms of the agreement with the Labor party in forming a coalition government. The differences between the views of Hertzog and Smuts on this issue were aired thoroughly in a debate not many months before the meeting of the conference and again after the conference. Hertzog admitted that Smuts held that South Africa possessed "a completely independent international status," that the Union was "as free as England." The difference between his views and those of Smuts was in regard to what was meant by completely independent international status. Hertzog believed it included the right of secession; Smuts did not. Here he inverted Smuts's implied argument about unity. According to Hertzog, Smuts emphasized the idea that there was "a super-authority whether acknowledged by legislation or only something which has been accepted by the Imperial Conference." Smuts contended that if there was no such authority the Commonwealth would fly apart, but Hertzog felt that "if we do not wish to fly apart we must give up the idea of a super-authority." Smuts wanted to leave everything to inference while Hertzog was convinced that if the relations between England and the Dominions were known precisely, there would be better mutual understanding and cooperation. There would be "a certain basis for the community of nations to stand by each other for the good of us all, and in the best interests of the world about us."[3]

In reply Smuts repudiated the ideas attributed to him by Hertzog. His idea of the Commonwealth was that it was "an organization or a combination of equal states, and nobody superior" and that this was also the view of the British prime minister and of the others. "There is no super-state, no super-authority. It is a meeting of equals under one sovereign, and they meet and discuss matters of common concern."[4]

Prime Minister Hertzog lost little time in preparing the British government for the steps he would take to clear up the confusion which existed in South Africa and which prevailed abroad as to the status of the Union. Since 1912 he had promised the people of the Union that the juridical status of South Africa would be clarified. Moreover, there was always the danger under a democratic system of government such as

[3] *Hansard*, vol. 7, cols. 2662–66, 22 April 1926.
[4] Ibid., col. 2667.

that of South Africa that if the status of the Dominions was not made clear to foreign governments somebody might come to power and permit the old position of subordination to return imperceptibly. In examining the records of previous imperial conferences he was struck by the number of most authoritative declarations with respect to dominion status made by very responsible leaders of Great Britain. If these had been announced officially and publicized, much of the bitter political wrangling in South Africa never would have taken place and the word *empire* would have acquired a totally different meaning.[5] Nevertheless, Hertzog let the British government and the world know that he expected the 1926 Imperial Conference to make a clear-cut declaration. Smuts stated that Hertzog had warned that if the conference would not act on his proposal, South Africa would make such a statement alone, which would mean the breakup of the British Empire.[6]

General Hertzog introduced a resolution in the Inter-Imperial Relations Committee of the conference that the prime ministers acknowledge that each of them separately are representatives of "independent states, equal in status 'and separately entitled to *international recognition, with governments and parliaments independent of each other, united by the common bond of allegiance to the King and freely associated as members of the British Commonwealth of Nations. . . . and* [that] *their relations as described above, formally and authoritatively be made known to their own communities and to the whole world.*"[7]

According to C. M. van den Heever, Hertzog ascribed his success to the support which Lord Birkenhead, secretary of state for India, gave him in his request for a declaration which would remove all future doubt.[8] In the beginning Lord Balfour, Amery, and Chamberlain had objections, but Birkenhead's influence brought the wavering conference members to the support of Hertzog's proposal. The Hertzog resolution became the basic draft and after many revisions was adopted.

Hertzog received the active support of Canada, another Dominion with a large non-English population group, for whom such a declaration

[5] The best account of Hertzog's work in connection with clarifying the imperial structure is to be found in C. M. van den Heever, *Generaal J. B. M. Hertzog* (Johannesburg, 1944), pp. 479ff.

[6] Ibid., p. 490.

[7] Ibid., p. 491. Italics are Hertzog's.

[8] Ibid., p. 493. Imperial Conference, 1926, *Summary of Proceedings*, Cmd. 2768 (London, 1926), pp. 24–25.

as that sought by Hertzog was important. Australia and New Zealand, on the other hand, were weak British communities, geographically far from the mother country and close to the populous Asian countries whose impoverished millions might cast a covetous eye on the sparsely settled wealthy British territories. These Dominions were more interested in imperial unity and defense. The Inter-Imperial Relations Committee, under the chairmanship of Lord Balfour, presented a formula which sought to satisfy both points of view. The Dominions were described as "autonomous communities within the British Empire, equal in status, in no way subordinate one to another in any aspect of their domestic or external affairs, though united by a common allegiance to the Crown, and freely associated as members of the British Commonwealth of Nations." The first part of the declaration expressed the Canadian and South African views, while the second stressed the Australian and New Zealand position. Prime Minister Hertzog was pleased with the results. At the conclusion of the conference he said, "I leave fully satisfied that whatever I wanted to have and attain has been attained at these meetings, and, what is more, that it has been attained with the full cooperation and sympathy of all when we have met together."[9] Upon his arrival at Cape Town, he said, "I have no fear of that Empire any longer . . . because of what has been done and achieved by the Imperial Conference."[10]

Hertzog viewed the results of the Imperial Conference as a Nationalist and personal triumph. His split with Botha and Smuts in 1912 was caused by opposing views on the nature of the Empire. He himself had never preached any other doctrine than that which had now been recognized by the conference, whereas the South African party and its leader, Smuts, had been preaching heresy all these years. He was glad that there now could be a "united sentiment and conviction" with respect to a question which had in the past given rise to so much that was "bitterly injurious to our country as well as our people."[11]

The first time Smuts spoke in this debate he admitted that he was in a difficult position. It was one of the misfortunes of South Africa that the subject under discussion for years had been a highly controversial issue.

---

[9] Imperial Conference, 1926, *Appendices*, Cmd. 2769 (London, 1926).

[10] Quoted by Smuts in Parliament, 16 March 1927, *Hansard*, vol. 8, col. 1496.

[11] *Hansard*, vol. 8, cols. 1477–83, 16 March 1927. The debate began on 8 March and continued intermittently until 26 March.

He hoped it would be different in the future. The question of the British Empire, its nature and its relations *inter se* and among the states of the world was one of the most puzzling questions in the whole range of international law. The Commonwealth was something new, something to which the categories of juridical science did not apply. At one of the imperial conferences held during the war, it was decided that after the conclusion of hostilities a constitutional conference would be called to deal with this question of relationship within the Empire. Smuts said he went to the 1921 conference fully prepared to press the subject, but he encountered grave difficulties. Other members of the conference thought it was premature to deal with the question. He did not want to belittle the importance of what the 1926 conference had done, but he did not think that anything had been changed. Participation by the Dominions in the peace conference and in the League of Nations had created the new situation. The Balfour Declaration merely stated the existing situation and practices, but it was salutary in that it removed an element of uncertainty and doubt in a very formal and authoritative manner.

Smuts cautioned care in interpreting the declaration. While there was an intention on the part of the statesmen at the conference to clarify certain matters "there was an equally deliberate intention to say nothing about other matters." Some of the most important questions in imperial and international relationships had been left "obscure and unsettled" by the declaration. It speaks of the Dominions as "autonomous communities within the British Empire," but the use of the word *independence* was carefully avoided. Smuts conceded that it was difficult to understand how a body of absolutely free and equal states could at the same time form a coherent entity. Smuts again asserted that he never was in favor of a superstate but that he desired the adoption of a common imperial policy which might guide the foreign relations of the Empire. He admitted that developments had reached a difficult stage. With the Locarno Pact a new departure had occurred, namely, for the first time the British government had deliberately made no effort to carry the Dominions with her in a joint policy, hammered out at conferences, for the Empire as a whole. England's preoccupation with European questions made it necessary for Britain to assume obligations on the continent of Europe which the Dominions did not want to underwrite. The conference, said Smuts, had not come to grips with the problem of how to keep an association of independent states together.

After the right of secession, dearest to the Nationalist heart was the right of neutrality. Hertzog argued that the Dominions had the right to individual neutrality. The denial of this right to Great Britain or the Dominions not only would imply a denial of national freedom in its full international scope but it also would assume the existence of "a collective state entity having the character of an international person, whose will over-rides that of each of the constituent members." Moreover, as a member of the League of Nations South Africa had the obligation under certain conditions to be neutral. Smuts was not prepared to concede this and reproached the prime minister for raising the question of the right of neutrality, since the conference report said nothing about neutrality. No neutrality was possible, argued Smuts, in a treaty of alliance and the Commonwealth was much more than that. The Commonwealth meant "a sense of trust and confidence, of safety and security for all its members. It means that behind our weakness there is real power." But if the members were one and all to assert and proclaim their right of neutrality before the world, "what would remain of this security and this assurance? . . . We are not a free individual State, but we are a free member of an association, an Empire."[12]

Smuts's position on the nature of the Commonwealth was not free of ambiguity and mysticism. The Empire, he argued, was a "new fact, a unique thing within the domain of constitutional law and theory. It is a new attempt at human government. . . . The old categories and reasonings of international law do not apply to such a case. The empire is not a logical construction." If the Empire succeeded it might become "a new landmark in human government" and point to "a future in which the sovereign international State of the past will have disappeared, and with it the international anarchy which has existed during the era of international sovereignty."

It was sometimes difficult to follow Smuts's arguments. He seemed to blur the distinction between constitutional principles and law and policy. When he denied that he had ever favored a central authority in the Commonwealth, Hertzog interjected to ask whether that was not the inevitable result of his group-unity idea. To this Smuts replied in the negative. Group-unity, he said, was nothing more than "consultative unity." He did not wish to consider what the situation would be if

[12] Ibid., vol. 10, cols. 2155–56.

consultation did not produce unity on a concrete policy. There was also an ambiguity about Smuts's views on the right of dominion neutrality. He recognized that legally there was such a right but that it would be fatal to the Commonwealth if it were exercised. Hertzog likewise blurred the lines between law and policy. He did not think that the continued presence of a British naval base (Simonstown) on South African territory would compromise the Union's neutral position in case of a war in which Britain became involved—as if foreign policy could be conducted without reference to international law. He wanted both British naval protection and the right of neutrality.

The two party leaders were a little less than completely honest about each other's position in this debate. Hertzog and the Nationalists naturally desired to make as much political capital as possible out of the Balfour Declaration, which led Smuts to seek to minimize its significance. He also had the problem of not alienating some extremely pro-British leaders in his own party and the Unionists. Hence Smuts's line was first to assert that the Balfour Declaration contained nothing new; it merely stated what was the existing situation in interimperial relations, and that he had been largely instrumental in winning for South Africa and the other Dominions what was now recognized in an imperial conference statement. He also sought to minimize Hertzog's role in the achievements of the conference, saying it was not fair to the other parts of the Empire or to their statesmen to represent the declaration as his work alone.[13] It was a valuable document, Smuts said, and the gratitude of South Africa was due the prime minister for his part in the work.[14] To Smuts surely belongs the credit for preparing the way for the Balfour Declaration, but it was due to Hertzog's initiative and persistence that the 1926 conference did produce the statement. As far as the legal, constitutional questions were concerned, the two leaders were not far apart; it was with respect to the policy that would follow the recognition of freedom and equal status that the two differed. Smuts feared the ends for which the Nationalists would use national freedom. He was so loathe to have the Union do anything which would weaken the Commonwealth that he sometimes appeared to deny South Africa's complete freedom of choice.

By the Statute of Westminster, 1931, the British Parliament gave the

[13] *Hansard*, vol. 8, col. 1488.
[14] Ibid.

force of law to the principle of equal status expressed in the Balfour Declaration. The statute stipulated that any alteration in the law governing the succession to the throne or the "Royal Style and Titles" would thereafter require the assent of the Dominion parliaments as well as that of the United Kingdom, and that no law made by the Parliament of the United Kingdom would extend to any of the Dominions other than at the request and with the consent of that Dominion. In 1934, after Smuts and his party had formed a coalition with Hertzog and his wing of the National party with Smuts as deputy prime minister and minister of justice, a bill on the Status of the Union was introduced in Parliament to bring the Union's legislation into harmony with the Balfour Declaration and the Statute of Westminster.[15]

While Hertzog was fighting and winning the battle for a formal recognition of the Union's independent and sovereign status, he was taking measures to bring practices into harmony with this status and to provide South Africa with the customary symbols of statehood. In 1927 he created a department of external affairs, with himself as head, and in 1929 diplomatic representation was exchanged with the Netherlands, the United States, and Italy. The status of the governor general was changed in 1927 and in 1937 the first South African citizen (Sir Patrick Duncan) to hold the office was appointed governor general. Already in 1925 Afrikaans, a semi-indigenous language, replaced Dutch as one of the two official languages of the Union. After two years of bitter debate a Union flag was adopted in 1927. About one half of the population was opposed to any flag which included the Union Jack in its design, while the other half would not accept a flag which excluded it. In the end a compromise design which included the flags of the two republics and the Union Jack was agreed upon, but the Union Jack also continued as the national flag and was used for certain occasions. *God Save the King* was the official anthem, but *Die Stem van Suid Afrika* was in effect the unofficial one for Afrikaner Nationalists. The problem of a national anthem remained.

[15] The debate began on 28 March 1934, when Oswald Pirow, minister of railways and harbors, introduced the bill. Smuts's support of the bill was complete. *Hansard*, vol. 23, cols. 2072–82.

THE INDIAN QUESTION

In dealing with the perennial Indian question the Hertzog government made advances in the conduct of its external relations. In an attempt to solve the problem South Africa entered into direct negotiations with India without Empire participation. Years later India was to assert that the agreement reached in these negotiations was an international treaty while South Africa held it was only an informal agreement.[16]

Patrick Duncan, Smuts's minister of the interior, early in 1924 introduced the Class Areas bill which would provide areas in the towns of Natal where Indians could freely reside, trade, and acquire property. The bill, if enacted into law, would in effect institute segregation for the Indians. Before the bill could be acted upon Smuts prorogued Parliament and precipitated an election campaign which he lost to the Nationalist-Labor coalition. Hertzog and Colonel Frederick H. P. Creswell, the leader of the Labor party, had made Duncan's bill an issue in the campaign, declaring that it did not go far enough. In 1925, D. F. Malan, the new minister of the interior, introduced a bill known as the Areas Reservation bill, which did not differ greatly from the Duncan bill. But the introduction of the bill raised a furor in the Indian community.[17] The South African Indians appealed to the Indian government for intervention in their behalf. India had come out of World War I with a heightened nationalism and sense of international importance and was sensitive to the treatment Indians received in the Empire to whose victory in the war it had made a substantial contribution. New Delhi suggested negotiations. The Pact ministry withheld its proposed legislation and agreed to a round table conference "to explore all possible methods of settling the Indian question in the Union in a manner which would safeguard the maintenance of Western standards of life in South Africa by just and legitimate means."

Before the conference met, South Africa allowed India to send a commission to study the position of Indians in the Union and to present their case before a parliamentary select committee. The round table conference, which met in Cape Town, concluded on January 11, 1927. In the agreement India recognized the right of South Africa to use

[16] See Chapter 14.

[17] Natal had in 1923 deprived Indians of the right to buy or lease municipal land and in 1925 took away their right to vote in municipal elections. In 1926 the Transvaal made it more difficult for Indians to obtain trading licenses.

proper means for the maintenance of Western standards of life while South Africa recognized that Indians domiciled in the Union should be enabled "to conform" to Western standards of life if they cared to do so. For those Indians who wished to return to India or to go to other countries the Union government would organize a scheme of assisted emigration. In view of the agreement, the Union government decided not to proceed further with the Areas Reservation and Immigration and Restriction bills. It requested the Indian government to maintain an agent in the Union to secure cooperation between the two governments.[18]

Minister of the Interior Malan who with Prime Minister Hertzog was the chief negotiator for the Union, stated that the agreement was "more in the nature of an honourable and friendly understanding than of a rigid and binding treaty." The Union government had not surrendered its "freedom to deal legislatively with the Indian problem whenever and in whatever way" it deemed necessary and just, nor had the Indian government bound itself "either permanently or for any limited period, to co-operate with us in any practical solution of our problem in the manner agreed upon."

The whites generally and in particular those in Natal were dissatisfied with the agreement. A representative of Natal characterized it as "half-baked, ill-considered, hare-brained"; it did nothing to protect white civilization so far as Natal was concerned. Under the agreement the Indian government was not even obligated to encourage repatriation. The agreement assumed that Asians could be assimilated into Western civilization, which most Europeans believed was utterly impossible. For the Indians who remained in South Africa, the government had promised a policy of "uplift." Natal resented this provision, for it shouldered the province with heavy burdens which would have to be borne largely by its small European population.[19] The Indians were pleased with the agreement, regarding it as their Magna Charta. They especially noted the chapter dealing with "Upliftment of the Indian Community" in which the Union government firmly declared its belief in and adherence to "the principle that it is the duty of every civilized Government to devise ways and means and to take all possible steps for the uplifting of every section of their permanent population to the full extent of their

[18] *Hansard*, vol. 8, cols. 508–14, 21 Feb. 1927.
[19] O. R. Nel. *Hansard*, vol. 8, cols. 1400–1408.

capacity and opportunities." This was indeed a remarkable declaration of principles from Nationalist leaders. This expression of generosity was based on the expectation that so many Indians would take advantage of the assistance offered them by the Union government to repatriate that the Indian problem would be reduced to manageable proportions, but this did not take place. With the Indians disappointed in the program for their uplift and the Europeans in the meager results of the assisted emigration policy, relations began to deteriorate again.

In accordance with the terms of the Cape Town Agreement, a review conference was held in 1932. The situation was little better than it was in 1927. Natal and the Transvaal continued to restrict Indian rights; Natal persisted in a policy of refusing trading licenses and Transvaal abolished the right of Indian traders to appeal to the Supreme Court thus depriving Indians of much of the little protection they had enjoyed. This was done with at least the acquiescence of the Union government, since all provincial ordinances required the assent of the central government. Though most Europeans had given up all hope of solving the Indian problem by emigration and Indians resisted it, the government desperately made another attempt to get the Indians out of South Africa. If they could not be induced to return to India, they might be tempted by colonization schemes in other countries. The Union government proposed a joint inquiry to explore this possibility for Indians in India as well as in South Africa. Pending the inquiry the Cape Town Agreement would continue. India agreed to the proposal but did nothing to carry it out.

The commission collected a mass of data on various British colonies, analyzed it, and presented the pros and cons of each for Indian settlement schemes. The continent of Africa was eliminated from consideration as reserved for Africans. The commission finally recommended British Borneo, British Guiana, and East New Guinea. The commission's labors went for naught; their recommendations were ignored and soon forgotten.[20]

GENERAL PEACE POLICY

South Africa under the Pact ministry strongly supported most movements for the pacific settlement of disputes and in support of peace. It

[20] G. H. Calpin, *There Are No South Africans* (London, 1941), pp. 75–78.

welcomed the Kellogg Treaty for the renunciation of war.[21] General Smuts, the internationalist, was not as enthusiastic about the treaty as General Hertzog, the nationalist. Smuts believed a new attitude toward war had been born and a new principle had been laid down. It represented an attempt by the American government to find a formula by which it could support the forces for peace though not a member of the League of Nations. But Smuts recognized that there were widespread doubts about the effects of the treaty. Although on its face the treaty purported to be an absolute renunciation of war, there was an informal reservation of the right of self-defense. Belligerents always claim that they are fighting in self-defense.[22]

The Union accepted the optional clause of the Statute of the Permanent Court of International Justice which provided for automatic or compulsory jurisdiction of the Court, with the reservation that it did not extend to disputes with other members of the League which were also members of the British Commonwealth of Nations.[23] But South Africa refused to ratify the League of Nations' General Act of 1928 for the settlement of international disputes. When Smuts asked why the government took this position, Prime Minister Hertzog replied that it was dangerous for South Africa to ratify the General Act in view of the Union's Asiatic legislation. While certain reservations were permitted, it would be difficult to draft them so as to make sure that the Union would not be brought before an arbitration court on a matter related to its special legislation for Asians, such as those dealing with residence restrictions.[24]

The Pact ministry loyally supported the League of Nations. Prime Minister Hertzog and Minister of Finance Havenga attended the 1930 session of the Assembly. In announcing to Parliament that the two planned to represent the Union at the Assembly meetings, Hertzog said: "I consider it a very favorable opportunity for going there. In that way we will show, as we have indicated from the beginning, that we are real supporters of the great institution."[25]

[21] *Hansard*, vol. 12, cols. 8–10, 28 Jan. 1929.

[22] Ibid., cols. 11–16.

[23] The date of signature was 19 Sept. 1929. The Union attached three other minor reservations to its acceptance.

[24] *Hansard*, vol. 17, col. 2792, 23 April 1931.

[25] Ibid., vol. 15, col. 3019, 10 April 1930.

Fusion
1933–1939

6

Uncertainty
in the Midst of
Rising World Tensions

Hertzog and Smuts decided to bury the hatchet and join in a coalition cabinet (March 31, 1933), with Hertzog as prime minister and minister of external affairs and Smuts as deputy prime minister and minister of justice. The country was experiencing a severe economic crisis and the world situation was becoming tense. Hitler had come to power in Germany, and Japan had withdrawn from the League of Nations. Hertzog seemed convinced that Smuts and his party had accepted the sovereign status of the Union as embodied in the Statute of Westminster and had also accepted the policy of "South Africa first," and that the English-speaking section of the population had recognized the equality of language rights. There were difficulties in arriving at complete agreement on a few points—the divisibility of the Crown, the right of neutrality, and the sovereign status of the Union—but coalition was achieved and in the general elections held in May 1933, the coalition won an overwhelming victory.[1] In June 1934 Hertzog and Smuts and their parties moved from coalition to fusion as the United South African National party. D. F. Malan with his Purified National party and Colonel Charles F. Stallard with his Dominion party did not join in fusion for exactly opposite reasons. The first represented the extreme wing of Afrikanerdom and the latter of British jingoism.

CONSTITUTIONAL REFORM:
RELATIONS WITH BRITAIN

Hertzog pushed on with his constitutional program. He was determined to gather the full fruits of his previous labors by implementing the Statute of Westminster as the constitutional law of South Africa. In his speech opening the debate Minister Oswald Pirow noted that constitutional doubts in South Africa very soon became "political issues—political issues, moreover, fought with extreme bitterness, and almost invariably along racial lines."[2] However, an English-speaking leader of the House heartily supported the bill.[3] He said he knew it would not satisfy the extremists. Hertzog was very sanguine about the results of such a bill. It would improve relations between the Afrikaners and the English, extinguishing once and for all the smoldering embers of racial strife; it would remove doubts as to the genuineness of the South African spirit of the English-speaking section of the population; it would strengthen and not weaken the ties of sentiment and interest which bound them to Great Britain; it would clear the decks for great economic advance.[4]

General Smuts also gave it his wholehearted endorsement.[5] The bill did no more than express the existing constitutional position. The Status of the Union bill was "a measure of common agreement on the vital issues of our constitution." As he saw it, the most important part of the Balfour Declaration of 1926 was found in the preamble which he called "the great equation of our Commonwealth, upon which our Commonwealth rests." Smuts ended with a passionate plea for the acceptance of the bill by all sections of the population. South Africa had had two roots of division, the one racial,[6] the other constitutional. The first was withering; he hoped that this bill would "cut the root of the constitu-

---

[1] 144 out of 150 seats in the House of Assembly.

[2] *Hansard*, vol. 23, col. 1864, 28 Mar. 1934. "Racial" refers in this case to English versus Afrikaner.

[3] L. Blackwell.

[4] L. Blackwell. *Hansard*, vol. 23, cols. 1879–87.

[5] Smuts's speech is found in *Hansard*, vol. 23, cols. 2072–82.

[6] Smuts here has reference to the relations between Afrikaner and English, not to the native problem.

tional controversies which, for a generation have divided South Africa, and convulsed it to its foundations."

The bill if enacted into law would not settle everything, Smuts intimated. He said he had told the prime minister that he stood precisely where he had stood earlier, and Hertzog had agreed. But to Smuts's mind, "these things, secession, neutrality and the like are impracticable and academic. I do not believe that anything we can say in a constitution will settle our attitude or influence it when we come to the day of secession or to the day to declare our neutrality. These events, if ever they come to pass, would shake the whole British Empire and perhaps the whole world to its foundations."

The Status of the Union Act in effect moved the issues of secession and neutrality from constitutional law to politics. In spite of Smuts's statement that "whatever can be said in human language" to affirm the British connection was said in this bill, the connection was broken three decades later. It was South Africa's racial policy with respect to non-Europeans which precipitated the issue.

With the appointment in 1937 of a South African as governor general, Hertzog had about completed his constitutional reforms. One anomaly remained—the right of appeal to the Privy Council. This was removed by the Nationalist government in 1950.

SOUTH AFRICA AND THE DETERIORATING WORLD SITUATION

Suspecting that there existed a basic difference in attitude on world politics between Hertzog and Smuts, Malan as leader of the opposition sought to drive a wedge between the two and make political capital out of it. In his speech in support of his no-confidence motion at the opening of Parliament in January 1935, he stressed external policy. He said that the position of the previous government had been that if Great Britain went to war South Africa not only could stay out of the war but that as a matter of policy it would remain outside; but what the position of the present government was it was impossible to find out. It spoke with two voices, according to Malan: the minister of justice (Smuts) says that South Africa cannot stay out of a war in which Britain is involved, but the prime minister says it can. So far the minister of justice has acted as minister of external affairs and the prime minister has never contradicted him in public. The future of cooperation between Afrikaners and English in South Africa depended on whether the Union was to become involved in the disputes of the world because England was involved. If that was the policy of the government it would cause a more serious division between the races than ever before. The problems of South Africa could be solved only in an undivided and unadulterated South African patriotism, such as was found in the National party.[7]

Oswald Pirow, minister of defense, told the delegates to the Fifth Imperial Press Conference which met at Cape Town in February 1935 that there was no anti-British feeling in South Africa; nevertheless, if war broke out and the government should rashly attempt to commit the country to participate in another overseas war, there would be large-scale disturbances, possibly even civil war. For this reason the government would not take part "in any general scheme of imperial defence." He observed that a large portion of Africa was being turned into a parade ground for militarized natives. South Africa's contribution to imperial defense was seeing that her ports were properly defended.[8]

ITALY, ABYSSINIA,[9] AND THE LEAGUE OF NATIONS

South Africa supported League of Nations sanctions against Italy for invading Abyssinia in October 1935. Hertzog and Smuts were in thorough agreement on this matter. South Africa was the first member of the League of Nations to announce that it would put into force all the sanctions the world organization should vote. Charles te Water, high commissioner at London, as South Africa's representative in the League of Nations Assembly appealed to Mussolini and the Italian people "to pause and consider, even at this eleventh hour."[10]

Most people in South Africa, including the Bantu, were in agreement with the government's policy of firm support of the League in the application of sanctions against Italy. The war in Abyssinia profoundly aroused the Africans. For them it was a case of black men defending their country against white aggressors and Haile Selassie was their

---

[7] *Hansard*, vol. 24, cols. 95–97.

[8] *The Guardian* (Manchester), 6 Feb. 1935.

[9] Prior to World War II, Ethiopia was generally called "Abyssinia."

[10] League of Nations, *Official Journal*, Special Supplement No. 138, p. 79. Te Water's speech was not free of racial overtones—Italy's action endangered white civilization. Te Water was honored with the presidency of the Assembly in 1933.

hero. The defeat of Abyssinia deeply depressed the African community.[11] Prime Minister Hertzog was as ardent a supporter of Great Britain and the League of Nations in this crisis as his anglophile deputy, General Smuts. Only D. F. Malan and his small band of Purified Nationalists were opposed.

A broad debate on the issue of support of League sanctions and of foreign policy generally was precipitated when on January 31, 1936, Malan moved that the House express itself as unwavering in a policy of peace as opposed to military or economic sanctions and in favor of neutrality in all wars in which South Africa had no direct concern. Sanctions were dangerous. They could cause a local war to develop into a European or world conflagration. The League of Nations had become an appendage of two great powers and was being used to serve as a bulwark of the Treaty of Versailles.[12] Hertzog replied that his government was following "a policy of peace, coupled with the honourable protection of our freedom, and the interests of the state." The attitude of Italy with respect to Abyssinia was to his mind "one of the most serious threats to our freedom, and to the interest of South Africa that has ever occurred in the past forty or fifty years." Malan's policy would make the application of sanctions impossible and destroy the collective security principle of the League of Nations.[13]

The Italo-Abyssinian conflict caused an important change in General Smuts's thinking about the League of Nations. In a speech in London in 1934 he had said that the League was a conference table, but in 1935 he said that sanctions were fundamental.[14] In the debate on the Malan motion Smuts argued that there was no alternative to the policy of the government: "fidelity to our engagements and loyalty to the League of Nations. That is our great bond and our great Charter. . . . This is not the time to desert the League. The stronger and the more effective the League is the better for us and for our future protection."[15]

These sentiments were anathema to Malan and his Nationalists. The Nationalists expected from Smuts the kind of sentiment he had ex-

[11] See Edward Roux, *Time Longer Than a Rope* (Madison, Wis., 1964), pp. 202–203.

[12] *Hansard*, vol. 26, cols. 30–31.

[13] Ibid., col. 57.

[14] W. K. Hancock, *Smuts*, 2 vols. (Cambridge, Eng., 1962, 1968), vol. 2: *The Fields of Force, 1919–1950*, pp. 272–73.

[15] *Hansard*, vol. 26, cols. 80–82.

pressed in the debate, but they professed disappointment in Hertzog, against whom they directed their most bitter attacks, asking whether the prime minister now characterized as ridiculous his former views in favor of a policy of neutrality in wars waged by England.[16] The Nationalists wanted a statement or a commitment from the prime minister as to what the policy of the government would be in case a general war should break out.

Hertzog was deeply disappointed when it became evident that League sanctions had failed and was loathe to accept the fact. If the League wanted to do its duty it would at least have to continue the sanctions which it had voted until the aggressor eventually gave in. "I say again that before it can be said that sanctions have been a failure it must first appear that the League of Nations has said that sanctions must not be proceeded with any more, but when that is stated, then the League of Nations will be dead."[17]

The South African representative at the League of Nations, Charles te Water, delivered a forceful speech in the Assembly in opposition to the relaxation of sanctions against Italy. He chided the great powers for their failure to press the issue to a successful conclusion. "Today we know that the Covenant is falling to pieces in our hands," he declared. "Fifty nations, led by three of the most powerful nations in the world, are about to declare their powerlessness to protect the weakest in their midst from destruction. The authority of the League of Nations is about to come to nought."[18]

SOUTH AFRICA'S ATTITUDE TOWARD IMPENDING WAR

In this debate Malan succeeded in getting a statement from a minister as to what the policy of the government would be in case of a future war. Minister of Defense Pirow made a statement (authorized by the prime minister) on May 6, 1936: "We are not bound directly or indirectly to take part in any war in Africa or elsewhere. We shall take part in no war except when the true interests of South Africa make such a participation inevitable. We as a Government will not even take part in an inevitable war, except after the people through its representatives

[16] Ibid., col. 90.

[17] Ibid., vol. 27, col. 3120, 6 May 1936.

[18] 1 July 1936. League of Nations, *Records*, Sixteenth Ordinary Session of the Assembly, Twentieth Plenary Meeting.

in Parliament have by means of the largest possible measure of unanimity given us unambiguous instructions to that effect."[19]

Hertzog at this time seemed to be deeply concerned about his country's security. In this debate he flared up at Malan's insistence on South Africa's becoming involved in England's wars. He said there was a time when Britain was his enemy and he had to fight her hard, but South Africa had acquired both its freedom and the friendship of the greatest country in the world. Among all the nations of the world there was not one which was prepared to come to South Africa's assistance, or would do for it what England had already done for it. Apparently realizing the political dynamite this remark contained, he went on to say, "I make my honorable friend, the Leader of the Opposition, a present of this, because I want the people in the country to have no doubt about my attitude and about the attitude of the Government in reference to this matter."[20]

There were similarities as well as differences in the foreign policy views of Hertzog and Smuts. Both regarded the Treaty of Versailles as the source of European tensions. Smuts had been opposed to many of its provisions and had hesitated to sign it.[21] Hertzog, who had been opposed to South Africa's participation in World War I, felt just as strongly about the Treaty of Versailles. When he was in London in May 1937 for the coronation and the imperial conference he said that European unrest was created by the Versailles Treaty. He advised that the injustice which still remained be abolished and to rebuild on a basis of "right and justice in a spirit of goodwill and cooperation."[22] Malan's views on the Treaty of Versailles were, if anything, even stronger. He branded it "that greatest, worst *heridites damnasa* of world history." Instead of the League of Nations being used to remove the inequities of the treaty, it was used to maintain the status quo in the interests of certain nations.[23]

South Africa undoubtedly exerted its influence in London for peace. War, if it came and whether South Africa remained neutral or participated in it, would bring an end to fusion and the Hertzog ministry.

[19] *Hansard*, vol. 27, col. 3120.

[20] Ibid., cols. 3120–21.

[21] W. K. Hancock and Jean van der Poel, eds., *Selections from the Smuts Papers*, 4 vols. (Cambridge, Eng., 1966), 4:174, 179.

[22] Quoted by Oswald Pirow, *James Barry Munnik Hertzog* (Cape Town, 1957), pp. 223–24.

[23] *Hansard*, vol. 32, cols. 3574–75.

Smuts was in agony trying to decide what his duty was.[24] Yet, in spite of his changing attitude Smuts supported Hertzog's peace and neutrality policy. So great was the tension in the country that had war broken out in 1938 at the time of the crisis in Czechoslovakia, the government with the support of Smuts would have tried to maintain neutrality. The Afrikaners just at this time were enjoying a national, republican festival in the form of the *voortrekker's* centenary celebrations, and emotions were running high. As late as September 1938 Smuts, with the other members of the cabinet, signed the strange document submitted by Hertzog calling for a status of semineutrality in the event of war in which the United Kingdom should be a belligerent.

Hitler's campaign for the recovery of the former German territories was a cause of embarrassment to the South African leaders, especially to Hertzog. Charles te Water, high commissioner in London and a devoted follower of Hertzog, while on a visit in Canada suggested an international conference, in which South Africa would participate, to consider Germany's colonial grievances and claims.

The South African response to Hitler's demand for the return of the German colonies involved strange and contradictory attitudes on the part of many of the Union's leaders. In 1935 Hertzog urged a plan for the cession of colonial territory to Germany, believing this would satisfy German demands and bring about a relaxation of international tensions. Probably realizing that this might result in pressure on the Union to return South West Africa, he suggested that Liberia would best serve this purpose.[25] Hertzog apparently favored a readjustment of colonial possessions provided it was not at South Africa's expense. The Nationalists were prepared to make peace with Germany in the hope that it would give them the republic. Smuts at first entertained the idea of a colonial resettlement, but as Hitler's purposes became steadily more clear he became opposed to any appeasement. Hertzog and Smuts and Pirow, the minister for defense, were agreed that they did not want Germany entrenched within bombing distance of the Rand mining area and the Simonstown naval base.

In October 1938 Pirow went to England to negotiate with the British War Office about military supplies. Smuts suggested to him that since he

---

[24] Hancock, *Smuts*, 2 vols. (Cambridge, Eng., 1962, 1968), vol. 1: *The Sanguine Years, 1870–1919*, p. 313.

[25] C. M. van den Heever, *Generaal J. B. M. Hertzog* (Johannesburg, 1944), pp. 654–55.

was *persona grata* with Hitler he should offer his services to Chamberlain as a mediator. Apparently it was also Smuts's suggestion that he relate the Jewish problem to the colonial question.[26] Pirow did go to Germany and conferred with Ribbentrop and Hitler. He emphasized that he greatly desired close relations with Germany but that unfortunately the treatment of the Jews in Germany was causing great difficulties. Something had to be done to solve the Jewish question. Hitler stated that Anglo-German relations could not be consolidated as long as Britain refused to accept Germany as a great power. This was tied up with the colonial question. Britain with forty-five million inhabitants required a quarter of the globe as living space and other states such as France, Holland, and Belgium regarded vast overseas areas as a vital necessity. "Nothing was granted to Germany, the greatest nation in Europe with her eighty million inhabitants. This was a state of affairs that could not last forever." When Pirow suggested that Germany help solve the Jewish question by offering one of the former German colonies as a place of settlement, Hitler replied that the German people never could be made to understand why areas "in which the blood of so many German heroes had been shed . . . should be put at the disposal of the bitterest enemies of the Germans."

From the interview with the Führer, it was obvious that South West Africa was the former colony which Hitler most desired. He chided South Africa for not being able to understand that South West Africa should be returned to Germany. Pirow explained that this territory was of great military and political importance for South Africa. While the Union did not want to go to war with Germany over South West Africa, it would rather obtain other areas for it in exchange. Hitler then asked about East Africa as a possibility. To this Pirow replied that East Africa was a country which was "already integrated as a result of its internal relations to the great stretch of territory of the Whites in Africa, which extended in a chain from Abyssinia to the Cape. This was a community of a white master race as opposed to the Negroes." Hitler concluded the conference with the observation that since the governments had all stated their attitude on the colonial question so decisively it was useless to raise the issue.[27]

[26] Pirow, *Hertzog*, p. 228.

[27] United States Department of State, R. J. Sontag and others, eds., *Documents of German Foreign Policy, 1918–1945*, Series D (Washington, D. C., 1951), 4:335–41.

South West Africa was giving the Hertzog government serious concern. Over 1,700 Germans remained in the mandated territory after World War I and became British subjects. There was no trouble with them until Hitler came to power, when a complete change took place. New German immigrants arrived and developed a concerted and determined movement to mobilize all the Germans and their social and cultural institutions for the Nazification of the whole white community. It was not a spontaneous movement of the Germans in South West Africa, but was inspired and directed from Berlin.[28] The prime movers and instigators seem to have been the German minister in Pretoria and the consul general in Windhoek. The Germans in South Africa as well as in South West Africa were dragooned into the movement. Recalcitrants were reported to the authorities in Germany and any one who had property or relatives in the fatherland was quickly brought to account. In response to intelligence reports that Hitler planned a coup in South West Africa in April 1939, Smuts, as minister of justice, sent a force of three hundred policemen to Windhoek, without consulting the cabinet. The opposition sharply criticized the stroke as an act that might provoke war.[29] Pirow thought Smuts had hoped for an attempted coup in Windhoek as this would have suited his war policy.[30] How Smuts viewed the situation is revealed by remarks he made to one of his biographers: "Austria and other small states had been invaded on the plea that they could not keep internal order." The Union would not lay itself open to invasion on that ground.[31]

Malan revealed later that as prime minister he learned from the then unpublished German documents that contact had been maintained between persons in South Africa with belligerent Germany. Information about the presence and movement of ships in Table Bay was sent by a member of the *Ossewa-Brandwag* in Cape Town along the organization's channels to the German consul general in Lourenço Marques, who sent it on by radio to Berlin. As a result German submarines were able to sink many Allied ships in the sea lanes around the Cape.[32]

---

[28] In a memo to the Permanent Mandates Commission (17 Mar. 1937) H. B. Hirsekorn of Windhoek, South West Africa, frankly stated that the Germans "submitted their political and especially their internal difficulties to official quarters in Germany" (Permanent Mandates Commission, *Minutes*, 33d Session, 1937 [Geneva, 1937], p. 138).

[29] J. C. Smuts, Jr., *Jan Christiaan Smuts* (Cape Town, 1952), pp. 372–73.

[30] Pirow, *Hertzog*, pp. 242–43.

[31] F. S. Crawford, *Jan Smuts* (New York, 1944), p. 280.

Hitler also tried to use the Germans in South Africa and he tried to propagandize Afrikaners. South Africa was bombarded by radio from Germany, "in a way more dangerous, subtle and insidious than any attack by armies."[33] Many Afrikaners fell under the spell of Hitler's national socialism.[34]

NEUTRALITY OR BELLIGERENCY

As the crisis in Europe deepened Hertzog and Smuts began to move apart in their views. According to Pirow, the idea of Germany as Europe's bulwark against Russia became one of the main principles of Hertzog's foreign policy.[35] It is clear that Hertzog and his government were under no duress from Britain to support it diplomatically in the deteriorating world situation. The contrary may have been true, that London was influenced by Hertzog's policy of appeasement. As late as April 12, 1939, the prime minister declared in Parliament, "We are acting precisely like friends, and let me say that those are the relations between ourselves and England, and I am proud of the relation of friendship, of the most intimate friendship, which there exists, but a friendship as between friends and not as allies who have entered into an alliance for a certain purpose."[36]

Smuts had believed in Hitler's good faith until the Czechoslovakian crisis but with the annexation of Bohemia and Moravia he lost all confidence in him and felt that South Africa had no other course but to stand by Britain.[37] In speech after speech in the year preceding the outbreak of war, Smuts declared this conviction in no uncertain terms.[38] On May 4, 1938, he said, "If one part of the Empire is in danger, then

---

[32] D. F. Malan, *Afrikaner Volkseenheid en my Ervarings op die Pad Daarheen* [Afrikaner National Unity and My Experiences on the Path Thereto] (Cape Town, 1959), pp. 222–23.

[33] Prime Minister Smuts to party meeting at Bloemfontein, 3 Nov. 1939, quoted by his son, J. C. Smuts, Jr., *Jan Christiaan Smuts*, p. 377.

[34] Malan, *Afrikaner Volkseenheid*, chapter 31. Even Prime Minister Hertzog fell under the influence of authoritarian ideas. In a speech on 8 Sept. 1934, he declared, "The party system is played out. The democratic system is past. More than half of the nations have already abolished it. In South Africa this must also happen" (Malan, *Afrikaner Volkseenheid*, p. 187).

[35] Pirow, *Hertzog*, p. 221.

[36] *Hansard*, vol. 34, col. 2779.

[37] Pirow, *Hertzog*, p. 245.

[38] *Daily Telegraph*, 13 Jan. 1939.

all the other parts will stand by the one that is in danger. The policy of South Africa is to stand loyally and faithfully by our friends. If England is attacked then I take it that our position is clear."[39] When Malan asked the prime minister whether he subscribed to Smuts's views he replied that when and if the occasion arose the government would do its duty and give leadership.[40]

Malan charged the government with having no external policy. The prime minister, asserted Malan, was keeping the House "completely and intentionally in the dark in relation to the policy or lack of policy on the part of the government." Because of the division in the party and the cabinet the government was seeking its "only salvation and refuge. . . . in a policy of ambiguity and bilateral statement, in speaking with two voices."[41] Hertzog, on the other hand, stated that what the leader of the opposition wanted was a statement that the government would remain neutral in all circumstances, so long as there was no actual military attack on South Africa. He was not prepared to make such a statement.[42]

When Great Britain declared war on Germany on September 3, 1939, the Union Parliament happened to be assembled in a brief special session. The issue of war or neutrality could not be evaded. Hertzog had repeatedly stated that if and when this issue should arise, Parliament would decide. Half of the cabinet followed Hertzog in support of a resolution declaring the Union neutral; the other half supported Smuts in calling for a declaration of war on Germany. Hertzog reported to the House that the division in the ministry was unbridgeable. The present government had split in two.[43]

In support of his position Hertzog declared that the government had promised the nation time and again that South Africa would not take part in any war unless its interests were so threatened that its existence was at stake. He would stand by that policy. Being dragged into the war would be a catastrophe. Two attempts had been made to bring together the Afrikaans and the English sections of the country to fuse them into

[39] Quoted by Malan, *Hansard*, vol. 32, col. 1667, 25 Aug. 1938.
[40] Ibid., col. 1683.
[41] Ibid., cols. 2716–17. *Die Transvaler* was suspicious even of Hertzog's proposed neutrality (1 Sept. 1939). Some Afrikaner Nationalists feared that involvement in war would lead to the military training of Africans.
[42] *Hansard*, vol. 34, cols. 2726–36.
[43] Ibid., vol. 36, cols. 18–19.

one nation; the failure of the second attempt would shock the people so deeply that it would take years for them to recover. For him to advocate a declaration of war would be disloyalty to the Afrikaner people.

Hertzog argued that the Union had no interest in the war between Germany and Poland. England had certain obligations toward Poland, but South Africa had none. He did not wish to question the sincerity of Chamberlain and other British statesmen who believed that Hitler wanted to dominate the world, but in his opinion there was no proof of this. He explained all the aggressive acts of Hitler and the German people as determination to free themselves from the humiliation of the provisions of the Treaty of Versailles.[44]

What General Hertzog proposed was a qualified neutrality; in effect what General Smuts proposed was a qualified belligerency. Hertzog said in his speech that the difference between him and his group and Smuts and his followers was that the latter proposed active participation in the war. That, however, was not an accurate description of Smuts's position. Smuts said that it would be wrong and fatal for this country to continue to treat Germany as a friend, "as if nothing had happened in the world." That was the issue, not South Africa's active participation in the war. The situation of South Africa might be such that an active participation as in the last war would not be possible. To look after South Africa's vital interests in Africa would probably engage all the resources and all the efforts of which the Union was capable.

The middle course of semineutrality which the prime minister proposed was one quite unknown to international law and would present South Africa with grave problems, Smuts believed. It would be respected by no state, and certainly not by Germany. South Africa would be forced out of this compromise course. It would be far better to adopt a clear-cut line recognized by international law and the usage of nations.

Smuts disagreed with Hertzog on the real cause of the war. Poland and Danzig were the immediate occasion of the war but not the real cause, which in Smuts's judgment went far beyond Poland and virtually touched South Africa. He regretted that the prime minister's statement read like a complete justification of Hitler. In September 1938 there was the feeling, not only in South Africa but universally, that Hitler had a strong case and that he simply wanted to unite a portion of German land with Germany and the people with their fatherland. Twelve months

[44] Ibid., vol. 36, cols. 19–23.

earlier they were prepared to accept his word and to make concessions, but following Munich most of the world had changed its ideas as to the aims and objectives of the German chancellor. The prime minister, Smuts said, was closing his eyes to these developments when he stated that there was no question of domination. Hitler had given due notice that after Danzig he would demand the return of the German colonies, an issue that virtually touched the interests of South Africa. If the course proposed by the prime minister were followed, South West Africa might as well be written off and the future security of the Union would be threatened. As Smuts saw it, the world was once more up against a fundamental crisis in human destiny, in the future of civilization.[45]

Another matter that distressed Smuts with respect to the prime minister's proposed policy was that, however disguised, it would practically dissociate them from the British Commonwealth of Nations. It was a question not only of loyalty and self-respect, but of national security. If the Union deliberately dissociated itself from the line taken by Britain and the other Dominions and continued with Germany on a friendly basis, "we are going to get what we deserve," and when the day of trouble comes, "as it is bound to come as sure as we sit here today, that claim for the return of South West Africa will be presented to us at the point of a bayonet. We have to say whether we are going to face that issue alone and stand alone against the odds which will then confront us."

Smuts moved an amendment to the prime minister's motion calling for severance of relations with Germany, continuance of cooperation with the British Commonwealth, all necessary measures of defense of its territories and also a provision not to send armed forces overseas.[46]

In this debate Smuts was not as fortunate in all his supporters as he was in his chief opponent, Hertzog, who alienated many by his all-out defense of Hitler. Heaton Nicholls presented an ultraloyalist British point of view. According to him the Union automatically was at war when Britain went to war. The prime minister by his motion was

---

[45] Later in a message to the people of South Africa Smuts stressed the moral issue. Nazism with its hostile attitude toward Christianity and its systematic promotion of a new paganism was in conflict with South Africa's spiritual outlook (*Die Transvaler*, 12 Sept. 1939).

[46] *Hansard*, vol. 36, cols. 23–31.

actually proposing secession from the Commonwealth, which would be fought by every loyal British subject in South Africa. The legal effect of the prime minister's motion would be to destroy the Act of Union.[47] Fortunately for Smuts's position, another English-speaking member of the House, B. K. Long, took a point of view diametrically opposite to that of Nicholls. He argued that under the Statute of Westminster as confirmed in South Africa by the Status of the Union Act the Union did have the right to declare its neutrality, and he was convinced that this was also the opinion of the very large majority of English-speaking South Africans. But he was opposed to the prime minister's proposal to attempt to take a middle course where no middle course was possible.[48]

Malan and his Purified Nationalists supported Hertzog's motion. Malan's argument was similar to Hertzog's, but better stated. "Suppose," said Malan, "the British connexion, as we know it, had not existed, and war conditions had arisen in Europe, would there have been any question on the merits of the case for our country to participate in such a war?" If the Treaty of Versailles had not existed, Germany would not have had a Hitler. If moral ties drew South Africa into all of England's wars, "then I say talk of freedom as much as you like, but we are a country of serfs." [49]

On the evening of September 4 the House adopted Smuts's amendment for entering the war on the Allied side by a vote of eighty to sixty-seven. There were a few English names among those who supported Hertzog's motion and about twenty-five Afrikaner names among the supporters of Smuts's amendment.

Prime Minister Hertzog asked the governor general, Sir Patrick Duncan, to dissolve Parliament, but he refused the request. He feared that a general election at that time would lead to bitterness and even violence. Moreover, the Parliament had been elected in May of the previous year and the question of South Africa's participation in a war in which England was involved had been put clearly before the electorate; the policy proclaimed by Hertzog and his ministers was that the question, if it should arise, would be decided by Parliament. Parliament had decided, and if Smuts could form a government which could

[47] Ibid., cols. 34–35.
[48] Ibid., cols. 37–43.
[49] Ibid., cols. 45–52.

command the support of the House he did not feel justified in dissolving Parliament.[50] On September 6 the Union severed its relations with the German Reich.[51]

[50] *Cape Times*, 5 Sept. 1939.

[51] Union of South Africa, *Government Gazette*, 6 Sept. 1939: The question of war and peace was not placed before the Senate until 30 January 1940. It confirmed the decision of the House with little debate (Union of South Africa, *Parliamentary Debates* (Senate), 1940, cols. 103ff.

World War II and Aftermath 1939–1948

7

The Resurgence
of Afrikaner Nationalism

Parliament's decision to enter the war marks a watershed in South African history. Smuts and his supporters won that victory, but they helped set the stage for the ultimate triumph of Afrikaner nationalism and republicanism. The movement begun by Hertzog in World War I, somewhat arrested by the Balfour Declaration and the Statute of Westminster, gathered momentum during and after World War II. Hertzog joined forces with Malan and the two issued a joint statement that "a republican form of government, separated from the British, was best suited to the traditions and aspirations of the South African people."[1]

In a speech to the crowds which saw him off at the railway station after his defeat on the war issue, Hertzog said that Afrikanerdom had found its unity, which would never again be taken from it.[2] D. F. Malan declared that their future course would be directed at one aim: the Republic of South Africa. Only then could the country exercise self-determination.[3] *Die Transvaler* stated editorially that the political struggle had finally assumed its natural character—that of a contest between republicanism and imperialism.[4]

While Smuts had succeeded in taking his country into the war on the side of Britain, his effort to mobilize the country for full-scale military participation in the war met with enormous difficulties. This was due to the mixed racial composition of the Union's population and the attitudes which obtained among the dominant whites, especially the Afrikaners. Most whites were opposed to enlisting non-Europeans for combat service.

The three whites who represented the natives in the House of Assembly had helped Smuts obtain his slender majority for his resolution for South African participation in the war. They did so because they believed Hitler represented dictatorship, aggression, and racialism. Most Africans were prepared to enlist and fight the Nazis, but because they were restricted to noncombat service their enthusiasm cooled. The African National Congress in December 1939 endorsed the war resolution but urged that all races in South Africa be admitted into full citizenship with equal rights and duties and declared that the country could be effectively defended only if all sections of the population were included on equal terms in the defense system.[5]

For a brief time it looked as if adverse developments in the war might bring about a change in racial policy. When the Japanese invaded Southeast Asia and captured Singapore it seemed possible that they might proceed against Madagascar and even attack South Africa. The coloreds did not share the alarm of the whites; they were plainly sympathetic with the Japanese. At this point Smuts made his amazing "retreat from segregation" speech.[6] He declared that isolation had gone and segregation had fallen on evil days. "How can it be otherwise?" he asked. "The whole trend both in this country and the African continent has been in the opposite direction, towards closer contacts between the various sections. Isolation has gone. The old isolations of South Africa have gone, and gone forever."[7] The Japanese were stopped and the tide began to turn in Europe, and Smuts's "charter" was forgotten.

[1] *Daily Herald* (London), 29 Jan. 1940.

[2] *Die Transvaler*, 7 Sept. 1939.

[3] Ibid., 6 Sept. 1939.

[4] 6 Sept. 1939.

[5] Edward Roux, *Time Longer Than a Rope* (Madison, Wis., 1964), p. 305. The South African government apparently also persuaded the British government not to use recruits from the Protectorates as fighting men, fearing the influence this practice would have on South African natives (ibid., p. 307).

[6] Cape Town, 21 Jan. 1942.

[7] Roux, *Time Longer Than a Rope*, p. 306; Alan Paton, *Hofmeyr* (London, 1964), pp. 353–54.

Malan justified Japan's aggression on the ground that it needed living space. To this Smuts replied that if Japan should seek living space in South Africa he would arm every African and colored person who could bear arms. Malan's response to this bold statement was that this was too high a price to pay to the Empire.[8] The pressing need for troops led Smuts in 1944 to propose arming the colored soldiers and using them in combat. The cabinet rejected the proposal.[9]

South Africa was unprepared for war.[10] Hertzog had been deeply concerned about formal recognition of the Union's sovereign status, but he made no effort to free the country from utter dependence on the British navy for the security of South Africa's long coastline and trade routes. The Union had only a token army and air force. Smuts held former Defense Minister Pirow responsible for the sad state of the country's defenses. He ascribed Pirow's inactivity to the fact that he expected South Africa to be neutral in the impending war.[11]

Another military problem which confronted Smuts's government was the commitment of troops outside the borders of the Union. There was much opposition to the use of troops beyond the Union's frontiers. Smuts proceeded cautiously. He declared that if the need arose for the defense either of the Union or of the British territories, his government would extend operations as far as Kenya and Tanganyika, but it would use only volunteers in these campaigns.[12] He reminded the opposition that Defense Minister Pirow had said repeatedly that South Africa's defense line extended to the equator and beyond. Pirow protested that his assurance to Kenya and Tanganyika to come to their aid if in danger had been misinterpreted. He had in mind only danger arising from attacks of blacks upon whites. South Africa regarded itself as the protector of white civilization.[13]

Italy's entry into the war in June 1940 brought the war nearer to South Africa, and troops were sent beyond the equator. South African forces took a leading part in wresting Somaliland and Ethiopia from the

[8] Paton, *Hofmeyr*, p. 353.

[9] W. K. Hancock, *Smuts*, 2 vols. (Cambridge, Eng., 1962, 1968), vol. 2: *Fields of Force, 1919–1950*, p. 412.

[10] "South Africa was militarily naked when the war broke out," writes Smuts's biographer, ibid., p. 331.

[11] *Hansard*, vol. 39, col. 5020, 15 April 1940.

[12] Ibid., vol. 37, col. 981. Three-fourths of the men in the armed forces volunteered for this service.

[13] Ibid., cols. 1029–30.

Italians and participated in the North African campaign against Rommel. A large force was sent to Egypt. A South African brigade took part in the occupation of Madagascar. This operation was in technical violation of the war resolution about the use of South African troops, but it could be argued plausibly that Madagascar was in the Union's defense zone. In February 1943 Smuts obtained authorization from Parliament for the employment overseas of armed forces on a voluntary basis. Smuts argued that though Africa had been cleared of the enemy the Union was not safe so long as the war might be lost elsewhere.[14]

How deeply and bitterly the country was divided on the war issue was revealed in nearly every debate in Parliament. When Smuts in February 1940 came before Parliament with a War Measures bill providing for sweeping, emergency powers the opposition was prepared to bombard Smuts and his government for being guilty of attacking the liberties of the people, but Smuts threw his opponents into confusion by withdrawing the most drastic provisions of the bill in his opening speech.

Several times more Hertzog pressed his isolationist, defeatist, and Nationalist views on Parliament and the country. On January 23, 1940, he moved that the war with Germany be ended and peace be restored. Germany was wrongfully accused of lust for world domination. Others argued that they were not hostile to England but Germany was a bulwark against Bolshevism and it was a pity that Britain had not cooperated with her.[15] The severe Allied reverses in April, May, and June 1940 were seized upon by Hertzog to demand again that South Africa get out of the war. On June 17 Hertzog addressed a public letter to Prime Minister Smuts and a few days later he and Malan signed a manifesto declaring continued participation in the war to be hopeless and calling on Afrikaners to demonstrate for peace. On August 29 he introduced a resolution in the House that "every effort be made forthwith and immediate steps be taken to restore peace with Germany and Italy." He asserted that British victory over Germany was an illusion; that the war was hopelessly lost.[16]

Prime Minister Smuts replied sharply to Hertzog's speech. South Africans were not deserters; they did not turn about and run away when things were going against them. There was no reason for changing

[14] Ibid., vol. 45, cols. 505, 1002.
[15] Ibid., cols. 38–137.
[16] Ibid., vol. 40, cols. 79–89.

their attitude and course of action. Hertzog had said nothing about the terms of peace the opposition would accept. Would it mean giving South West Africa and Tanganyika back to Germany? Kenya and Tanganyika "are our northern boundaries so far as defence is concerned. . . . We know that if those British colonies in the north fall into the hands of Italy, then a deadly attack will be made upon us, on the defence of South Africa. We cannot wait until the enemy reaches the Limpopo."[17]

Smuts further argued that the war was more than a military struggle. It went much deeper. It touched the foundations of humanity and human existence. It would be treasonous and cowardly to withdraw from the struggle. He warned that speeches like those of General Hertzog encouraged underground movements to take over the government by force.

Pirow, the former minister of defense who had organized a group—the New Order, somewhat after the manner of the Nazis—attacked the government in a clever, pro-German speech.[18] "The Prime Minister," he said, "cannot tell us why we are fighting but he says that he is determined to fight to the end." Pirow prophesied that South Africa would soon reach the stage in which "resistance to the unscrupulous and cruel sacrifice of the interests of South Africa for the sake of the Empire will be regarded as high treason."

The Nationalist opposition used the debate to air again all the grievances of the Afrikaners against the British. The Boer War was refought and the old Boer grievances against the English were paraded again. The Afrikaner had no interest in the war and would not support it. They were being forced to support it, they were harassed and even persecuted, and treated as Nazis.[19] Peace should be concluded because the war was driving a deep wedge between English-speaking and Afrikaans-speaking peoples of the country, causing extremely bitter relations.

The Nationalists used every possible opportunity to attack the government's war policy. The same arguments were made in debate after debate, with few new points introduced. The character of the debate varied only with the changes in the fortunes of the Allies in the war. The debate that followed the no-confidence motion introduced by Dr.

---

[17] Ibid., cols. 89–101.
[18] Ibid., cols. 103–10.
[19] Ibid., cols. 133–39, for the speech by Capt. G. H. F. Strijdom.

Malan in February 1941 was the longest in the history of the House up to that time. It was a rambling debate. The government was charged with wholesale prosecution of people who did not support the war. There were occasional expressions of anti-Semitism.[20] Frequently there were expressions of concern about the use of non-Europeans in the armed services.[21]

The brutal German invasion of the Netherlands came as a severe jolt to the Nationalists. Smuts must have hoped that it would change the attitude of many of them toward support of the war. The Afrikaners had maintained close cultural and religious relations with the Netherlands. Many of their leaders had acquired their higher education in Holland.[22] They had pointed to the Netherlands policy of neutrality as a model for South Africa. Smuts was not the man to neglect so fine an opportunity either to win converts to his cause or to embarrass his political enemies. When the Netherlands was invaded Smuts made a national broadcast in which he gave expression to a feeling of profound sympathy with the Dutch nation in their hour of suffering. Malan reacted to the broadcast in a speech in the House. In view of the difficulty he was in, Malan's speech was a masterful performance. "Whatever the attitude of hon. members may be in connection with the question of our participation in the war," he said, "we are in agreement with each other on one point, and that is that we have the greatest sympathy and fellow-feeling with Holland in the disaster it has met with." News had come that the Queen of Holland had taken refuge in another state. Afrikaners felt that they stood in a special relation toward her, for "she, more than anyone else showed her sympathy in a practical way with South Africa and the people of South Africa when Paul Kruger had to leave his country, sent a man-of-war to take him overseas. It was she also, when he drew his last breath in exile, who again placed a Dutch man-of-war at the disposal of South Africa to take his earthly remains to South Africa, so that he could rest not only in the bosom of his fatherland, but that he could rest among his own people."[23]

Malan then proceeded to deal with the embarrassing questions. Ag-

---

[20] Ibid., vol. 41, cols. 2177–2455.

[21] Ibid., vol. 44, cols. 5305–5306.

[22] Hertzog studied law at the University of Amsterdam; Malan obtained his doctorate in theology from Utrecht; Verwoerd (later prime minister) was born in Holland.

[23] *Hansard*, vol. 39, cols. 7566–67, 14 May 1940.

gression was wrong and he frankly condemned it, but he condemned it on all sides. The Allies also were guilty, for they had violated the neutrality of Iceland and Norway. The question was not whether the opposition condemned aggression—they did—but whether the circumstances which had developed should induce the Nationalists to alter their position on the war. The aggression against Holland was not sufficient reason to abandon the example that Holland had set and for South Africa to become involved in the wars of Europe.[24]

Smuts in reply to Malan cleverly exploited the situation. He and his supporters shared the sympathy for Holland expressed by Malan. If it should become necessary for the Dutch royal family to find a home, Smuts said, the people of South Africa would regard it as the greatest honor and privilege to welcome it. The House of Orange occupied a tender spot in their hearts. It was a royal house for which they had the greatest honor and sympathy. When the freedom of humanity was at stake, it "fought to the uttermost, and maintained the struggle for eighty years, and in that way preserved the liberty of conscience and religion and the freedom of parliamentary institutions."[25]

The opposition supported a Parliamentary grant of assistance to Holland, but the leaders did not waiver in their position toward the war. Some of their followers deserted, however, and the government's position was strengthened.[26] There was political confusion in the ranks of the opposition. The alliance between Hertzog and Malan became increasingly strained and broke up in November 1940. Hertzog and his righthand man, N. C. Havenga, resigned their parliamentary seats in December.[27]

A considerable number of Afrikaners were attracted to Hitler's national socialism. Hitler's Germany was their ideal, and their organizations faithfully followed the Nazi models and practices. They rejected democracy and capitalism and played on the Afrikaner's anti-British feeling and his yearning for the return of Boer republicanism. Even Hertzog in his last years leaned toward National Socialism which, he

[24] Ibid., cols. 7567–71.

[25] Ibid., vol. 39, col. 7573.

[26] Ibid., cols. 7573–76. When Japan invaded the Dutch East Indies in the early months of 1942, Smuts had another opportunity to express his deep sympathy with the Netherlands.

[27] Hertzog lived only a year after he retired from public life. He died 21 November 1942.

believed, conformed to the moral and religious life and world view of the Afrikaner people and whose basic principles were embodied in the constitution of the old Orange Free State and inspired all the social legislation of this small model republic. Liberal capitalism, according to Hertzog, was responsible for the obliteration of the Boer republics and was also responsible for the impoverishment and decline of the Afrikaner people.[28] Fortunately for the government these extremists were badly divided. There was the Steyn-Vorster group in the Transvaal; there were the Grey-Shirts, Brown-Shirts, and Black-Shirts; and there were the *Ossewa-Brandwag* (Oxwagon Fire Guard) and Oswald Pirow's New Order, to say nothing of the twilight Afrikaner *Broederbond*, of which Malan himself was a member. Fortunately, also, since these groups rejected the party system, they were almost as hostile to Malan and his National party as to the government. Malan fought them bitterly,[29] but in order to weaken their effect he took positions which he otherwise probably would not have taken and which were an embarrassment to him later. There was considerable sabotage after South Africa entered the war. The situation might have been even worse if the government had not called in all private rifles.

In January 1942, when Allied fortunes were very low, Malan moved in the House that in view of the serious crisis in which South Africa found itself as a result of participation in the war, the House declare its support for converting the country into a republic, dissociated from the British Empire. The republic should not be cast on any foreign model and should spurn the false and dangerous elements of British "liberalistic democracy," but should be based upon the principles embodied in the two former South African republics. It should be made safe for the European race and its civilization in accordance with the guardianship principle.[30] Smuts characterized the republic as outlined by the motion as a declaration of war on all sections of the population which did not agree with the ideas of the Nationalists. A republic so intolerant and exclusive could never be achieved, declared Smuts.[31]

[28] Hertzog inclined toward the Salazar-Portuguese type of national socialism (C. M. van den Heever, *Generaal J. B. M. Hertzog* [Johannesburg, 1944], pp. 753ff.).

[29] See D. F. Malan, *Afrikaner Volkseenheid en my Ervarings op die Pad Daarheen* [Afrikaner National Unity and My Experiences on the Path Thereto] (Cape Town, 1959), Chapter 31.

[30] Ibid., vol. 43, cols. 33–34.

[31] Ibid., cols. 53–56.

South Africa made a significant contribution to the Allied victory in World War II, though the number of its soldiers was not great.[32] During the early years of the war the Cape route was of the utmost importance in the war strategy. Without it the Commonwealth might have collapsed, or at least been rendered militarily impotent, and without the Commonwealth the Allies might not have won the war. South Africa contributed greatly to driving the enemy out of Africa, thus helping to reopen the Mediterranean, which was an important factor in reversing the tide in favor of the Allies. However, the clearing of Africa of the enemy and the reopening of the Mediterranean to Allied shipping and the increasing military strength of the United States greatly reduced South Africa's role in the war.

[32] Early in 1944 South Africa had between 60,000 and 65,000 men in North Africa and Italy (Hancock, *Smuts*, 2:412).

8

The New World
and Storm Signals

As early as May 1941 General Smuts began to outline his hopes for the new world order.[1] He believed that the day of the small state had passed. The pressure of the times was irresistibly forcing the free democracies into a great world organization, of which the British Commonwealth was undoubtedly a precedent and prototype. Closest to this inner circle was the United States, which had the same ethic of life and philosophy and a common language and a literary culture. The states arrayed against Hitler would at the peace naturally form a world society "which would provide for effective action by the society in all important matters affecting future security and reform. In this way an effectively functioning organ of the world community would arise, capable of binding the component nations in the paths of peace and ordered progress and arranging its relations with other States not members of the association." The mistake of the League of Nations had been to attempt too wide and universal a membership on too loose and nebulous a basis of organization and duties. In that common world authority the United States would have to play a leading part.

Smuts was deeply concerned about the military, economic, and political developments in the war from the point of view of world politics. He explained his concern in an "explosive" address[2] before a gathering of members of the British Parliament. The great lesson taught by the war, said Smuts, was that peace not backed by power remained a dream. In a new world organization provision would have to be made not only for freedom and democracy, but for leadership and power. This could be done more effectively than was done in the Covenant of the League of Nations "by giving a proper place to the three great Powers that are now at the head of our United Nations." Smuts thought that the reason why everything had gone wrong in the end was that in the League insufficient recognition was given to leadership and power.[3] Another flaw in the League, Smuts felt, was that it followed too exclusively political lines. The new organization would have to give more attention to economic questions.

The old map of Europe was being rolled up, said Smuts, and a new map was being unrolled. At the end of the war three of the great powers would have disappeared, leaving the trinity of Great Britain, Russia, and the United States. What troubled Smuts was that two partners in this trinity had immense resources while the third, Britain, was impoverished. This, he feared, was an unequal partnership. He saw no solution to the problem in a closer union with the United States, since it would create a lopsided world. As a solution to the problem he suggested that Britain work intimately with the small democracies of Europe.

Smuts's explosive speech furnished the Nationalists with much grist for their mill. They had argued that it was a mistake to weaken Germany as it was a strong bulwark against Communist Russia; Smuts now in effect admitted the validity of the Nationalists' warnings. He expressed his concern about the greatly strengthened position which Russia would occupy in Europe after the impending crushing defeat of Germany, yet he had repeatedly argued that South Africa was too exposed and weak to stand alone in the world and therefore it must

[1] In a broadcast May 12 and published in J. C. Smuts, *Plans for a Better World* (London, 1942), pp. 274–81.

[2] 3 Dec. 1943.

[3] For the text of the speech see Nicholas Mansergh, ed., *Documents and Speeches on British Commonwealth Affairs, 1931–1952* (London, 1953), pp. 441ff. Smuts suggested that there might never be a peace conference but only an armistice on a basis of unconditional surrender. This was prophetic as far as Central Europe was concerned.

remain closely aligned with Britain and the Commonwealth. But if the prime minister was correct about the economic exhaustion of England, then England could no longer protect South Africa. Malan moved that the House agree with the prime minister about the relative positions of Russia, England, and the United States after the war and that the House express its deep conviction that any war which contemplated the "destruction, crippling or elimination" of such countries as Germany, Italy, Poland, the Baltic States, or Finland was in conflict with the true interests of Europe and Western European civilization, and that in view of England's changed international position and the Union's internal situation South Africa's constitutional status should be changed into that of "a free independent Republic separated from the British Crown and Empire."

This republic, said Malan, should be based upon the principle of popular government and the equal language and cultural rights of both the English and Afrikaans sections of the population. It should be "anti-capitalistic and anti-communistic by nature and made safe for the European race and Christian civilisation as well as for the development of the non-European population according to their own character and ability by the loyal maintenance of the principle of separation and trusteeship."[4]

THE UNITED NATIONS CHARTER

Before leaving for the San Francisco conference as South Africa's principal delegate, Smuts discussed the problem of organizing for peace. The League of Nations had been an organization simply for consultation, and not for action. It had no machinery for the actual prevention of war. The new arrangement was to be different. A Security Council was to be empowered to resort to force to prevent war. War had become man's greatest enemy. Small nations, said Smuts, can no longer defend themselves. "Unless some method is found to render war obsolete, the future of the human race is dark beyond measure." The great powers would have to undertake to protect the world peace.[5]

[4] *Hansard*, vol. 47, cols. 75–76, 25 Jan. 1944.

[5] Ibid., vol. 52, cols. 3675–77, 3723–25. In this debate Smuts also said that in view of all the difficulties in Europe he did not see how peace could be made in a moment. It would take place over a long period through consultation and experimentation.

Malan, the leader of the opposition, was concerned about the preliminary Dominion conference at London, fearing that it would impair the autonomy, the independence of the Dominions, and especially their status as international entities.[6] Eric Louw, who was later to become South Africa's first minister of external affairs, asserted that Smuts would go to the United Nations conference not as the representative of South Africa, but as a member of the British Empire's delegation, and would be concerned not so much with the interests of South Africa as with the interests of the British Empire.[7] Another member warned against relying exclusively on any world organization. Smuts agreed. South Africa had put its faith in the League of Nations, in disarmament, and in a number of very idealistic principles but, notwithstanding, had been plunged into the most devastating war the world had known. "I think one of the lessons we have learnt," said Smuts, "is not to put our faith merely in documents and organizations, but to look after ourselves and to keep well armed."[8] Yet at the beginning of the debate Smuts had declared that small states could no longer defend themselves and that neutrality was a thing of the past.

Smuts was not the influential figure at San Francisco that he was at Paris a quarter of a century earlier. This was probably due to the nature of the United Nations conference whose work was restricted to drafting a constitution for the new world organization, and most of the work on that had already been done; Smuts was in substantial agreement with the proposals of the sponsoring states. He wanted a world organization "with teeth," yet he did not want it to be a superstate. He was honored with the chairmanship of one of the four commissions into which the conference was divided. Though the representative of a small or intermediate power, Smuts supported the demands of the great powers. This put him out of line with the representatives of the other Dominions, who fought tenaciously to reduce the special position accorded the great powers in the United Nations Organization. The South African delegation presented a text for the preamble to the Charter. Smuts, in offering it, stressed the need for a statement that would rally world opinion in support of the Charter. It was adopted in principle as the basis for the preamble, but after a subcommittee had revised it Smuts commented

[6] Ibid., vol. 52, cols. 3678–79.
[7] Ibid., col. 3681.
[8] Ibid., cols. 3845–46.

ruefully that it was "very nice as father of the baby still to recognize it after others had the handling of it."[9]

The South African government ratified the Charter on October 9, 1945, and on February 6, 1946, it placed the instrument before Parliament for concurrence of this act. Smuts explained the main provisions of the Charter. Under modern conditions a great war can take place only between great powers. Since they alone have this power the responsibility for peace must be placed in them. To carry this responsibility the great powers must be accorded a special position in preventing war, but also everything must be done to keep them together. To create the conditions of unanimity the veto was necessary. Smuts admitted that that arrangement involved a risk. The veto cut both ways. It was intended as a bond to keep the great powers together, but by its very nature it was also an instrument that could be abused and wreck the working of the whole scheme. "That is the cloud that hangs over the whole scene," admitted Smuts.[10]

Smuts stressed the social and economic provisions of the Charter. The League of Nations was almost wholly a political institution. The great depression had demonstrated the confusion and bitterness economic problems and social conditions could cause. The economic and social provisions would help strike at the roots of war; therefore the Economic and Social Council might become as important as the Security Council, predicted Smuts.

Malan declared that Smuts's outline of the United Nations was characterized by an absence of enthusiasm. The National party did not stand for isolation, declared Malan; in principle it was in favor of world organization, but the new world organization was, in his judgment, "a bad thing."[11] Malan feared that under Article 34 of the Charter the Security Council might investigate South Africa's racial policy. To Smuts's motion to approve the Charter, Malan offered an amendment protesting the exclusive character of the organization, the veto right of the great powers, and the inferior and dependent position accorded the community of smaller states.[12]

When asked by a member if he would take South Africa out of the

[9] United Nations, *Documents of the United Nations Conference on International Organization* (New York, 1946), 6:365.
[10] *Hansard*, vol. 55, cols, 1155–73.
[11] Ibid., col. 1183.
[12] Ibid., col. 1191, 6 Feb. 1946.

United Nations if his party came to power, Malan replied that since the choice was between a bad thing and nothing, it was better to accept the United Nations and seek to improve it. All the small states thought the Charter was bad, but they accepted it. However difficult it might be, a Nationalist government would try to improve the United Nations. But, he added, if the country should find continued membership in it intolerable or involve a danger for South Africa he would withdraw from it.

It was not only Malan and the Nationalists who feared that the United Nations might be used to intervene in the Union's racial policy. Even government supporters were not free of this. One, Charles F. Stallard, a former member of Smuts's ministry,[13] pointed to the bias of the Charter against racial discrimination.[14] He foresaw the possibility of questions involving racial policy coming before the General Assembly and the Security Council. South Africa would maintain that racial policy was a purely domestic question, but Stallard doubted that this position could be successfully maintained.

The prime minister sought to reassure members of the House by pointing to Article 2, paragraph 7, which prohibits the United Nations from intervening "in matters which are essentially within the domestic jurisdiction of any state" or requiring members to submit such matters to settlement under the Charter. This article, originally in the body of the Charter, was moved up to Article 2 dealing with principles, so as to restrict all the powers and activities of the United Nations. Smuts disposed of the question rather easily, much too easily, as time was to show.

AGAIN THE INDIAN QUESTION

The Indian problem in South Africa had become increasingly acute and had become an international question before the Nationalists under Malan came to power. The Smuts government appointed commissions to ascertain the facts and make recommendations. The first reported that in the years from 1927 to 1940 there had been 512 cases of Indians' purchasing land in predominantly European areas in Durban, followed by Indian occupation in about a third of them. The second reported in

---

[13] Col. C. F. Stallard, leader of the Dominion party.
[14] Art. 1, par. 3; Art. 55 (c).

early 1943 that the number of purchases of land in European areas by Indians had increased greatly in the past two and a half years. The Smuts government felt it had to act. Reluctant to attempt a permanent solution, especially in wartime, it asked Parliament to pass the "pegging Act,"[15] and promised a full judicial inquiry into the Indian situation in Natal. The act passed in 1943 "pegged" the situation for three years.[16]

The Indians, understandably, did not like the pegging act and asked for another way of dealing with the situation. In response Smuts, with a number of white leaders met with representatives of the Natal Indian Congress in 1944. From this meeting came the Pretoria Agreement which declared the matter could be regulated best by the Natal Provincial Council. A bill, known as the Occupation Ordinance, was introduced in the Natal Provincial Council but failed to get the approval of the Select Committee of the House of Assembly to which it had been referred. The bill, which had the approval of the Natal Indian Congress, was unacceptable to most Europeans in Natal. The Indian community protested this proposed ordinance as a breach of the spirit of the Pretoria Agreement. Caught in an impasse, the Union government withheld the necessary consent to the Residential Property Regulation Ordinance, which had been passed by the Natal Provincial Council, and issued a statement that it intended to find a solution other than that of the Pretoria Agreement; it asked the third commission to complete its inquiry and report. The South African Indian Congress reacted to this move by reiterating the Indians' claim to full parliamentary and municipal franchise on the common role. In protest the Indian members of the commission resigned from that body and the Indian community boycotted it.

The third commission presented an interim report in June 1945. It declared that racial animosity in Natal seemed to make friendly negotiations and compromise impossible, and it strongly criticized the attitude of politicians in India who had encouraged the South African Indians to put forward unreasonable demands. The problem could not be solved

---

[15] The full title was "Trading and Occupation of Land (Transvaal and Natal) Restriction Act."

[16] See G. H. Calpin, *Indians in South Africa* (Pietermaritzburg, 1949); also pamphlet issued by the Union of South Africa Government Information Office, New York, *The Indian in South Africa* (New York, n.d. [ca. 1947]); also W. K. Hancock, *Smuts*, 2 vols. (Cambridge, Eng., 1962, 1968), vol. 2: *The Fields of Force, 1919–1950,* chapter 26.

by the compulsory repatriation of the Indians nor by their complete and immediate assimilation with the Europeans. A middle course would have to be found which would enable the two elements to live and to develop with a minimum of friction. In seeking a solution it would be helpful to consider the point of view of the Indian government. The commission therefore recommended that an agreement be reached by negotiation with the government of India. It declared its belief that the only practical basis for negotiation and agreement was more restrictive qualifications for suffrage for Indians than for Europeans.[17]

These developments placed Prime Minister Smuts and his government under severe pressure. The farmers of Natal now joined the Natal urban dwellers and businessmen in an insistence upon restrictive legislation, while the South African Indian Congress had moved toward a more uncompromising position. It demanded the adult franchise on the common roll, the unconditional repeal of the pegging act, nullification of the Housing and Expropriation Ordinances, a policy of no segregation in housing schemes, free and compulsory elementary education for Indians, and a round table conference with the Indian government. Smuts rejected nearly all of these demands. He declared it would be a departure from fixed principles to invoke the assistance of a foreign government to solve an internal problem. The South African Indians had to make up their minds whether they were South Africans or Indians and stop acting as if they were both. Smuts also rejected the demand for the franchise on the common role, pointing out that communal representation was an Indian system. The government presented a bill that tied together the two questions of land tenure and political rights. The bill, which became the Act of 1946, replaced the temporary pegging act, which had expired. It established areas in the cities of Durban and Pietermaritzburg and in other parts of Natal where Indians could acquire and occupy property. Outside of these areas Indians could buy or occupy land only by permit from the minister of interior. The act further provided that the Indians in Natal and the Transvaal would be represented in Parliament by two senators, one elected by Indians and one appointed by the governor general, and by three representatives in the House of Assembly, to be elected by Indians. Both senators and representatives had to be white, as the constitution restricted member-

[17] Union of South Africa Government Information Office, *The Indian in So. Africa,* pp. 23–25.

ship in Parliament to Europeans. The Indians in Natal were also to elect two members to the Natal Provincial Council.

This device of uniting economic restriction with political concession failed to satisfy either Indians or Europeans in Natal. The former branded the proposed legislation as the Ghetto bill, the latter hated the concession.[18] Smuts had difficulty in persuading his own party caucus to support him. He warned that the question of South West Africa would be raised in the United Nations. It would be difficult to argue for the incorporation of that territory into the Union after South Africa had segregated Indians without compensation and withdrawn rights from them without according them any political participation.[19] Passage of the act was greeted with resistance by the Indians in South Africa, with scorn from Indians in India, and with sharp criticism in the press throughout the world. Some two thousand Indian resisters were put in jail for brief sentences. India recalled its high commisioner from Pretoria and broke trade relations with South Africa; on June 22, 1946, India made application to the secretary general of the United Nations to inscribe the treatment of Indians in South Africa on the agenda of the General Assembly. South Africa was to be arraigned before the United Nations.

[18] Malan in this debate argued that the race question was of one piece: "Those three sections (Natives, Indians, and Coloureds) of the colour problem are an interdependent whole. If you break down the dividing wall at one place it is ever so much harder to protect it at another place" (quoted by Calpin, *Indians in So. Africa*, p. 229).

[19] Ibid., p. 220.

The Foreign Policy
of Apartheid
1948–

9

Nationalism
and Foreign Policy

The triumph of the Nationalist and allied Afrikaner parties in the parliamentary election of May 26, 1948, came as a surprise to everybody, including the Nationalists. The elections of 1943 had been favorable for Smuts and his United party, at least so it seemed superficially. The United party had increased the number of its seats in the House of Assembly from seventy-two to eighty-nine. The United party's gains, however, were not won at the expense of the Nationalist party, which actually gained two seats to increase its strength to forty-three. The New Order and Afrikaner parties were wiped out with a loss to the opposition of twenty-four seats. While the United party succeeded in increasing its strength in Parliament, it suffered a setback in popular votes.

From the point of view of popular votes the 1948 election was not a victory for the Nationalist party. The United party received nearly 50 percent of the votes cast, as against less than 40 percent for the National and the allied Afrikaner parties. However, from the point of view of the number of parliamentary seats won, the results were an unmistakable triumph for the Nationalists. They won seventy seats in the House of Assembly and the Afrikaner party nine, to only sixty-five for the United party. This perverted result was made possible by the inequality in population between the rural and urban districts. The *platteland* was predominantly Afrikaner. The National and Afrikaner parties carried the less populous rural and urban districts by narrow margins while the United party won the larger city districts by substantial majorities. Smuts himself went down to defeat in the district he had represented for years. The election results indicated a trend which was to become stronger in the following years.

The Nationalists conducted an astute and vigorous campaign. They dropped republicanism and secession as issues by pledging not to move in this direction until after the people had declared by a decisive vote in a special referendum that they desired a republic. They also dropped isolationism by declaring that South Africa could not be neutral in the event of war between Communist and non-Communist blocs. Communism was made an issue. Smuts was charged with a heavy responsibility for the bad situation in the world. He had yielded to Russian pressure to ruin Germany, the bulwark against Russian Communism. Communism was infiltrating Western countries; there were Communist activities even in South Africa.[1]

The Nationalists made racial policy the chief issue in the campaign, using for the first time the term *apartheid* to describe their policy of segregation, now to be more comprehensive and purposeful. *Die Transvaler* summarized the issues as "Liberalism, Communism and Equality," which in Nationalist language means white supremacy. Malan opened the campaign with his motion in Parliament declaring that the act to give Indians representation in that body should be repealed, that native representation in the House should be abolished and that the Natives Representative Council should likewise go.[2] For reasons of political strategy, the Nationalist attack was centered not so much on Smuts as on Jan H. Hofmeyr, his deputy. The former was seventy-eight years of age and would in the normal course of events have to turn over the leadership of his party to his able lieutenant. Moreover, Smuts's views on racial policy did not differ greatly from their own, while Hofmeyr's were much more vulnerable. Smuts emphasized the enormous difficulty of the racial problem; he accepted the policy of white supremacy but warned his fellow countrymen to proceed cautiously. In the debate on

[1] The Nationalists began pressing this offensive early. See the foreign policy debate of April 1947, *Hansard*, vol. 60, cols. 237–85.

[2] Ibid., cols. 62–74, 20 Jan. 1948.

the representation of Indians and natives which took place in the House in January 1948, Smuts referred to the enormity of his country's racial problems: "We have perhaps the most difficult position of any country in the world, but I do not believe that any country in the world has achieved the success with these difficult problems that South Africa has achieved." In other countries it was a question of mixing or of extermination, but South Africa chose to ensure the survival of both sections.[3]

When asked about the demand for equality, he said that it was unreasonable. He warned of a worldwide interest in what is described as human rights and the human standpoint, and that must be kept in mind.[4]

An increasing number of Afrikaners regarded Smuts's position on racial policy as ambivalent and hence did not fully trust him. Malan's explanation of why so distinguished a man as Smuts should have trouble with the South African electorate was that "on the Colour problem he has never sounded a clear note."[5]

With respect to the racial problem, Smuts could carry water on both shoulders and with some degree of success, but Hofmeyr found it increasingly difficult to equivocate on this issue of such vital concern to South African society. Moreover, Hofmeyr was moving steadily away from the traditional South African position. In an address in 1946, he declared, the plain truth "is that the dominant mentality in South Africa is a *Herrenvolk* mentality—the essential feature of our race problems is to be found in that fact."[6] Shortly thereafter in the debate in the House on the Indian representation bill he said, "I take my stand for the removal of that colour bar from our constitution."[7] He added defiantly that if his political adversaries wanted "to use it to make political capital against me, they are free to do so."[8] The Nationalists charged him with being in favor of racial equality and alleged that he was a Negrophile and was prepared "to plough the Afrikaner under."

It is widely believed that Hofmeyr cost his party the election, but this

[3] Ibid., col. 83.

[4] Ibid., col. 88.

[5] Ibid., col. 120.

[6] See Alan Paton, *Hofmeyr* (London, 1964), p. 422.

[7] *Hansard*, vol. 56, col. 4436. He was referring to the color bar in parliamentary representation.

[8] Alan Paton states that while Hofmeyr condemned white domination, "he could not see what to go forward to except white leadership, based on merits and deserts." (Paton, *Hofmeyr*, p. 520).

is an oversimplification. The white South African electorate turned against Smuts and his party as an answer to the attack on the Union's racial policy in the United Nations. South African whites felt that a hostile world was threatening their supremacy in their own country. Smuts's government had helped create the international situation which Afrikaners believed to be thoroughly hostile to their interests. A leading student of South African politics concludes, "Apartheid overthrew Smuts. It was the result of adverse world criticism of the Union's racial policy and not its cause. It was the last desperate attempt of Afrikanerdom to stem the rising tide of colour."[9]

Upon assuming office the new prime minister, who was also minister of external affairs, D. F. Malan, in a nationwide broadcast (June 4, 1948) outlined his government's foreign policy. The interests of South Africa would always be placed first, he said, but the new ministry did not subscribe to an isolationist policy. However, Dr. Malan declared that South Africa had accepted membership in the United Nations "on the unequivocal understanding that there was to be neither external interference in our domestic affairs nor any tampering with our autonomous rights." The new ministry also wished to continue friendly relations with Great Britain and other members of the British Commonwealth, but the prime minister emphasized that cooperation with them would be possible only if it did not detract from South Africa's status and freedom as a sovereign state, and only if it involved no intervention in their domestic affairs.[10]

This statement by Prime Minister Malan foreshadowed events to come. Concerned about the image of his government abroad, Malan appointed Charles te Water, former high commissioner to London and Union representative at the League of Nations, as a roving ambassador. Malan said that there was great prejudice against South Africa, based on misconceptions.[11] Te Water lamented that South African policies were being challenged at the bar of world opinion, and into this difficult and dangerous situation "we have now unhappily intruded our domestic party quarrels, with inexcusable shortsightedness and to the delight of our detractors. We have exported our disunity to the world."[12] In every

---

[9] D. W. Kruger, *The Age of the Generals* (Johannesburg, 1961), p. 226.

[10] Union of South Africa, State Information Office, *Foreign Policy of the Union of South Africa* (Pretoria, n.d.), pp. 4–5.

[11] *The Star*, 13 May 1949.

[12] *Cape Times*, 2 Feb. 1949.

important debate on racial policy the National party spokesmen sought to silence critics of the government's racial policy by charging them with giving aid and comfort to hostile forces abroad. Often it was made to appear that foreign hostility was not due to the policy itself, but to the opposition's representation and criticism of it.[13]

In an address to the Senate just before his departure for London to attend the 1949 Commonwealth prime ministers' conference, Malan again emphasized that his government was not in favor of isolation.[14] He pointed out that the National party had supported the League of Nations and was not in principle opposed to the United Nations. But the United Nations had revealed serious weaknesses, the first of which was the great power veto which threatened to paralyze the organization. Another weakness, and one which touched South Africa closely, was United Nations intervention in the domestic affairs of its members. The organization was concerning itself with the Union's domestic affairs in connection with the Indian question. South Africa was not the only country which was complaining about intervention in domestic matters, or which feared such intervention. A third weakness was that the meetings of the organization had become only a platform for propaganda. Scarcely any matter was discussed or decided on its merits, but most were determined by negotiation and trading behind the scenes. "Nevertheless," concluded Dr. Malan, "I say that U. N. O., if it can be relieved of its shortcomings—and we should like to assist in bringing that about—will be not only a useful but also a necessary organization for maintaining the peace and cooperation of the world."

Malan discussed at some length the threat of Communist aggression. Berlin was a focal point; if the Allies had to withdraw from Berlin he feared Germany would be lost to the West, and nothing would "be able to check the Communist tidal wave in Europe and in the world." For that reason South Africa was giving military aid to the Allies in maintaining their position in Berlin. He heartily endorsed the formation of the North Atlantic Treaty Organization (NATO) and implied that if South Africa were invited to join it would do so.

Lastly, Malan discussed the situation in Africa and how it affected the Union. He reiterated the idea that a war between Communist and

---

[13] *Hansard*, vol. 66, col. 313. The debate took place on 25 Jan. 1949.

[14] Union of South Africa, State Information Office, *Foreign Policy of the Union of South Africa*.

anti-Communist countries would create a dangerous situation in South Africa which would be more threatening than for any other country because Communist propaganda in the Union was effective with the non-European population. For this reason South Africa could not remain neutral in case of war between Communist and non-Communist countries. He hoped that since the North Atlantic powers would need South Africa and South Africa would need the Atlantic Pact, there would be an opportunity for an agreement on an African policy.

The prime minister regarded the Middle East as the weakest, most vulnerable point since the Russian bases were nearby and those of the Allies were far away. The Suez Canal might even be destroyed, in which case the passage around the Cape would become absolutely necessary to the West if it wished to retain contact with Asia. In such an event the NATO powers would need South African cooperation and goodwill. "But," he concluded, "it may also be that, in view of the dangers to which I have referred, here within our borders, we too may need those Powers, or other Powers that have interests here in Africa."

Not many months before his death (September 11, 1950) General Smuts warned the House, of which he had been a member for over forty years, that the course on which Malan's government had started South Africa could only bring harm to the country. South Africa was becoming increasingly isolated from world public opinion. South Africa had strong friends but Smuts believed that the apartheid policy was alienating them. As a small minority in a black continent trying to build a European civilization South Africa needed the world's support and sympathy, but its official racial policy made that support impossible.[15]

VERWOERD'S BASIC VIEWS

Hendrik F. Verwoerd was the ablest, most forceful, and most revolutionary of the Nationalist prime ministers. He gave expression to his views on foreign policy in a brief, impromptu reply to British Prime Minister Harold Macmillan's speech to the members of the South African Parliament at Cape Town on February 3, 1960. He said that his country's objectives were the same as those of Great Britain: peace and the continued existence of Western ideas and Western civilization. South Africa wanted to be on the side of the West in the tense division which

[15] *Hansard,* vol. 70, cols. 36–37, 24 Jan. 1950.

existed in the world. The white man in Africa was as entitled to justice as the black man. South Africans called themselves Europeans, but in reality they were representatives of the whites of Africa, who brought Western ideas to Africa and were responsible for the awakening of the Africans. The whites came to South Africa to stay; South Africa was their fatherland. They believed in giving Africans the full measure of rights which belong to all people, but they believed in balance. Each race was to enjoy those rights in its own area.

South Africa regarded itself as indispensable to the white world, but desired at the same time to make friends of the black states of Africa so that they would add strength. "We are the link. We are White, but we are in Africa. We have connections with both and this lays upon us a special obligation and we understand this. . . . If our methods differ let us try to understand each other and may we find in the outside that trust in our uprightness which must be the basis of all goodwill."[16]

In 1963, after five years as prime minister, Dr. Verwoerd made a notable and revealing speech on his government's racial and foreign policies. The speech was characterized by a strange mixture of boastfulness and frustration.[17] During the years of his leadership South Africa had seen great economic progress. South Africa had become a republic and left the Commonwealth, and the white groups were growing into "a single nation with greater, stronger and more lasting bonds of unity." Its defense, both internal and external, had been greatly strengthened. Great projects for the future development of the country had been undertaken.

"Our major task," said Verwoerd, "is to ensure that a White nation will prevail here." But the great and complex problem of race relations made this task very difficult. In its aim to survive and prosper as a white nation South Africa had no desire to suppress "those entrusted to [its] care," nor to deny them the opportunity to develop fully. The purpose of apartheid was constructive, born of goodwill. Yet almost every nation and the United Nations condemn South Africa's policy.

Verwoerd then went on to point out that it was easy to understand why South Africa was condemned by the Communist countries. "South

[16] A. N. Pelzer, ed., *Verwoerd aan die Woord* [Verwoerd Speaking] (Johannesburg, 1963), pp. 317–20.

[17] Given in Pretoria 3 Sept. 1963 and published by State Department of Information, *Fact Paper 107*, "Crisis in World Conscience" and "The Road to Freedom for Basutoland, Bechuanaland and Swaziland" (Pretoria, n.d.).

Africa is unequivocally the symbol of anti-Communism in Africa. Although often abused, we are also still a bastion in Africa for Christianity and the Western world." Leaders of African and Asian states attack South Africa in order to divert attention from their own shortcomings. The Afro-Asians aspire to share in South Africa's wealth by the device of the one-man-one-vote principle.

More difficult to understand was why the Western countries, "from whom we are descended and with whom we have such close cultural ties, turn against us." The reason was not to be found in any conviction that South Africa was wrong or was an oppressor; it was out of considerations of self-interest. In the struggle between East and West the Afro-Asians hold the balance of power. This was especially true in the United Nations. It was to further their political and economic interests that the Western countries joined in the attack on South Africa.

It was obvious, he said, that South Africa could conciliate the world only by handing over the country "to black domination." The issue at stake was the "self-preservation of a nation—nothing more and nothing less." It was dangerous even to make concessions because they could lead eventually to the loss of "everything we cherish, and which will ultimately prove to be of importance to others: the West and also our non-White wards."

At this point Verwoerd put the world conscience to the test. When freedom was multilated in Ghana or remained illusory as in Liberia and Ethiopa, he said, these conditions were tolerated or ignored, but when aggression against South Africa was planned openly it was not condemned. The United Nations did nothing to stop these hostile maneuvers and even associated itself with attacks on South Africa. The world conscience was silent about the oppression of the Baltic states at the hands of Russia. There was slavery in some countries of the Middle East, but no effort was made to put an end to it. Minorities were oppressed in many countries. "What is world conscience doing in all these cases, apart from washing its hands in innocence like Pontius Pilate?" he asked.

If South Africa's policy in trying to solve the racial problem by separation was wrong, did the United States or Britain have a better solution? "Here in the Republic we have greater peace and order. We have much less rude handling, or oppression, and far less ill-feeling between Black and White. . . . For this country we have no doubt that our methods alone can ultimately prove fair to all races, including the Whites. Other countries must choose for themselves."

Prime Minister Verwoerd ended with a note of warning. The attitude of the West was not based on "principle, farsightedness or self-reliance. If Southern Africa should be lost to the West then I am convinced that this will upset the balance of military and strategic power in the world."

10

The High Commission
Territories

Though interested in the expansion of the Union territory, Botha and Smuts did not press Britain to transfer the Protectorates. When the National party leader Hertzog became prime minister in 1924 at the head of a government in coalition with the Labor party he at first took a somewhat ambiguous position on the matter. While he declared that he favored the incorporation of the Territories only if their populations desired it, he, nevertheless, reopened the question with the British government. In the beginning he seemed interested only in Swaziland, which had considerable resources. He became more insistent and his demands were extended to all three Territories. He assumed that the South Africa Act gave the Union a right to the Protectorates, that the Union government merely had to ask for their transfer, which then would take place automatically. As Hertzog held republican sentiments and was a determined segregationist, both the British government and the inhabitants of the Territories had little desire to yield to the South African prime minister's demands. These reactions only made Hertzog more insistent. He declared in Parliament that the right of the Union to the Territories had never been questioned, that the time for transfer had arrived.[1]

Hertzog thought he had reached an agreement with Secretary of State for Dominion Affairs J. H. Thomas for cooperation in the development of the Territories and their early transfer to the Union. Subsequently it appeared that the two principals interpreted the agreement quite differently. Thomas reminded Hertzog that when the South Africa Act was passed the British government made the pledge not to transfer the Territories until the inhabitants had been consulted and Parliament had been given an opportunity to express its views. The British government did not think the time was ripe for consulting the inhabitants. Under the circumstances a consultation would be "embarrassing and undesirable."

The secretary concluded that the policy of both governments for the next few years should be one of encouraging the inhabitants to join the Union.[2] Hertzog interpreted the agreement to mean that the officials in the Territory "should actively discourage agitation against joining the Union," and that they should also be instructed "to inculcate in the inhabitants ideas favorable to transfer."[3]

Hertzog made some progress in discussions with Thomas's successor, Malcolm MacDonald, during the years 1937 to 1939. They agreed to set up a Joint Advisory Committee composed of three representatives of the Union government and the three resident commissioners. This committee had hardly begun its work when war put an end to the interesting development.

South Africans made many complaints about the situation in the Territories. The Protectorates exported cattle diseases and locusts to the Union. People from the Territories came to the Union to work but the reverse was not permitted. The situation could not be remedied so long as the Union had no control over the Territories.[4] It was generally admitted, even by those who opposed incorporation of the Protectorates in the Union, that conditions in these Territories were a discredit to the British.[5]

The Smuts government from 1939 to 1948 did little to secure the

---

[1] *Hansard*, vol. 23, cols. 2759–61, 25 April 1934.

[2] Great Britain, Parliamentary Papers (Commons), Cmd. 4948.

[3] This correspondence was revealed by Prime Minister Malan in Parliament on 13 April 1950, *Hansard*, vol. 71, cols. 4199–4205.

[4] See ibid., vol. 23, cols. 2745ff., 25 April 1934, for an expression of these complaints.

[5] M. Perham and Lionel Curtis, *The Protectorates of South Africa: The Question of Their Transfer to the Union* (London, 1935).

incorporation of the Territories. When questioned in Parliament in 1944 Smuts stated that South Africa had cooperated cordially with them and presently was treating them as virtually a part of the Union. The internal administration was left to the British, but in regard to customs, posts, railway traffic, and general treatment, they were on the same footing as if a part of the Union. The question of their transfer would be resumed after the war.[6]

When the National party came to power in 1948, pressure on Britain for the transferral of the Territories was resumed, but in view of the new government's racial policies opposition in Britain and the Territories was greater than ever. Prime Minister Malan took up the matter with Philip Noel-Baker, minister of Commonwealth relations, and Ernest Bevin, minister for foreign affairs, at the time of the 1948 Prime Ministers' Conference. He bluntly told the British ministers that the people of South Africa were becoming impatient, and he repeated Hertzog's threat of closing the Union markets to the Territories if they wished to remain under British rule. He warned the British ministers that if there was no change of course the Union government would eventually have to proceed in accordance with Section 151 of the Constitution and ask Parliament to petition for the transfer.[7] Smuts, now the leader of the opposition, protested that it was not right to represent Britain as continually seeking excuses for not transferring the Territories. Virtual agreement had been reached before World War II. He pleaded for negotiations in a peaceful spirit.[8]

Addressing a dinner in Cape Town in February 1951 honoring Patrick Gordon Walker, British minister of Commonwealth relations, Malan expressed South Africa's dissatisfaction. "Within her embrace and even actually within her borders, South Africa was compelled to harbour territories entirely dependent on her economically and largely also for their defence, but belonging to and governed by another territory."[9]

When Malan in Parliament in 1951 threatened to impose economic measures against the Territories if they were not transferred, he received a quick response from London. Winston Churchill, prime minis-

[6] *Hansard*, vol. 48, col. 3954.
[7] Ibid., vol. 71, cols. 4192–4205, 13 April 1950.
[8] Ibid., col. 4210.
[9] *Rand Daily Mail*, 10 Feb. 1951.

ter at the time, sharply commented in the British Parliament that there could be no transfer "until the inhabitants of the Territories had been consulted and Parliament had had an opportunity of expressing its views."[10]

More than three years later, having made no progress in acquiring control of the Protectorates, Malan expressed his fear that Britain might grant the Protectorates independence. The Union could not "permit Negro States, Bantu States, to arise within our borders, States which are free and independent and which can lay down their own policy in every respect." For over forty years the British government had been hiding behind its promise to consult the natives with respect to incorporation, interpreting it as tantamount to giving the natives a veto. South Africa's patience "is coming to an end." The British attitude indicated a lack of confidence in South Africa and "we do not intend to continue living under a cloud of suspicion."[11]

Mrs. Margaret Ballinger took issue with the prime minister's arguments. She asserted that the crux of the situation was that the British government was committed in its own territories to the principle of the progressive enfranchisement of the African while the Union was moving farther and farther away from that idea. She agreed with Malan that the Protectorates in fact belonged to South Africa, that they were economically dependent on her and that their future lay with the Union. But politically they did not belong to South Africa, and she asked the prime minister what he was prepared to do to persuade the British government to hand the Protectorates over to his government and what offer he was prepared to make to the South African native population to persuade the British electorate that these territories would be properly treated if incorporated in the Union.[12]

Finally, in April 1954 Prime Minister Malan introduced in Parliament a resolution calling for the transfer of the Territories "as soon as possible." The leader of the opposition moved an amendment condemning the attempt to reinforce diplomatic negotiations by parliamentary pressure. After a lengthy and heated debate the resolution was adopted by a vote of seventy-five to thirty-one. The United party was in agree-

[10] Great Britain, *Parliamentary Debates* (Commons), 5th ser., 494 (1951): 559–60, 22 Nov. 1951.

[11] *Hansard*, vol. 82, cols. 1328–29, 11 Aug. 1953.

[12] Ibid., vol. 82, cols. 1333–35.

ment with the position of the government on this issue, but it wanted to avoid offending the British government.[13]

On the day that the resolution was passed, Prime Minister Churchill, in the House of Commons, reaffirmed the pledge of the British government given in 1909 that the High Commission Territories would not be transferred until their inhabitants had been consulted and Parliament had expressed itself on the matter. "It is in the interest," he said, "as it is also the desire, of this country and of South Africa, that the friendship which has developed so strongly between us over the years should remain unbreakable. I therefore sincerely hope that Dr. Malan and his Government, with whom we have hitherto happily cooperated on so many problems we share in common, will not needlessly press an issue on which we could not fall in with their views without failing in our trust."[14] In the Union Parliament Malan replied sharply that South Africa wanted to retain British friendship but where their interests clashed he was not "prepared to crawl. . . . I want to negotiate on an equal footing."[15] Malan retired from office in November 1954 and was succeeded by Johannes G. Strijdom, who also made an effort to secure the Protectorates, but with no success.[16]

In the course of the various debates it had been argued that incorporation of the Territories was necessary for the defense of South Africa. Malan pointed out that in Basutoland there were headwaters of rivers which could be used for the development of large-scale irrigation projects. One member of the House contended that it was absolutely essential that the Protectorates be transferred to the Union because they constituted a danger to South Africa in time of war; they were centers for Communist propaganda; and they might apply for independence.[17]

TRANSITION

When Prime Minister Verwoerd in 1959 announced his government's Bantustan policy, the situation underwent a complete change. Verwoerd declared that the Bantustans could have independence if they wanted it and were ready for it. At about the same time the British government

---

[13] Ibid., vol. 85, cols. 3796ff.

[14] Great Britain, *Parliamentary Debates* (Commons), 5th ser., 526 (1954) : 966.

[15] *Hansard*, vol. 85, col. 3970.

[16] *Hansard*, vol. 94, col. 5272.

[17] J. H. Fouché, ibid., col. 5462.

instituted a policy of economic development and preparation for self-government in the Territories. The implications of the new situation were quickly raised in Parliament. The prime minister was asked how he related these new constitutional developments in the Protectorates to the Union's right to incorporate them. R. G. Durrant, who raised the question, summarized the changed situation: "The present theories of the Prime Minister have altered completely the traditional policy of South Africa in regard to the incorporation of the Protectorates, and that affects the vital interests of South Africa."[18]

Verwoerd admitted that the situation had been altered. Nevertheless, there could be no reconsideration of the Union stand since 1910 that the fate of the Territories was linked with the fate of South Africa. Now that the Union was giving the Bantu increasing control over their own areas, the misconception and doubts that the idea of cooperation with the Union created in the minds of the people of England and the Territories should disappear. It was a pity that the Union government did not have the opportunity to tell the Bantu in the Territories clearly what its aims were. Verwoerd pointed out that the Protectorates had two guardians. Britain was their guardian in the governmental sphere and the Union in the economic, and of these two, economic guardianship was the greater. It was essential that the economic guardian should be also the constitutional guardian so that the process of preparation for independence might be guided harmoniously. South Africa should be made the protector of the Protectorates.[19]

Four years later Verwoerd elaborated these ideas in a speech, directed at England and the Protectorates.[20] He said that sometimes things happened in these territories which hurt South Africa or seemed undesirable, and which could be avoided by the protecting power. The situation became very trying at times, as when South African air space was violated by aircraft transporting "fugitives and offenders" from the Republic between the Territories.

Great Britain, as the guardian of these Territories, was aiming at granting them self-government, which was exactly what the Republic was achieving in the Transkei. Great Britain had been advised "from all sides" not to free these territories lest they fall under the control of

[18] *Hansard*, vol. 101, cols. 5233–35, 4 May 1959.

[19] Ibid., vol. 100, cols. 5254–57.

[20] Union of South Africa, Department of Information, *Fact Paper 107*, "Crisis in World Conscience" and "The Road to Freedom" (Pretoria, n.d.).

South Africa. Verwoerd emphasized that the Republic had no territorial ambitions. "Indeed, were they under her guardianship, South Africa would free them stage by stage, just as she is now doing in the Transkei." The Republic as "guardian, . . . protector . . . [or] helper . . . [could lead the people] far better and much more quickly to independence and economic prosperity" than could the United Kingdom. If the administration of these Territories were made the responsibility of South Africa, it would aim at leading the whole people into democratic rule through natural native democracy. To help them advance economically it would apply its border-industry policy, so that their people could work near home. "Such measures," said Verwoerd, "would result in satisfied neighbors in states which would no longer be like overfilled dams continually flooding South Africa." Included in a common market with the Republic, there could be long-range planning for economic development over a large area with a large population. Finally, it would enable the Republic to move more rapidly by creating other Bantustans, by joining peoples ethnically linked but divided by the borders between South Africa and the Territories.

Verwoerd challenged Britain to allow the Republic to put the essentials of his policies before the people of the Territories. He was convinced that if his suggestions were placed before the people they would agree to them. If South Africa was not given the opportunity to put to the inhabitants of the Territories "our plans for a great consultative and cooperative future they would have no real self-determination." Let the people decide. They should have the chance "of knowing what a good friend the Republic of South Africa can be and wishes to be. . . . If they decide to go their own way, in growing isolation from South Africa, so well and good."

One reason for the Verwoerd proposal probably was that his policy of Bantustans encountered grave difficulties which control over the Protectorates could help solve. The Tomlinson Commission, appointed to examine the socioeconomic development of the Bantu reserves, concluded that "the present geographical pattern of the Bantu Areas is so fragmentary that it will not be possible to carry out in all respects the programme of [separate] development proposed by the Commission."[21]

[21] Union of South Africa, *Verslag van die Kommissie Vir die Socio-Ekonomise Ontwikkeling van die Bantoegebiede Binne die Unie van Suid Afrika* [Report of the Commission for the Social-Economic Development of the Bantu Territories

THE NEW SITUATION

Bechuanaland became independent on September 30, 1966, under the name of Botswana; Basutoland became independent on October 4, 1966, and adopted the name of Lesotho; and Swaziland became a sovereign state on September 6, 1968. All three have been admitted to membership in the United Nations, swelling the ranks of ministates in that organization. They are also members of the Commonwealth and the Organization of African Unity.

Botswana has an area of 275,000 square miles but its population is less than 600,000. Most of the country is arid or semiarid; devastating droughts are often ruinous to cattleraisers. Cattle and beef are chief exports, but some manganese and asbestos are also produced. There are considerable copper and nickel deposits in the northeast, but industrial development of the country has only begun. The annual per capita income is estimated at only fifty-five dollars. The value of exports in 1965 was less than $16 million while imports totaled over $23 million. About two-thirds of Botswana's imports come from South Africa and nearly a third from Rhodesia. Some 30,000 Botswanas work in South Africa and South West Africa, accounting for 10 percent of Botswana's export earnings.

Lesotho has an area of 11,716 square miles and a population approaching 900,000. Its mountainous territory is completely surrounded by South African territory. The country's natural resources are meager; its economy is largely dependent on the earnings of an estimated 200,000 Lesotho migrant workers in South Africa. About a third of Lesotho's national income is derived from wages paid in South Africa. The value of its exports ($6.1 million in 1966) is less than a fifth of the value of its imports. Surrounded by South Africa, Lesotho is wholly dependent on trade from or through South Africa. The annual per capita income is estimated at fifty-five dollars. Lesotho's share of the receipts from the customs union constitutes about 36 percent of the government's total income.[22]

Swaziland has an area of only 6,704 square miles and a population

---

inside South Africa], 7 vols. (Pretoria, 1955). See also D. Hobart Houghton, *A Summary of the Findings and Recommendations of the Tomlinson Report* (Johannesburg, 1956).

[22] See A. J. Van Wyck, *Lesotho: A Political Study* (Pretoria, 1967).

approaching 380,000. It is rich in mineral deposits. Iron deposits are conservatively estimated at 60 million tons and coal (anthracite) at 50 million tons. A railroad has been built between the iron mines and Lourenço Marques. Swaziland, with an annual per capita income estimated at $240, is undergoing rapid industrial development. The percentage of whites in the population is much greater than in either of the other two countries. They number about 8,000 and own 46 percent of the land.

The dependence of the three ex-Protectorates on South Africa is so great that they have been called "almost permanent adjuncts of the South African economy." They continue to be in a customs union with South Africa.[23] Conservative parties are in power in all three states; their leaders realize that they must cooperate with South Africa if their countries are to survive. A leader of the opposition in Lesotho expressed it simply but bitterly when he said, "What happens if we aren't good boys and we go against South Africa? We pay for it—and with South African currency, too."[24]

At first glance it would seem that by granting them independence Britain had placed the Territories at the mercy of South Africa since the latter can crush them by economic power alone. However, the situation is not altogether one-sided. South Africa can hardly allow her neighbors to sink into hopeless poverty nor seek to impose her racial policies on these nonracial states without drawing to itself the heightened hostility of the world. As Anton Rupert, the South African industrialist who serves Lesotho as economic adviser, put it, "If they do not eat, we do not sleep."[25] Swaziland can probably make it on its own, but it will be a long time, if ever, before the other two can be made self-supporting. South Africa must help these countries economically or run the risk of an infectious running sore on its borders. Indeed, South Africa may find itself with a burden it cannot get rid of. Moreover, South Africa is eager to use her black neighbors to establish better relations with the other African countries. To serve that end these neighbors must be both friendly and prosperous.

[23] The customs receipts were distributed as follows (1966) : Basutoland—0.88575 percent ($3,472,000); Swaziland—0.149 percent ($658,000); Bechuanaland—0.27622 percent ($5,320,000) (*Hansard*, Vol. 15, col. 1768).

[24] *New York Times*, 30 Sept. 1966.

[25] *The Star* (Johannesburg), Weekly Air Edition, 29 Oct. 1966.

"In our position we can act as a bridge between the North and the South," observed M. P. Nwako, Botswana minister of state. Moderate spokesmen at the United Nations and the Organization for African Unity would be of great value to South Africa. But traffic over a bridge is rarely all in one direction. The traffic toward South Africa is not altogether to South Africa's liking. Because President Seretse Khama married a white (English) girl, he was prohibited for seventeen years from entering South Africa. Now South Africa invites him and entertains him as a distinguished guest. Prime Minister Vorster's outward policy is certain to produce internal strains.

11

Rhodesia:
South African Protégé

Conditions in South Africa and Rhodesia were too similar for the two countries not to feel an attraction for each other.[1] In addition to similar conditions and problems there was the presence in Rhodesia of a considerable number of South African whites, both Afrikaner and English. If we use membership of the Dutch Reformed churches as the basis, the Afrikaners constituted 17.7 percent of the total white population in 1931, but only 13.5 percent in 1951. As in South Africa there was tension between the two linguistic groups. The Afrikaners were considered by the English-speaking Rhodesians to be backward. The earlier Afrikaner immigrants came to Rhodesia to work on the roads, railways, and in the mines, though many of the later settlers became farmers. As a cohesive linguistic and religious group with demands for state financial support for their Afrikaans-medium schools, they were regarded with suspicion and dislike by the English-speaking majority. The Afrikaners were suspected of harboring republican sentiments and of loyalty to the Afrikaner Nationalist party of South Africa. When the Nationalist party came to power in South Africa in 1948, a similar party was organized by Afrikaners in Rhodesia.[2]

In 1953 Southern Rhodesia entered into a federation with Northern

Rhodesia and Nyasaland. It has been suggested that a motive in the formation of the short-lived association was "to resist the fatal southward pull of Malan's Nationalist Union."[3] Albert Hertzog bluntly asserted in the Union Parliament that the federation was not formed for the well-being of the natives, but to prevent the development of unity between the Europeans of Rhodesia and the Union.[4]

Events took a strange turn when Rhodesia in November 1965 announced its unilateral declaration of independence from Britain. All the things which the Rhodesians feared might happen in South Africa and which had led them to reject joining the Union, had come to pass. Afrikaner Nationalism had triumphed, had made the country a republic and taken it out of the Commonwealth of Nations. These ideas which were so repugnant to Rhodesians in 1922, they themselves put into practice in 1965.

The beginning of decolonization in Africa and the movement to form a federation in south central Africa precipitated a debate in the Union Parliament on the relation of South Africa to its neighbors to the north. On March 4, 1952, a member of the House introduced a resolution calling upon the government to negotiate with the two territories "with a view to their joining the Union in the formation of a greater Union of Southern States in Africa."[5] The author of the proposed resolution spoke of "the idea of a great African federation," composed of all the "national elements which have come out from Europe to establish civilization on this continent." In view of the trends throughout the world, "the solidarity of European civilization on this African continent, together with America, will be the only bulwark against aggression from Asia in the future."[6] The sponsor of the resolution recognized that there were obstacles to unification, chiefly the language and native questions, but he did not believe they were insuperable.[7] The seconder of the motion pleaded for greater cooperation between the Union and

---

[1] See Chapter 4 for the history of the early relations between the two neighbors.
[2] See Colin Leys, *European Politics in Southern Rhodesia* (Oxford, 1959). On the role of the Afrikaners in Rhodesia see also L. H. Gann and M. Gelfand, *Huggins of Rhodesia: The Man and His Country* (London, 1964), pp. 59–62.
[3] Eric A. Walker, *A History of Southern Africa* (London, 1962), p. 797.
[4] *Hansard*, vol. 85, col. 4432, 3 May 1954.
[5] *Hansard*, vol. 77, col. 2177. S. J. Tighy (United party) was the mover.
[6] Ibid., col. 2178.
[7] Ibid., col. 2184.

the Rhodesias. He admitted that there were great differences between South Africa and the other African territories but there was one great similarity between the Rhodesias and the Union: their common belief that they were "the permanent pillars of White civilization in Southern Africa."[8]

Prime Minister Malan was highly critical of the motion. It was unrealistic; it could do no good and might do harm. The Union had once made an offer to Southern Rhodesia and it had been rejected. Negotiations for a greater Union of South Africa should, therefore, be initiated by Rhodesia. Contrary to what had been said, the Rhodesias were not looking to the south, but to the north. Any suggestions from South Africa would be regarded as intervention. Moreover, fear of the Union had been used to promote federation in the north.[9]

But this did not mean that Malan personally was not interested in what was happening in the north. "Our whole existence and future depends on maintaining the Western European Christian civilization in the Union of South Africa." Cooperation was in the interest of all the countries of southern Africa but it should come not by establishing a constitutional association but by good understanding and cooperation by the conference method. He repeated the desire he expressed in 1945 for a Charter of Africa.[10] A Rhodesian federation which tries to maintain Western European Christian civilization would form "a bulwark between us and the northern part of Africa with the pressure coming from that direction." But if the Rhodesias abandon the preservation of this civilization and the supremacy of the European the result would be the very opposite, and they could become "a bridge between us and the territories farther north, thus endangering our position in the south."[11]

SOUTH AFRICAN REACTION

The situation created by Rhodesia's declaration of independence was delicate, if not embarrassing. Prime Minister Verwoerd discussed the problem from his government's point of view in the House in January 1966. Nobody could be more sympathetic with the white people of

[8] Ibid., col. 2191.
[9] Ibid., col. 2194.
[10] Ibid., col. 2196.
[11] Ibid., cols. 2196–97.

Rhodesia than the members of the government.[12] But, however they felt about the British policy, it was not for South Africa to interfere or do anything about it. The whole situation was delicate. It was in South Africa's interests to stay out of the conflict as long as possible and to restrict the conflict to the United Kingdom and Rhodesia. South Africa would permit no interference in her own affairs; to be true to this principle it would not interfere in those of others. A second major principle of South African policy was that the country would, under no circumstances, participate in either boycotts or sanctions. South Africa had repeatedly been threatened with both and to a degree had experienced both. His government would uphold this principle equally toward all sides. South Africa's position was, in fact, of great value to Rhodesia, which, fighting boycotts and sanctions, found continued economic and trade relations with her neighbor a great advantage.[13]

The opposition was critical of the government for not going further —for not extending the revolutionary government de facto recognition and for not giving it unusual assistance. If the Rhodesians were forced to their knees and chaos should take over, South Africa's security would be vitally affected. If Rhodesia fell to militant black nationalism both Angola and Mozambique would be outflanked and weakened.[14]

In reply to Sir De Villiers Graaf's argument that South Africa should commit itself openly to Rhodesia's cause rather than play the part of a benevolent neutral, the prime minister pointed out some difficulties and dangers. It is questionable whether South Africa, if led into a state of siege, fighting boycotts and sanctions, would be a more valuable neighbor to Rhodesia than she was at present. Rhodesia undoubtedly wanted to remain free from interference from a stronger party. Moreover, Rhodesia's racial policy was different from South Africa's and much nearer to the British and American views. In this respect Rhodesia would have an advantage over the Republic in arriving at a settlement —"Why, then," said Verwoerd in an amazing lapse of detachment, "should Rhodesia allow herself to be attacked as if she were a supporter of the apartheid policy, to call it by that name."[15]

[12] B. J. Schoeman, minister of transport, declared that the South African government was wholeheartedly behind Rhodesia, which it regarded as the "White frontier" on the Zambesi (*Sunday Times* [Johannesburg], 14 Nov. 1965).

[13] *Hansard*, vol. 16, cols. 49–57, 25 Jan. 1966.

[14] Ibid., cols. 40–44.

[15] Ibid., cols. 54, 56.

However much white South Africans sympathized with the whites in Rhodesia they strongly advised the Rhodesian government against a unilateral declaration of independence. The political columnist of *Die Burger* warned that it would let loose "a handful of devils" in and around southern Africa. He feared it would precipitate an international crisis and that South Africa would be drawn into it.[16] Verwoerd wrote to both Prime Minister Harold Wilson and Prime Minister Ian Smith urging a solution of the problem.[17]

When Balthazar J. Vorster succeeded to the prime ministership on September 13, 1966, he continued Verwoerd's policy. He declared that the issue was a domestic and not an international problem and urged Rhodesia and Britain to seek "an honourable, acceptable, and realistic solution."[18] Again on December 6, 1966, Vorster made a strong appeal to Britain and Rhodesia to settle their dispute. He sharply criticized Britain for taking the dispute to the United Nations and asking for the application of sanctions against Rhodesia. Sanctions could only create bitterness. They would serve no one's cause.[19] Smith visited Pretoria in October 1967 and after the meeting of the two prime ministers, Vorster stated that he still believed that the issue had to be solved and that it could be solved, if there was goodwill on both sides.[20]

Rhodesia's unilateral declaration of independence had created a strange triangular situation between South Africa, Britain, and Rhodesia. South Africa tried to maintain normal, friendly relations with both. Yet South Africa was refusing to enforce the United Nations sanctions which Britain had called for, and the trade lost by Britain, which it badly needed, was gained by South Africa. Rhodesia's ability to withstand the sanctions was in large part due to the policy of South Africa of doing business as usual, which really became an unusual business with Rhodesia. Britain's stake in South Africa in trade and investments was so great that it could not afford to alienate that country nor embroil her in hostile action. But South Africa was not happy about Rhodesia's position. One reason for Verwoerd's and Vorster's reserve toward the

---

[16] 2 Oct. 1965.

[17] *Hansard*, vol. 17, col. 2546, 21 Sept. 1966, statement by B. J. Vorster after he became prime minister.

[18] *The Star* (Johannesburg), Weekly Air Edition, 10 Dec. 1966.

[19] *New York Times*, 7 Dec. 1966.

[20] *The Star*, Weekly Air Edition, 28 Oct. 1967.

Smith government may have been that it followed a policy of nonracial-
ism and not of apartheid.

South Africa had a number of important interests in Rhodesia. It had
an emotional interest, since many of the Rhodesians were related to
Afrikaners and English-speaking South Africans. Second, South Africa
had an intense interest in keeping a hostile African regime from being
set up on its border. Third, it was in its interests to have a convincing
demonstration that sanctions would not work. This would reduce the
danger of sanctions being applied against South Africa.

Rhodesia was holding out, yet South Africa was far from happy
about it. South Africa was giving Rhodesia so much economic support
that Afro-Asian resentment against the Rhodesian government was
turning against South Africa as well, and there was danger that matters
might get out of hand. For South Africa the Rhodesian affair came at a
most unfortunate time; Pretoria had enough foreign complications
without becoming involved in Rhodesia's problems and it had begun a
counteroffensive against Pan-Africanism. Prime Minister Vorster had
placed a high priority on a policy of improving relations with southern
African countries. A plan for a coprosperity sphere, with the great
economic power of South Africa at its center, had a strong magnetic
attraction for the weak developing neighbors whose economic dependence on South Africa gives them limited freedom in any case.[21] The
Rhodesian dispute constitutes a grave threat to the delicate harmony
that has been established in southern Africa under Pretoria's leadership. An intensification or widening of the conflict centering on Rhodesia, and involving racial policy, would make it more difficult for South
Africa not to become more directly and deeply involved and upset the
advances made in South Africa's counteroffensive, if it did not reduce
southern Africa to chaos. So South African policy continued to be one
of ignoring calls for sanctions against Rhodesia or anybody else, of
giving as much unofficial aid to Rhodesia as possible to keep it from
collapse, of avoiding recognition of Rhodesia as a fully legal state and
of exerting pressure on both the United Kingdom and Rhodesia to settle
their dispute. South Africa's fear of attracting sanctions against itself

[21] Even Zambia, which is very hostile to both Rhodesia and South Africa, does
increasing business with the latter. South Africa's exports to Zambia between 1964
and 1967 increased in value from R27.5 million to R61.7 million (*The Star*, Weekly
Air Edition, 10 Aug. 1968).

was not unfounded. On November 7, 1968, the United Nations General Assembly adopted a resolution calling for stronger sanctions against Rhodesia and the extension of them to South Africa.[22]

GUERRILLA THREATS

In May 1967 clashes between Rhodesian forces and African nationalists occurred near the Zambian border. These hostilities became more serious and in August a battle took place in which South African forces were involved. In July 1968 a South African policeman was killed and three were wounded. Rhodesian and South African forces maintain four joint command posts on the Zambesi.[23] At a press conference, Prime Minister Vorster declared that South Africa would fight terrorists wherever it could fight them. When asked if that included Portuguese territories, he said that he had reference to South African terrorists, that is, people who originally came from South Africa and had been trained elsewhere with the object of coming back. South Africa could not expect others to fight her battles.[24] Popular feeling that Rhodesia and the Portuguese were fighting South Africa's fight was expressed in various forms such as the Friends of Rhodesia Association and the Mozambique Fund. Individuals and local governmental units made contributions to these funds.

The new developments were a cause of embarrassment to the British government. A Labor member of Parliament, Andrew Faulds, who was also chairman of the Anti-Apartheid Movement, wrote a letter to Prime Minister Harold Wilson urging him to act on what he called South Africa's armed intervention in Rhodesia in support of the illegal Smith regime and white supremacy. The South African action created a serious challenge to Britain's authority and responsibility in Rhodesia, yet the government made no protest nor had taken any steps to put a stop to it. The visits of British warships to South Africa indicated growing military ties with that country. South Africa's armed forces had entered British territory to bolster a regime that was in rebellion against British authority. Moreover, he noted, "South Africa remains the principal economic support for the illegal Smith regime. Its counter

---

[22] *New York Times*, 8 Nov. 1968.

[23] Ibid., 2 Aug. 1968, article by Lawrence Fellows.

[24] *The Star*, Weekly Air Edition, 30 Sept. 1967.

sanctions policies have destroyed much of the effectiveness of Britain's sanctions measures."[25]

The British government found itself in an uncomfortable position in this strange diplomatic situation. The captured men apparently were all South African terrorists. They were on their way to South West Africa or South Africa, with no intention of causing damage in Rhodesia. South Africa was careful to treat its action as a police and not a military matter. Pretoria, after asking the Rhodesian government for permission to cooperate with its forces, informed the British government of its move, thus recognizing British sovereignty in Rhodesia while at the same time accepting the de facto authority of the Smith regime. London may have registered a protest at Pretoria but it could not have been a strong one, for it was in a weak position. As the sovereign authority over Rhodesia it had responsibility to prevent the passage of armed bands through its territory to attack a friendly state, which it obviously could not do.

THE FUTURE OF SOUTH AFRICAN-RHODESIAN RELATIONS

The situation between South Africa and Rhodesia is today quite different from what it was in 1923. The former has adopted territorial separation of the races as its national policy. The Afrikaner Nationalists have been in power for two decades and the English-speaking elements of the population have moved in increasing numbers to the support of the Nationalist government. Having established a republic and withdrawn from the Commonwealth, the Nationalists have become less anti-British while the Rhodesian whites have developed a bitterly anti-British attitude. Every day that sanctions continue the two countries move closer to each other economically and psychologically. Prime Minister Ian Smith and members of his party are moving in their thinking toward the South African pattern. On a visit to South Africa, Smith said, "I don't think there is necessarily only one road. We may solve our problems in different ways. On the other hand, we may ultimately find that one common road is the answer."[26]

[25] Ibid., 9 Sept. 1967.
[26] Ibid., 1 April 1967. See also the account of an interview, ibid., 6 Mar. 1967. Smith is not a stranger in South Africa; he is a graduate of Rhodes University College. White Rhodesians are moving toward a racial policy like that of South Africa.

If sanctions ultimately grind down its economy, and if Rhodesia seeks a solution to its desperate problem through union with South Africa, what would be South Africa's response? And the world's reaction? Prime Minister Hertzog declared years ago that "neither of us can run away from each other,"[27] and Winston Churchill nearly half a century ago said that there was ultimately only one destination for Rhodesia: union with South Africa,[28] but neither envisaged the strange circumstances which are bringing the two countries into closer relations.

[27] *Hansard*, vol. 19, col. 3313, 18 April 1932.

[28] At the 1921 Imperial Conference. He added, "One wants Rhodesia to be at man's estate before she joins the Union, and to join it willingly and as a partner. After all, Rhodesia is an enormous factor in the whole South African situation" (Imperial Conference, 1921, *Summary of Proceedings and Documents*, Cmd. 1474 [London, 1923], p. 37).

12

The Lands
Farther North

The question of the use of South African troops beyond the border of the Union was an issue that gave the Smuts government considerable trouble in the Second World War. The defense limits of the Union had been an issue in debates even before the war. Defense Minister Oswald Pirow planned a coordination of the defense of the Union with that of Kenya, Tanganyika, Uganda, and Nyasaland. Smuts emphasized the defense of white civilization as the criterion that should determine the defense limits of the Union. This criterion was acceptable to the Nationalists, but they were uncertain as to where the frontiers of white civilization were. They agreed that South Africa's defense frontier extended at least to the Zambesi, but were reluctant to see the armed forces used beyond that line and were bitterly opposed to their employment in the Middle East or outside of Africa. The government partially solved this problem by using only volunteers in its northern African expeditions. Smuts knew the danger of arousing Afrikaner isolationist sentiments and proceeded cautiously. He resisted the proposal of the British defense minister to move the troops from East Africa to Egypt, influencing Lord Wavell, the commander-in-chief, to finish the campaign in Abyssinia before shifting the troops to the Middle East.[1]

General Smuts contended that it was South Africa's task to clear Abyssinia and British Somaliland of the enemy.[2]

In his remarkable speech delivered before the Empire Parliamentary Association on October 25, 1943, on the future of world politics and Great Britain's role in it, Smuts suggested the reorganization of the Empire by grouping the colonies in a region and bringing them into a closer relationship with a neighboring Dominion, thus making the Dominions "sharers and partners in the Empire."[3] This suggestion reveals the thinking not only of Smuts the holistic imperialist but also of Smuts the Afrikaner. Under this scheme British territories in Central and East Africa would, even if not placed under the guardianship of the Union, follow its leadership. Thus a common racial policy, that of indefinite white tutelage of the Africans, would be guaranteed in all southern Africa.

As the Nationalists began to note that new winds were blowing in Africa, they developed second thoughts about the Union's relations with the other African countries. They began to see, as Smuts had seen much earlier, that the native policy of the colonial powers in Africa could have an unfavorable repercussion in South Africa. An interesting debate was precipitated in March 1945, when a member of Parliament urged Smuts to bring about a federal State of South Africa of which the Union, the Rhodesias, Kenya, Basutoland, Swaziland, and other British territories would be members.[4] In reply Smuts stated that the member was correct to assume that the whole of his striving had been to ensure the knitting together of "the parts of Southern Africa that belong to each other, parts that must necessarily work together for a stable future on the continent of Africa."[5]

Johannes G. Strijdom, who was to succeed Malan as leader of the Nationalist party and as prime minister in 1954, expressed concern about the danger of eventual domination by the native African over the white man in South Africa. He wished to know what the prime minister's attitude to this problem was.[6] Another member warned against the Union's entering any arrangement which would unite South

[1] J. C. Smuts, Jr., *Jan Christiaan Smuts* (Cape Town, 1952), pp. 408–409.
[2] *Times* (London), 13 Jan. 1941.
[3] Smuts, Jr., *Jan Christiaan Smuts*, p. 447.
[4] *Hansard*, vol. 52, cols. 3718–19, 19 Mar. 1945.
[5] Ibid., col. 3720.
[6] Ibid., col. 3962.

Africa and the rest of Africa in such a way that South Africa would no longer control its own policy.[7] In his statement Strijdom touched upon the basic dilemma of South Africa in this matter: How an arrangement could be set up which would give South Africa the power to influence the native policy of the other African territories without the possibility of its being used against the Union.

Malan suggested an African Charter, a pronouncement by all the powers having territories and interests in Africa, that the continent be preserved in its development for the Western, European, Christian civilization. This declaration should be made at once while the native population was still under the trusteeship of the Europeans, where they would have to remain for years to come. A necessary provision of the Charter should be that the natives would not be armed nor used in war.

Mrs. Margaret Ballinger declared that although she thought that it was a legitimate ambition on the part of South Africa to play a leading role on the African continent, she felt impelled to point out that there were obstacles to the realization of that ambition. The native population of the Protectorates was opposed to incorporation of their territories in the Union because they feared the native policy of South Africa.[8] Captain F. A. Joubert in 1933 had declared that in adopting a native policy South Africans would have to recognize that African and world opinion would have to be considered.[9]

In summarizing the debate, Smuts stated that he had only suggested a system of conferences, but the ideas which had been advanced in the debate were of great significance. The suggestion of an African Charter "to stand side by side with the Atlantic Charter," indicated how "the idea of the importance of this continent . . . has taken root." But he warned that there were difficulties. He could give no answer to many questions raised in the debate; history would have to give the answer. The racial problem was "the most difficult with which we can cope. We have not yet a direction in connection with it on this continent. We are still searching. . . . We have here the boiling pot of racial questions and there is no doubt—I feel it—that this greatest problem of mankind is the problem of race and color, and will remain a question in Africa for many years to come. I do not know whether we shall find a solution. It

[7] Ibid., col. 3971, 22 Mar. 1945.
[8] Ibid., col. 3864.
[9] Ibid., vol. 21, col. 471, 7 June 1933.

may be that the problem is unsolvable and lies outside the capacity of man. . . . This continent is the continent of racial problems; which is the greatest problem of humanity, and on it depends the whole future of the human race. One cannot solve it, but one can approach a solution."[10]

NATIONAL POLICY

When the National party unexpectedly won the parliamentary elections in 1948 the world was stunned, for Malan and his party had acquired a reputation for extremist views on racial and foreign policies. Probably for this reason Prime Minister Malan made a special effort to allay fears at home and abroad about the policies which his government would pursue. Very shortly after coming to power he sent Charles te Water on a mission abroad to improve the image of the new government. In April 1949 Malan sent him on a second mission, this time to the countries of Africa and the European countries with special interests in Africa. The prime minister had said in Parliament in September 1948, "We are part of Africa. . . . Whatever happens to the rest of Africa must have repercussions here."[11] In pursuance of these views te Water was to seek to establish friendly relations and to promote cooperation with the leaders and governments of these territories. Since the Rhodesias, Nyasaland, Tanganyika, Kenya, and Uganda were not yet independent he could make only informal courtesy calls on these governments. The white settlers in these territories looked to South Africa for leadership.[12] However, such leadership could not be given without British cooperation and Britain, twenty-five years earlier in connection with the situation in Kenya, had announced the policy of the paramountcy of native interests.

After a visit to Cairo, te Water said that there should be an organic rather than a political approach to African problems.[13] He had found an interest in discussing coordination in transport, soil conservation, and

[10] Ibid., vol. 52, col. 3975, 22 Mar. 1945. The question was raised again in 1949 in the debate on the imperial conference report, 12 May 1949 (ibid., vol. 68, cols. 5640ff.).

[11] *Cape Times* (Cape Town), 23 April 1949.

[12] Sir Alfred Vincent, leader of the elected members of the Kenya legislature, declared that the Union of South Africa was the natural leader of Africa (ibid., 23 April 1949).

[13] *The Star* (Johannesburg), 25 May 1949.

economic problems. A few days later he said that defensive alliances were in the forefront of Union policy and suggested that the Atlantic Pact should be reinforced by African and Mediterranean defensive alliances. He sought an exchange of views on this subject, particularly with the governments of Mediterranean countries.[14] The coolness with which this approach was received probably accounts for his suggestion of an organic rather than a political approach to African problems.

Malan's chief concern seemed to be the threat of Communism.[15] He regarded the South African situation with respect to Communist propaganda and activities as definitely serious and dangerous. No reliance could be placed on the United Nations for security. South Africa was "anxious to remain associated with the other members of the Commonwealth" if the Commonwealth did not interfere in the internal affairs of its members. A war between Communist and anti-Communist countries would create a danger in South Africa, since the Communists for a long time had been propagandizing and "it is taking root among the non-European population of the country." The extent to which the Union would be able to take part in such a war would depend on its internal situation. The countries of Europe which have possessions in Africa should have a conference in regard to a general policy for Africa. He hoped that since South Africa and the Atlantic Pact countries needed each other the opportunity would be created to reach an agreement. Malan concluded: The Suez Canal might be destroyed. In that case the passage round Africa would become necessary to the West if it wished to retain contact with the East. They would then "need our cooperation, our goodwill. But it may be also that in view of the dangers to which I have referred, here, within our own borders, we too may need those Powers, or other Powers that have interests here in Africa."

At least one conference to consider the defense problems of Africa was held. According to a statement by T. E. Donges, minister of economics and head of the South African delegation to the Sixth Session of the General Assembly of the United Nations, the South African government in conjunction with the British government had convened an African defense facilities conference at Nairobi in August 1951, to which all powers with African interests had been invited. The

[14] *Times*, 21 June 1949.
[15] The address was distributed as a pamphlet by the Union of South Africa, State Information Office, *Foreign Policy of the Union of South Africa* (Pretoria, 1949).

conference, whose object was "facilitating the movement of troops and supplies in time of war or emergency," was pronounced "an unqualified success."[16]

There was much discussion of African policy in the 1953 session of Parliament and Prime Minister Malan replied to questions at some length.[17] He began by saying that it was clear that the interests and future of South Africa were closely connected with what happened further north. South Africa had interests not only in southern Africa, but in all of Africa. He went on to say that there had been an awakening of nationalism. While he admitted that the African countries wanted to be free and completely independent, he was convinced that this was not the whole picture. There were "influences and powers" behind the awakening of this feeling. These influences were first of all Communist activities. Russia was exploiting the desire for more freedom. Second, there was the unfortunate experiment on the Gold Coast. The British gave that territory freedom based on an unqualified franchise. Ninety percent of the voters were totally uneducated—"near a state of barbarism." As a result of this example British territories in Africa now demand a Gold Coast constitution. Third, there was India. She stood for anticolonialism, demanding that the Europeans get out of Africa. Wherever there was trouble, or trouble might arise, between European powers with possessions in Africa or in South Africa, "India intervenes and takes sides against the European."

As a solution to these problems Malan had long advocated an African Charter, which should stress the following points: 1) protection of the indigenous people of Africa against penetration by the peoples of Asia, 2) the guidance of Africa along the road to European civilization, 3) the suppression of Communist activities, and 4) the prevention of militarization of Africans. Malan was not clear about it, but he also seemed to suggest a defense agreement.[18]

In March 1954, R. B. Durrant introduced a resolution in Parliament urging the government to initiate discussions with other governments and administrations in Africa for the purpose of bringing under centralized control existing spheres of cooperative efforts, adequately combat-

---

[16] United Nations, General Assembly, Official Records, 6th Sess., Plenary Meetings, Verbatim Record, 14 Nov. 1951, p. 153.

[17] *Hansard*, vol. 82, cols. 1205–1326, 11 Aug. 1953.

[18] In an interview with C. L. Sulzberger of the *New York Times* on 17 Jan. 1953, Malan had listed the same four points.

ing the spread of Communist propaganda, exchanging information on non-European populations, developing adequate defense measures, and developing trade and industry. Durrant believed that if white civilization was to be preserved the different territories should adopt a uniform outlook.[19] Malan agreed that steps had to be taken in that direction but this was not the right time for South Africa to take the lead in calling a conference. A better method was that of developing closer relations through cooperation. He hoped that eventually they could agree on a broader basis in regard to an African policy. He was not prepared to say that South Africa should take the lead. England should take the lead as it had more influence in Africa as a whole.[20]

The prime minister's speech and those of his supporters came in for sharp criticism. With respect to the nonmilitarization of Africa, it was pointed out that South Africa had the only white army on the continent. Was it suggested that Egypt, Ethiopia, and the Gold Coast should be asked to have white armies? All the colonial powers in Africa used African troops; hence nonmilitarization would mean demilitarization. He questioned whether that was possible and whether South Africa would also demilitarize. Malan saw only one hope, one ally, and this was British imperialism, and yet he urged Britain not to arm its natives. Another glaring inconsistency was pointed out: while the National party government in desperation turned to Britain, Nationalists were violently hostile to Britain and all things British.[21] Mrs. Ballinger chided the prime minister for saying that he could do little about threats to Africa because the people of Africa and the rest of the world did not like South Africans. "The real reason why the rest of the world does not like us," declared Mrs. Ballinger, "and the real reason why the British Press does not like us is that our own African population on the whole does not like us. That is our real difficulty."[22]

When Strijdom succeeded Malan as prime minister[23] he did not, as his predecessors had done, keep the portfolio of external relations for himself. He chose Eric H. Louw as minister for external affairs. Strijdom and Louw were regarded as belonging to the extremist wing of the

---

[19] *Hansard*, vol. 84, cols. 2163–74, 16 Mar. 1954.

[20] *Hansard*, vol. 85, cols. 4491–97, 4 May 1954. Malan in this speech said, "I say here deliberately that Nehru is the enemy of the white man."

[21] Ibid., cols. 4500–4501.

[22] Ibid., cols. 4504–4505.

[23] 30 Nov. 1954.

National party. During the four years of Strijdom's premiership, Nationalist leaders slowly began to recognize what some members of the opposition had seen fairly early, namely, that colonialism in Africa was rapidly on the way out and that plans for an African Charter and continental cooperation would in a few years be possible, if at all, only on an entirely different basis. Strijdom was slow to see this. In August 1954 he made a statement which reasserted the old purpose of seeking to win the colonial powers in Africa to a policy of white supremacy. "It is our task," he said, "to win their [neighboring states] support for our standpoint that white rule must be maintained and that otherwise they, as well as we, are doomed to disappear."[24]

If Pretoria made any further moves to induce other governments to join it in an African Charter or an agreement for cooperation for defense as well as other purposes, it must have suffered rebuffs. In spite of all the big talk in Parliament and outside about the necessity for such negotiations, nothing came of it. The governor general's speech opening Parliament in January 1955 said merely that "sound and friendly relations continue to exist between the Union and its neighbors as well as with other territories in Africa south of the Sahara. It is the aim of the government to promote co-operation with these territories on matters of common concern by means of mutual consultation."[25] Members of Parliament felt that the time for tentative approaches was past, that the time had come for issuing a formal invitation to establish an African Organization.[26] They were disappointed that the government promised only "to do everything in our power to keep in close contact with the various White communities, . . . to obtain the co-operation of the other territories in Africa, especially in Southern Africa, in regard to scientific conferences or conferences in regard to joint action and the coordination of transport, or even agriculture."[27] This policy statement appeared very feeble in view of Strijdom's analysis in the same speech of the dangers which faced South Africa. He asserted that the Union, alone and isolated, could not hope to maintain White civilization in South Africa. There would therefore have to be the greatest possible

[24] *New York Times*, 18 Aug. 1954. Prime Minister Malan had suggested a North Atlantic Treaty Organization guarantee for South Africa and the Indian Ocean two weeks earlier.

[25] *Hansard*, vol. 87, col. 3.

[26] Ibid., vol. 88, col. 4068.

[27] Ibid., col. 4025.

degree of understanding and cooperation between the various white communities in southern Africa in regard to many things if they wanted to ensure their existence in Africa. "That is what we generally mean when we talk about an Africa policy."[28]

Strijdom was frank about the necessity of aid from Western countries if the position of the white man in southern Africa was to be fulfilled. Several members of the opposition again pointed out the dilemma which confronted the government in its aims and policies. South Africa's place was beside the Western democracies, but the government was pursuing aims which tended to cut if off from the Western powers and Western trends and would reduce the country to an unwanted isolation. The epoch of white domination was over. The Western powers would not involve themselves in a conflict in order to maintain white domination. They would certainly "not lift a finger to preserve South Africa as the last stronghold of white *baaskap*." In their struggle against world Communism it was of vital importance to keep the nonwhite races on their side, and they could do this only by offering the black peoples of Africa a constructive and democratic alternative to Communism. "South Africa, under this government with its White baaskap policy," concluded B. Friedman, "is an embarrassment to the cause of the Western powers."[29]

Mrs. Ballinger said that the rest of the continent saw South Africa as the Achilles heel of African defense, "because we can offer them no guarantee in the present situation, that our non-European population will not be a fifth column when the disaster becomes an immediate one."[30]

But this presented the South African whites with a cruel dilemma. Said B. Coetzee, a radical Nationalist, "if we are to give up our position of domination in order to gain the friendship of the West, why do we really want their friendship? . . . What will that friendship help us thereafter?"[31] When confronted with these alternatives, the Nationalist had no doubt about which of the unpleasant courses he would choose. And when pushed into a corner the members of the United party and the vast majority of the whites had to admit, sometimes very reluctantly, that they really were not prepared to surrender "White leadership," as

[28] Ibid., cols. 4024–25.
[29] Ibid., cols. 4113–15, 19 April 1955.
[30] Ibid., col. 4125.
[31] Ibid., col. 4133.

they preferred to call it. They resolved the moral problem involved by pressing the policy of apartheid and separate development, which was in the interests not only of the white man but also of the natives.

By 1955 the prime minister began to make his adjustment to the trend toward the decolonization of Africa. In a speech outside of Parliament from which he quoted in addressing the House, he said, "As far as the non-White States with their millions of inhabitants are concerned, our attitude towards them as co-interested parties in Africa will have to be such that we do not regard each other as enemies but as nations and governments acknowledging and respecting each other's right to exist." He continued by saying that "we in the southern part where we still have White States, will not be able to treat these non-White states as enemies." Having regard for the dangers threatening Africa from the outside, he called for cooperation among the white states of southern Africa.[32]

The difficulties of implementing these policies appeared in different ways. Strijdom and Louw boasted about the number of agencies for cooperation in the scientific and technical fields in which South Africa was actively participating. A member of the House observed that none of these organizations had a secretariat located in any of the countries south of the Sahara, with the exception of the Tsetse Fly Bureau. When the prime minister spoke about the large number of conferences which were planned and in which South Africa would participate, the leader of the opposition asked how many of these conferences would be held in South Africa. Strijdom replied that they would probably be held in other territories. South Africa did not have the facilities for holding such conferences. In view of the creation of more and more nonwhite states, increasingly more nonwhite delegates would attend the conferences. The government was investigating the situation so as to create facilities which would make it easier for them to attend.[33] This matter of entertaining in segregated South Africa officials of African countries became a delicate problem.[34] The government could easily lose the support of its right-wingers on this issue.

The government could not decide on the direction in which it should go. All the talk about an African Charter had been based on the idea of

[32] Ibid., vol. 91, cols. 4104–4105, 23 April 1956.
[33] Ibid., cols. 4126–27.
[34] Ibid., vol. 95, cols. 7618, 7635, 10 June 1957.

forming a white bloc in Africa, but in rapid succession the African territories were becoming independent states. The formation of a white bloc could no longer succeed. As a member of the House had warned, "any attempt to establish . . . a White bloc would . . . merely be interpreted as proof of hostility towards the non-White States or the States which accept partnership as a basis. It would be accepted as proof that we do in fact want to export our racial policy outside our borders."[35] But the government was not ready to become friendly with the African states as this would offend the rank and file of the National party members. To make this policy acceptable would require a period of preparation. A member of Parliament admonished the government and his fellow South Africans that "one cannot be a leader if one is not accepted as a leader or even as a colleague if one's relations with the other States are not genuine and hearty and are not founded on the basis of respect and equality."[36] Repeatedly, Nationalist leaders declared that they were not prepared to relinquish their traditional attitude.[37]

It appears that Louw received a rebuff from London with respect to his ideas of African conferences and his proposals for a common racial policy. He told Parliament that he wanted to make clear "that the proposal which I made amounts to no more than that the representatives of countries concerned should have discussions. There is no question whatsoever of the establishment of any organization, such as the Pan-American Union, for example, nor is there any idea that there should necessarily be regular discussions." South Africa did not wish to interfere with the policy of any of those countries. He hoped that "where there is perhaps still some misunderstanding in the United Kingdom as to what we actually contemplate, that misunderstanding will be removed."[38] This was a big retreat from the Pan-African Charter talk of Smuts, Malan, and others. The British may have distrusted South African motives and they understandably would not want to be caught in discussions on racial policy with South Africa.

The opposition in Parliament sought to prod the government into greater cooperation with the new African states. This was generally done in the debates on the budgets of the prime minister and External

[35] J. D. du P. Basson, ibid., col. 7650.
[36] Ibid., col. 7649.
[37] J. H. Steyn in the House, ibid., vol. 91, col. 4413, 26 April 1956.
[38] Ibid., col. 4509, 27 April 1956.

(later Foreign) Affairs Department, and sometimes also in the no-confidence debates. In February 1961 one of the leaders of the United party introduced a resolution declaring that the House was of the opinion that the government should propose the establishment of an Inter-State African Development Association which would have "as one of its main objectives the raising of the living standards of the African masses with a view to ensuring their acceptance of Western democratic standards as opposed to Communist ideology." Minister Louw had stated some time earlier that South Africa should form a permanent link between Western and African states south of the Sahara. The policy had failed, declared the mover of the resolution, because the great Western powers did not accept South Africa as a link between the West and black Africa, nor did the emergent nations of Africa accept her as a go-between. South Africa was giving some economic assistance but what was needed was a forum to discuss "common problems in Africa, and active machinery whereby states could obtain the necessary economic assistance on the basis of cooperative effort."[39] As the most highly industrialized country on the continent, South Africa had an obligation to take the lead in cooperation for economic development.

The motion evoked a lively debate. Many suggestions were made: that South Africans should move away from a somewhat patronizing attitude toward the African nations; that they could not go on thinking of nonwhite people as being uncivilized; that they must realize that communication with sister states in Africa would henceforth be direct and not through the European colonial rulers; and that they should develop a truly African mentality. There was general agreement that South Africa's racial policy posed a serious obstacle to friendly relations with the African states. Most thought it was the chief barrier, but the minister for external affairs seemed to think it was the only obstacle. He cited a number of instances of hostility on the part of African states. Said Minister Louw, "what the African states demand from South Africa is that there should be equality of voting, that there should be no discrimination on social or other grounds, and that the Bantu should by virtue of their huge majority in numbers be in a position to govern the country. They have said it again and again at the U. N." It was naïve to believe that the African states would be willing to follow South Africa's

[39] Ibid., vol. 106, cols. 1923–35, 24 Feb. 1961.

lead in the establishment of a development corporation.[40] If the minister's analysis was correct there were three alternatives: 1) the African peoples would change their views about South African policy, which seemed very unlikely; 2) white South Africans would change their racial views and the government change its policy; or 3) South Africa would be isolated. The government was not prepared to change its racial policy to satisfy African states.

But since the government was unwilling to accept isolation as a fact or a policy, its position was not consistent. Sometimes it denied the facts: South Africa had powerful friends, it asserted. At other times, when forced to acknowledge the existence of general hostility toward South Africa, it argued that South Africa was strong and could defy the world. In time the world would see the justice and wisdom of South Africa's racial policy. They also sought comfort from the belief or hope that the Western powers would not themselves, nor permit others to, destroy South Africa which was a strategic bastion of the West against Communism and Asia. In any case, so argued the Nationalists, to abandon its racial policy would mean the certain end of the white South African nation. This was an impossible price to pay for the friendship of the world.

There was heightened uneasiness in South Africa in 1960 and 1961, due to the occurrence of a number of disturbing events. In February 1960 British Prime Minister Harold Macmillan made his "Wind of Change" address to the South African Parliament; in February and March there was serious racial tension culminating in the great tragedy at Sharpeville, followed by the proclamation of a state of emergency; in April there was an attempt to assassinate Prime Minister Verwoerd; and on October 5 a referendum was held on whether South Africa should become a republic; in January 1961 Dag Hammarsjkold, secretary general of the United Nations, conferred with the South African government about the purpose and principles of the Charter in relation to South African racial policies; and in March South Africa withdrew from the Commonwealth. The situation in the Congo was disturbing. The great concern was expressed in a resolution introduced in Parliament by Dr. Carel De Wet, a member of the government party. The resolution declared that consideration should be given to the dangerous

[40] Ibid., cols. 1936–41.

threat to South Africa of Communistic ideology and activities in Africa. The sponsor of the resolution was of the opinion that the nationalization of the Suez Canal gave encouragement to Communist activity in Africa. Communism and Communists should be exposed; whites and nonwhites should be indoctrinated against Communism; and stricter action should be taken against Communists. South Africa's primary international task was to make the world understand that the Union was "the indispensable bulwark against Communism in Africa. We must make the world realize that if the South African White democracy is not preserved, Western influence in Africa will to a large extent disappear." An ideology such as Communism could be combated only with another ideology. South Africa had that ideology: "separate development, not merely between Black and White, but between all the peoples of the world, as being above all others the only real antithesis of the Communist ideology."[41]

The introduction of this resolution gave the opposition an unusual opportunity to attack the Nationalist government's policy. Members of opposition parties declared that they were as opposed to revolutionary Communism as anybody, but they found the motion "vague, ambiguous and pointless." They contended that great mistakes were made by South Africans when they talked about Communism in Africa. The first was to confuse Communism with other ideologies such as socialism. This was to make enemies unnecessarily, since there were several socialistic governments in Europe and in many other countries in Europe the socialist parties were strong. A second mistake was to describe as Communist things which in fact were not Communist. Statements were frequently made that equal treatment for white and black, giving increased rights to nonwhites, and liberalism and anticolonialism were Communist. Such loose talk could only alienate the free world. A third mistake was to think that by forbidding Communist ideas they could be suppressed. A fourth mistake was the belief that South Africa could continue its present approach to its problems and in the event of war be sure that the Western countries would assist it in the struggle against Communism. In a struggle against Communism a country such as the United States might be forced to choose between India and South Africa. There was no guarantee that America would choose South

41 Ibid., cols. 2337–57, 3 Mar. 1961.

Africa. The fifth mistake was to blame Communism for what are often our own shortcomings.

The speaker for the opposition in the debate then made some suggestions with respect to the problem of Communism in Africa. The government was making a mistake in always talking about a struggle between the white and black countries. "In fighting against Communism we are not fighting for White civilization; we are not fighting for a White skin, we are fighting for a certain outlook and a certain idealism. Let us emphasize that and do not let us make potential enemies of non-White countries." He also pleaded for a policy of promoting diplomatic as well as economic and scientific cooperation with the African states, however difficult it might be.

The opposition spokesman ended his speech by suggesting similarities between certain practices of the Nationalist government and those of Communist countries. In the Communist state a citizen could be locked up without trial, the court was an instrument of compulsion, with no protection for the accused, with the trial held behind closed doors. Under Communist regimes banning without trial was a political weapon, the press was the lackey of the government, and free criticism was punishable by imprisonment. The state was everything and the individual nothing. "Do we realize," he concluded, "how far we have progressed along that road in South Africa, bearing in mind the effect of some of our laws, particularly our pass laws? Let us make a start, however small, to get a different spirit here so as to show the world that in this country anti-Communism has a strong moral basis."[42]

The opposition's prodding to make greater contact and establish friendships with the African states was of no avail. In June 1965 South Africa had few diplomatic and consular posts outside of Western Europe and the United States. It had three in the whole of Africa: one in Angola, one in Mozambique, and one in Rhodesia. It had only two contacts in Asia: Lebanon and Tokyo, and two in South America: Argentina and Brazil. A member of the House complained that the bulk of the Foreign Affairs budget was spent in Europe, "trying to convince White people that the policies of the Government are acceptable."[43]

South Africa hesitated about taking an active part in the Economic

---

[42] Ibid., cols. 2367–79.
[43] Ibid., vol. 15, col. 7695, 9 June 1965.

Commission for Africa, apparently for the reason that since it was a part of the United Nations system it permitted non-African states to intervene in its activities. South Africa preferred to cooperate in giving economic and scientific assistance through C.C.T.A. (Committee for Technical Cooperation in Africa) and F.A.M.A. (Foundation for Mutual Assistance in Africa) of which only African states and states with colonial responsibilities in Africa were members, but its contribution to these bodies was not large. After some delay South Africa did become a member of the Economic Commission for Africa, but the African members did not welcome its presence. The Commission recommended to the Economic and Social Council that South Africa be deprived of its membership until it set a time limit to its policy of racial discrimination. Pretoria then announced that it had decided "not to attend any activities of the Commission while the hostile attitude of the African States towards South Africa persists." The Social and Economic Council adopted a resolution which excluded South Africa from taking part in the work of the Commission until the Council, on the recommendation of the Commission, should find that conditions for constructive cooperation had been restored by a change in its racial policy.[44]

Government leaders engaged in much fine talk about friendly relations and cooperation with the African states, but they were handicapped and restricted by the policy and practice of racial social segregation at home. The problem came to a focus in the matter of diplomatic representation. Prime Minister Strijdom declared in 1957 that as the African states developed there would have to be ordinary relations "and even diplomatic relations." South Africa should not be overhasty but eventually there would be no other course than increasing consultation and cooperation with the nonwhite countries on matters affecting common interests.[45] This was a new development and the government would have to act carefully. But because of racial views and practices implementation of this policy ran into difficulties. In an interview with the press in Paris, External Affairs Minister Louw, when asked about diplomatic relations between his country and Ghana, replied that while there was no intention for the time being of having diplomatic relations

---

[44] United Nations, Official Records, ECOSOC, 36th Sess., Resolution No. 974, DIV (XXXVI), 30 July 1963.

[45] *Hansard,* vol. 94, col. 5220.

with African states, it probably would come sometime in the future, after a period of preparation.[46]

When six years later there still were no direct normal diplomatic relations with any African state, Prime Minister Verwoerd was asked in Parliament whether it was the policy of his government to have diplomatic relations with other African states. He made a lengthy reply which by implication indicated that the matter was one of great difficulty for the National government. First he tried to explain why there was still no exchange of diplomats with African states. Diplomatic relations were based usually upon friendship and harmonious relations. There were "various countries in Africa who were not only intent on undermining the policy of the South African Government but who were training people to do so by force of arms." But if African states really wished friendly relations, South Africa was willing to enter into diplomatic relations with them. But if we become so friendly, Verwoerd told the prime minister of Nigeria, there would be an understanding of the difficulties and of the best way to maintain diplomatic relations.[47] Here Verwoerd seemed to suggest that an accommodation was possible, but in a letter to Prime Minister Menzies of Australia he implied that any yielding on South Africa's rigid practices of the social segregation of the races would undermine its racial policy and eventually lead to the "swallowing up of the Whites."[48]

Verwoerd went on to say in Parliament that though South Africa was a prosperous country it could not maintain resident diplomatic representatives in all countries of the world and that with the large number of states that were coming into being in Africa it would be impractical to have diplomatic posts in all of them. Nor could the African states afford to have diplomatic representation in all the other African states. He had therefore suggested that some cheaper method be found. For example, the states which could reach South Africa within a day by air could establish contact through the appropriate cabinet minister "when they considered it necessary and important to do so." He also suggested the appointment of "a traveling ambassador who,

[46] Ibid., vol. 107, cols. 2373–74, 18 Aug. 1958.

[47] Ibid., vol. 10, cols. 4900–4901, 24 April 1964.

[48] Robert Menzies, *Afternoon Light: Some Memories of Men and Events* (New York, 1967), pp. 198–202.

when any problem presented itself, would be available to visit the country concerned. . . . We are near enough for all of them to follow this cheaper method."[49]

It is clear that leaders of both the government and the opposition feared the reaction within South Africa that almost certainly would follow the presence in Pretoria of a considerable number of Africans who lived among whites and were not subject to the restrictions of racial segregation.[50] This would constitute a formidable breach in the segregation front. When in 1958 the government entertained a representative of Ghana, put him up at the best hotel, and put at his disposal a white chauffeur to drive him around, even members of the United party were not above making political capital out of it.[51] In the search to solve this problem the government seized the suggestion that an area ("park") be set aside for diplomatic representatives and their families. Foreign Minister Muller announced in September 1967 that an examination of plans for the establishment of diplomatic suburbs in Cape Town and Pretoria had reached an advanced stage.[52] Special arrangements, however, might not be acceptable to African states or their diplomatic representatives. As summarized in an influential South African paper, the government "was sacrificing an essential component of the country's foreign policy on the altar of domestic apartheid." There is no substitute for the accredited diplomatic representative; "in emergent Africa his appointment signifies respect for the dignity of a new state, just as failure to appoint is an affront to that dignity."[53]

The opposition recognized that it was difficult to have "these diplomatic exchanges of persons of other colours," because of "the historical background of the Union and because of the susceptibilities and prejudices of certain of our people," but it was critical of the external affairs minister for doing nothing to prepare the way for this sort of

[49] *Hansard*, vol. 10, cols. 4901–4902.

[50] In a speech in April 1959, Minister of External Affairs Louw said that the exchange of diplomatic relations with the emerging states of Africa was sure to come, but not in the near future. Old established customs in race relations could not be changed overnight. (South African Institute of Race Relations, *Survey of Race Relations in South Africa, 1958–1959* [Johannesburg, 1960], p. 328).

[51] Complaint by Louw, *Hansard*, vol. 97, cols. 2439–41, 18 Aug. 1958.

[52] South African Institute of Race Relations, *Survey of Race Relations in South Africa, 1967*, p. 89.

[53] *The Star*, 23 Mar. 1959.

representation.[54] In a speech at the University of Pretoria, Minister Louw had declared that South Africa should serve as a link between the West and black Africa. A member of the House commented on this ambition of the minister by saying that he should realize an obstacle in his way was "the almost fanatical fear of his Government to meet, mix with or even to inter-change ideas with any man of colour, on any other basis than that of master and servant. . . . While the idea of such contact is repugnant to them; while they refuse to civilize themselves in this respect; while they fear the man of colour, the man of colour will hate and avoid them."[55]

Finally, toward the end of 1967, diplomatic relations with an African state were established. In September of that year it was announced that South Africa and Malawi would open legations in Blantyre and Pretoria. The first head of the Malawi mission was a British civil servant, but the first secretary was an African. President Banda, in making the announcement, said that the South African government had agreed that a Malawian of "full African blood and colour" should occupy the post as soon as possible and convenient and that all Malawian diplomats would be accorded full diplomatic treatment.[56]

[54] H. G. Lawrence, *Hansard,* vol. 100, col. 5435, 6 May 1959.

[55] Ibid., col. 5451.

[56] Walter Rosenberger and Herbert Tobin, eds., *Keesing's Contemporary Archives* (London, 1931–), 16 (1967–1968) : 22502.

13

Expulsion
from the Commonwealth

Before departing for London to attend the 1949 Commonwealth Prime Ministers' Conference, Malan made an important statement on South Africa's relation to the Commonwealth.[1] So long as nothing detrimental was done to the free, independent rights of the separate units of the Commonwealth his government had no intention of withdrawing from that association. South Africa was absolutely free and independent.

Upon his return from London, Malan made a statement to the House of Assembly on the work of the Conference.[2] The only matter before the meeting, he reported, was India's request to continue as a member of the Commonwealth after it had become a republic, a course on which it had firmly decided. India had given notice that it wished either to be an ordinary member of the Commonwealth or to be completely outside of it. Had India desired to become associated with the Commonwealth on a treaty basis, Malan would have opposed this as it would put India in a position to impose conditions, "and those conditions, in connection with India's relations with us could cause great difficulties, especially for South Africa." But if India's request for continued membership had not been granted, that great country and its goodwill would have been lost to the Commonwealth and the West. It would have meant also, according to Malan, "that if India could not be on friendly terms, as a fellow-member of the Commonwealth, with the other members of the Commonwealth—and every country must have friends nowadays—she would seek her friends elsewhere." India was anti-Communist and "in the present dangerous state of world affairs, that means a great deal to us."

The decision of the Conference to allow India, as a republic, to remain a member of the Commonwealth meant that a change was being made in its constitutional structure. It involved a change in the position of the Crown. The king would continue to form part of the governments of all the members of the Commonwealth, except India. This problem was solved by India's "acceptance of the King as the symbol of the free association of its independent members and as such the Head of the Commonwealth." Prime Minister Malan had objections to the phrase "Head of the Commonwealth." He feared that it might create the impression that members were to a certain degree in a subordinate position. In response to his request, the conference declared that "the designation of the King as Head of the Commonwealth does not connote any change in the constitutional relations existing between the members of the Commonwealth, and in particular does not imply that the King discharges any constitutional function by virtue of that Headship."

The prime minister was obviously pleased with the results of the conference. The conference not only acknowledged the right of secession, but a republic would soon be a member of the Commonwealth in good standing. The Union could become a republic and still continue as a member of the Commonwealth. The fullest right of neutrality when other members of the Commonwealth became involved in war was clearly established.

The National party had changed its position with respect to membership in the Commonwealth. Previously branded as "the fatal British connection" which dragged South Africa into the war, the Commonwealth was now extolled as "a world power, a Power that will exercise tremendous influence in the interests of security in the present dangerous state of world affairs."[3] The reason for the change of attitude was

[1] In the Senate, 8 April 1949 (see Union of South Africa, State Information Office, *Foreign Policy of the Union of South Africa* [Pretoria, n.d.]).

[2] *Hansard*, vol. 68, cols. 5551–65.

[3] Union of So. Af., St. Information Office, *Foreign Policy of the Union of South Africa*, p. 26.

revealed in the prime minister's speech, namely, the threat of aggression from Russia. "We on this side of the House," Malan declared, "have adopted the attitude that our sympathies lie with the Western Powers. We are anti-Communist and we want to throw in our weight with the anti-Communist countries."

Malan's statement on the Commonwealth conference led to a sharp debate on the merits and demerits of a republic for South Africa. Smuts, the leader of the opposition, asked Malan what the position of his government was with respect to the establishment of a republic. Malan replied that the views of the National party and his own personal views had not changed. They were convinced that unity of South Africans could be achieved best by establishing a republic, and while a republic was the ideal of the party, it would not create one unless approved by a majority of the voters in a referendum free from all other issues.[4]

As could be expected from his views on the Commonwealth, Smuts was not altogether happy about the concession which had been made to India in order to keep it in the association. In view of India's strategic, economic, and political position in the world he could appreciate the reasons why it was allowed to remain in the Commonwealth. While the members of the Commonwealth enjoyed the fullest liberty and freedom of development, the king was nevertheless something of a reality in the system, not merely a symbol. Smuts feared that the disappearance of the common allegiance would weaken the position of the Commonwealth considerably. He was anxious that the exception which had been made for India should not become a precedent.[5]

The attitude of Malan and his government toward the Commonwealth was determined by a number of factors. They feared isolation. South African society, in particular its huge African base, they feared, was vulnerable to Communist infiltration, as was the whole continent. In 1949, when the Cold War seemed about to develop into a test of military strength, this consideration was dominant. They felt that support of the

[4] Ibid., p. 28.

[5] *Hansard*, vol. 68, cols., 5565–92. Sir Robert Menzies, long prime minister of Australia, shared Smuts's views. "In one stroke," he wrote, "the common allegiance to the Crown ceased to be the bond of union, and the 'British Commonwealth' became 'the Commonwealth'" (Robert Menzies, *Afternoon Light: Some Memories of Men and Events* [New York, 1967], p. 188).

West against the Communist countries was decidedly in their interest. But unfortunately for the whites of South Africa, their native policy came increasingly under criticism, even at Commonwealth conferences. As Britain adopted a policy of rapid decolonization, the old Commonwealth composed of white or white-controlled Dominions became transformed into a multiracial association. The Commonwealth, like most of the world, was turning against South African racial policy.

The dilemma facing South Africa was poignantly expressed in an exchange between Smuts and Malan in Parliament a few months after the latter had succeeded the former as prime minister. Smuts asked what the position of the new government was going to be at the United Nations on South West Africa and the Indian question. World opinion on the Union's racial policy was hardening, said Smuts, and South Africa cannot isolate itself from it, nor defy it. South Africa should keep in step with world opinion as much as possible and avoid actions which look like defiance. Withdrawal from the United Nations would not help, but only make South Africa's position worse. India was already applying sanctions against the Union, fortunately without much damage, but sanctions imposed by the United Nations might be a matter of life and death.[6] Prime Minister Malan did not dispute Smuts's argument, but in reply asked him how far he would go in meeting world opinion. The Nationalist government was "not going to surrender our interests. We are not going to lie down for others to trample on us. We are not going to commit suicide."[7]

When it became clear that Britain was going to grant its African colonies independence and that these would swell the ranks of the Commonwealth as independent members on an equal footing with the older Dominions, Malan began to lose his enthusiasm for the Commonwealth. In 1951 he made a statement in which he criticized Great Britain for adding new members to the Commonwealth, "acting on her own accord and without consultation with or approval of the other group members . . . and now she intends to continue the process without limitation." Among the old members there existed a feeling of oneness, derived from specific common interests and a large degree of political and cultural identity. With the enlargement of the membership

[6] *Hansard*, vol. 64, cols. 1273–74, 31 Aug. 1948.
[7] Ibid., col. 1292.

this had been lost. The necessary conditions for cohesion were no longer present in the Commonwealth.[8] Jacobus G. N. Strauss, Smuts's successor as leader of the opposition, strongly supported Malan's views.[9]

The Malan government lost little time in attenuating the ties with Great Britain. In 1949 it put through Parliament a Citizenship bill which practically eliminated the advantages which British subjects had enjoyed over aliens with respect to South African citizenship. In 1950 the right of appeal to the Privy Council was abolished. Relations with Great Britain were deteriorating. Strauss declared that the British action in granting self-government to the Gold Coast was precipitate. The United party thought that the natives of Africa had "only the vaguest conception of democratic franchise and of democratic institutions" and felt that "European trusteeship and guidance" was necessary for the unforeseeable future.[10]

The Nationalists were avowed republicans and had been strongly opposed to membership in the Commonwealth. Apparently, out of fear of isolation, Malan and his government decided to remain in the Commonwealth, but their ardor for establishing a republic did not cool. When the National party in the general elections of April 1953 won a much larger popular vote and greatly increased their strength in Parliament, the United party feared that the Malan government might use its new strength to convert South Africa from a monarchy to a republic. Apparently in an effort to block this expected move, Strauss, at the opening of the first session of the new Parliament, moved that the House express its conviction that "continued membership in the Commonwealth by the Union under its present Constitution is in the best interests of the Union."[11]

In support of his motion, Strauss stressed the necessity of a common approach to external affairs; the necessity of full cooperation of all states south of the Sahara to deal effectively with the dangers of nationalism and Communist propaganda; the great strategic importance of South Africa in any world conflict because of its command of the

---

[8] The statement was made in Cape Town on 23 Feb. 1951 and was published in *Die Burger* (Cape Town) the following day. Extracts from Malan's statement are given in Nicholas Mansergh, ed., *Documents and Speeches on British Commonwealth Affairs, 1931–1952* (London, 1953), 2:1278–88.

[9] *Hansard*, vol. 75, col. 6787, 16 May 1951.

[10] Ibid., vol. 74, cols. 6785–86.

[11] Ibid., vol. 82, cols. 40–41, 7 July 1953.

Cape sea route and the production of strategic minerals and raw materials; and the dependence of South Africa upon external trade and capital for development. Strauss welcomed the rejection by the government of the myths of neutralism and isolation advocated by its supporters when they sat on the opposition benches.[12]

Prime Minister Malan saw the motion as a maneuver to bind the Union permanently to the Commonwealth and the monarchy. He branded it as an antirepublican motion. Since the Commonwealth offered the greatest freedom there was no reason to withdraw from it. However, there were reasons for concern. Injudicious extension of membership was weakening the unity of the Commonwealth. He pointed to the development of an unfortunate phenomenon. The Commonwealth did not permit interference in the internal affairs of its members, but the United Nations did, in violation of its constitution. And all the members of the Commonwealth were also members of the United Nations. "The result will be that unless a stop is put to it, U. N. O. will break down the Commonwealth." In spite of these misgivings and anxieties about the Commonwealth, the prime minister concluded that membership in it was of great value. It was a valuable source of information on world conditions.[13] He concluded, "We need friends in the international world. Not only do we need direct friends, but we also need the friends of our friends."[14]

The prime minister turned the tables on the opposition by offering an amendment which converted the motion from an antirepublican to a republican declaration. In the amended motion, the House approved the government's policy of "close consultation and cooperation" with the members of the Commonwealth, expressed its "conviction that such cooperation may also in the future prove to be possible and desirable irrespective whether South Africa is a Republic or not and irrespective whether she is a member of the Commonwealth or not." The House affirmed that establishment of the republic and withdrawal from the Commonwealth were two separate questions "which need not be answered simultaneously" and that the latter issue should be "judged and

[12] Ibid., cols. 41–50.

[13] "We are not at the hub of the world," he stated. "We do not have all the contacts in every direction, but other members of the Commonwealth have, and especially the Prime Minister and his cabinet in England."

[14] *Hansard,* vol. 82, col. 56.

decided at any given time in the light of the then existing circumstances and South Africa's interests and position in the international world."[15]

Malan's successor, J. G. Strijdom, took essentially the same position. It was no longer necessary for a country to withdraw from the Commonwealth upon becoming a republic.[16] The National party was adhering to its republican policy "but whether it will be a republic inside or outside the Commonwealth will be decided with a view to circumstances then prevailing."[17] In principle he had no objection to attending the prime ministers' conferences when circumstances demand and make it possible for him to do so, but if they were to be regarded as "a body which lays down policies for other countries," including his own, he would have nothing to do with them.[18]

Members of Parliament were very slow in seeing what was happening in Africa. In discussing an African Charter and the defense of Africa, members on both sides of the House assumed continued European control of the African territories. Even after Britain allowed the Gold Coast to gain self-government and Commonwealth membership, few saw the inevitable development toward African control, or they failed to make an adjustment to it in their views. One member, however, in 1954 asked the prime minister if he was prepared to make a statement on what the attitude of South Africa would eventually be toward a Commonwealth in which black-controlled African states became full members.[19] He received no answer to his question.

In spite of the fact that the two issues of converting the monarchy into a republic and of continuing membership in the Commonwealth had been separated by the decision in 1949 to permit India to remain a member after it became a republic, they could not easily be kept separate in South Africa. Most of the English-speaking South Africans believed that the two issues were associated and they feared that the Nationalists were determined to change the Dominion into a republic and also to take South Africa out of the Commonwealth. Malan and Strijdom had dissociated the two issues, but in his speech to the House

[15] Ibid., cols. 58–60. The debate on the motion extended over 7 and 8 July 1953, cols. 40–82 and 83–146 respectively. Most of the debate was on the issue of a republic rather than on Commonwealth membership.

[16] Ibid., vol. 91, cols. 4183–84, 23 April 1956.

[17] Ibid., col. 4129.

[18] Ibid., vol. 88, col. 4108.

[19] Ibid., vol. 85, col. 4480.

announcing a forthcoming referendum on the republican issue, Prime Minister Verwoerd promised that before the referendum was held the country would be told whether or not it would be the policy of the government to remain a member of the Commonwealth.[20]

Verwoerd sought to assure the English-speaking people that the good relations between South Africa and the United Kingdom would be strengthened.[21] The prime minister pointed out that South Africa was already a republic in all but name as a result of the legislation passed under the National governments.[22]

Sir De Villiers Graaf, who had succeeded Strauss as leader of the opposition, feared that the price for a republic might be loss of membership in the Commonwealth, with the loss of economic and defense advantages, since there was good reason to believe that many Nationalists wanted a republic outside of the Commonwealth.[23] He also contended that if the Union became a republic another barrier would be created between the Union and the Protectorates and also between the Union and the countries to the north (Rhodesia and Kenya, both dominated by white settlers) where there was great attachment to the monarchy.

Signs of approaching difficulties for South Africa in the Commonwealth began to be very visible in 1960. In an address to both houses of Parliament in Cape Town on February 3, 1960, British Prime Minister Harold Macmillan warned of the "wind of change" which was blowing through Africa. While a basic principle of the Commonwealth was respect for each other's sovereignty in matters of internal policy, it was necessary at the same time to recognize that "the internal policies of one nation may have effects outside it." He went on to say that as a fellow member of the Commonwealth the British government always tried to give South Africa full support and encouragement, but there were aspects of its policies which made it impossible to do this without being false "to our own deep convictions about the political destinies of free men. . . . I think, therefore," he concluded, "that we ought as friends to face together—without seeking, I trust, to apportion praise or blame—

[20] Ibid., vol. 103, cols. 106–107, 27 Jan. 1960.
[21] Ibid., col. 108.
[22] Ibid., vol. 103, cols. 105–106.
[23] Ibid., vol. 105, cols. 5891–92. He quoted statements made by Nationalists and *Die Transvaler* (Johannesburg).

the fact that in the world of today this difference of outlook lies between us."[24]

The Prime Ministers' Conference held in London in May 1960 gave clear indications that there was trouble ahead for South Africa. Serious racial disturbances had occurred at Sharpeville in March with the loss of sixty-nine lives and there was talk of expelling South Africa from the Commonwealth. In responding to an address of welcome by Macmillan, the Tungku Abdul Rahman of Malaya raised the South African problem and stated that he wished to have it debated.[25] Prime Minister Menzies objected on the grounds that the conference never before had discussed such matters. It was agreed unanimously not to discuss South Africa's racial policies, but Louw[26] offered to discuss the matter with limited groups of prime ministers.

When Kwame Nkrumah applied for permission for Ghana to remain in the Commonwealth after it had become a republic, his request was approved unanimously, but when Louw made a similar application, reservations of opinion were expressed.[27] Macmillan suggested that it would be inappropriate for the conference to express itself on this matter in advance of the referendum, lest it "appear to intervene in the domestic affairs of South Africa." The final communique gave little assurance that South Africa's request, if made after a successful referendum, would be granted. Its language on this matter was ambivalent.[28]

The referendum, which was held on October 5, 1960, gave a majority in favor of a republic.[29] At the opening of the next session of Parliament

---

[24] Nicholas Mansergh, ed., *Documents and Speeches on Commonwealth Affairs, 1952–1962* (London, 1963), pp. 347–51.

[25] The fullest account of what happened in the conferences, which are private, of 1960 and 1961, aside from the report of Verwoerd to his Parliament, was given by Prime Minister Robert Menzies of Australia, first in his own Parliament and later in his memoirs, *Afternoon Light*, pp. 186–229.

[26] Prime Minister Verwoerd was unable to attend the meeting as he had not recovered sufficiently from wounds inflicted by a would-be assassin. South Africa was represented by Minister of External Affairs Eric Louw.

[27] Shortly before, Louw had asked the conference whether the continued membership of the Union as a monarchy was unwelcome and the answer after a "very brief discussion" was " 'No' " (Menzies, *Afternoon Light*, p. 196).

[28] Extract from final communique of the Commonwealth Ministers' Meeting held in London, 3–13 May 1960, Mansergh, ed., *Documents and Speeches on Commonwealth Affairs, 1952–1962*.

[29] The vote was 850,458 for and 775,878 against. Only in Natal was there a majority against; in the Cape the vote was only slightly in favor. Only whites were eligible to vote.

when the prime minister moved that leave be granted to introduce a bill to Constitute the Republic of South Africa, the leader of the opposition moved an amendment that such leave be declined unless and until it was "unequivocally established that the proposed republic will remain in the Commonwealth."[30] He argued that the overwhelming majority of people who had voted for the republic did so "in the hope or in the belief that that republic would be within the Commonwealth" and they had been left in that hope and belief by the propaganda of the government spokesmen.

The prime minister branded the move of the opposition as "an attempt to stop us becoming a republic or otherwise to make it difficult for us to become a member of the Commonwealth." He recognized that practically everybody in the country wanted South Africa to remain in the Commonwealth and he had given the assurance in the campaign that he would do his best to achieve that and remain a member as long as the Commonwealth remained what it was. But the government had also made clear that if the Commonwealth should refuse South Africa membership or grant it only subject to humiliating conditions, "we will still become a republic but not a member of the Commonwealth." Those who voted for a republic did so with that understanding.[31]

One of the European representatives for the coloreds pleaded on behalf of his constituents that there should be no steps toward establishing a republic until there was an assurance that South Africa would be permitted to remain in the Commonwealth. The coloreds had not been permitted to vote in the referendum; they could make their views known only through their representatives in the House. They wanted South Africa to remain a member of the Commonwealth. They also wanted "to retain the friendship and the cooperation and the understanding and other links with the Western world."[32]

Technically South Africa withdrew from the Commonwealth, but in fact it was expelled. The government had set May 31, 1961, as the day for the inauguration of the Republic, and in view of this it applied for continued membership after that date. When the application was considered by the Prime Ministers' Conference which met in London March 8–17, several ministers sharply attacked South Africa's racial policy

[30] *Hansard*, vol. 106, col. 17.
[31] Ibid., cols. 25, 26.
[32] Ibid., cols. 27–31.

and asserted that an unqualified consent to its request would be taken as approval or condonation of the policies of apartheid. Verwoerd argued that the constitutional issue should be dealt with separately and that on the basis of precedents the application was a mere formality and approval should be automatic. Menzies, and Macmillan less fully, supported this position. But to all the prime ministers it seemed that no agreement on South Africa's membership was possible without an expression of strong disapproval of that country's racial policies. In effect, the multiracial Commonwealth adopted racial equality as a principle of its association, and the policy of the South African government was not compatible with it.

Most of the prime ministers, even Nehru and Nkrumah, thought that the break could have been avoided by concessions from Verwoerd.[33] Nehru said that the South African prime minister was "completely unwilling to make the slightest change in the policies pursued by them."[34] Nkrumah stated that his government had offered to exchange diplomatic representatives with South Africa, saying, "we continued negotiating with South Africa on the issue for over three years. It became quite clear, however, that the South African Government would never accept diplomatic representatives from any indigenous African state."[35] Macmillan believed that if Verwoerd had shown any understanding of the views of his Commonwealth colleagues, or made any concession, or had given anything "to hold on to or any grounds for hope," the break could have been avoided. "But the Prime Minister of South Africa, with an honesty which one must recognize, made it abundantly clear beyond all doubt that he would not think it right to relax in any form the extreme rigidity of his dogma, either now or in the future."[36]

Prime Minister Menzies observed that Nkrumah, Ayub Khan, and Tungku Rahman all followed a moderate line. They appreciated the position of the European population in South Africa. They did "not expect for one moment the immediate adoption of policies which would

[33] Extracts from several of the reports of the prime ministers to their parliaments are given in Mansergh, ed., *Documents and Speeches on Commonwealth Affairs, 1952–1962*, pp. 365–400.

[34] Ibid., p. 390.

[35] Ibid., p. 400.

[36] Ibid., p. 374. The speech was given 22 March 1961 (Great Britain, *Parliamentary Debates* [Commons], 5th ser., 637 [1961]: 441–46, 448–49).

put the position of the white population at risk." But they were very critical of the policy in the way it was applied, and in particular, they reacted sharply to the treatment in South Africa of visiting non-Europeans, whether official or unofficial. In a long letter[37] to Verwoerd, Menzies stressed this point, which he thought was the most important in their minds.[38]

In his letter, Menzies urged Verwoerd, as he had urged Louw privately at the 1960 conference, to exchange diplomatic missions with the Asian and African countries. He believed that if this were done and their diplomatic representatives were treated in exactly the same way as those of European states "a lot of the heat would be taken out of the present conflict." The Australian prime minister at the conference asked Verwoerd why his government had refused to exchange diplomatic representation with other Commonwealth countries. In his reply Verwoerd gave several reasons.[39] First, South Africa did receive diplomatic missions from Afro-Asian countries. India had had representation in the Union but had withdrawn it; Egypt currently had a mission in Pretoria; there were Chinese consular officials in South Africa; and representation from Japan was being considered. Second, South Africa could not establish diplomatic relations with unfriendly countries. Before there was any talk of representation, Nkrumah had made known that Ghana would do everything in its power to aid black men everywhere to take over the government. "Apart from all other considerations, it could not be expected that we would receive a mission which could easily become the centre of agitation where those would foregather, White and non-White, who wished to create a multi-racial or Bantu government here." Moreover, he argued, it was not a principle of Commonwealth membership that there must be an exchange of diplo-

---

[37] Menzies, *Afternoon Light*, pp. 198–202. Prime Minister Menzies made a rather lengthy statement to the Australian Parliament on 11 April 1961 (Australia, *Parliamentary Debates* [Assembly], 30 [1961]: 649–56), but his memoirs contain additional material.

[38] "They took great exception to personal discriminations," wrote Menzies, "and gave some instances of them. What rankles, for example, in the Tungku's mind is that should he visit South Africa in any capacity other than his present official one, he believes that he would be denied entrance to first class hotels and other wise treated differently from a white visitor" (*Afternoon Light*, p. 200).

[39] Verwoerd on 23 March 1961 made an extensive report and defense of his conduct at the conference, which was followed by discussion. *Hansard*, vol. 107, cols. 3482–3544.

matic representatives. For example, South Africa and New Zealand had friendly relations but no exchange of diplomatic representatives.

However, it is clear from his further explanation that this was not the decisive factor in the refusal to enter into diplomatic relations with sub-Sahara African states. In his letter to Menzies he stated that important nonwhite persons who visited South Africa suffered no discrimination or discourtesy, though under, it is true, special arrangements by their hosts or the government. At present, similar treatment for all nonwhite people who might wish to visit South Africa could not be arranged. To treat all nonwhite visitors as whites would undermine the policy of segregation, and in the end full social integration would necessarily follow. "Here again we are dealing with a possible thin edge of the wedge," said Verwoerd.[40]

Prime Minister Menzies characterized Verwoerd as "a man of high character, but unbending in his beliefs" and Macmillan spoke of him as honest but dogmatic. The Nationalists, and many English-speaking South Africans, are convinced that they have a solution to the race problem; a solution without injustice or subordination of one race to the other, and which would make coexistence possible, without losing the identity or culture of any race. During the transition there would inevitably be some inequalities and harshness, but the end would justify the means. As Verwoerd saw it, the small concessions which were demanded of South Africa were to be made not only to overcome an immediate problem, namely, to keep them within the Commonwealth, but also with the ultimate object of "the domination of superior numbers in the name of full equality and therefore, eventual victory over the Whites by forcing out or swallowing up the Whites."[41]

With his convictions, which were a true reflection of those of his followers, Verwoerd could not do otherwise than withdraw his country's application for continued membership in the Commonwealth. Most of the prime ministers felt that an unqualified consent to the Union's application would be to condone its racial policies. Nehru had declared that he would at the first opportunity raise the question of the compatibility of the policy of apartheid with membership in the Commonwealth, and Nkrumah said that he would reserve the right to attack South

[40] This fear that concession anywhere in the policy may lead to the breakdown of the whole structure accounts for "petty" as well as "big" apartheid.
[41] *Hansard*, vol. 107, cols. 3491–92.

Africa's policies. Minister for External Affairs Louw revealed statements by the nonwhite prime ministers on the issue. The views of the political leaders of India, Pakistan, Ceylon, Malaya, and Nigeria can be summarized by the statement of Pandit Nehru that "the principle of racial equality was fundamental to the Commonwealth association."[42] Prime Minister Macmillan summarized the situation as follows: "Most Prime Ministers find themselves in a dilemma. Either to continue to accept South Africa as a member of the Commonwealth, which would seem to be approval of her racial policy; or, on the other hand, a situation might arise in which South Africa would feel best to withdraw her application for continued membership, or the other Prime Ministers might feel that they have no other alternative but to ask South Africa to leave the Commonwealth."[43] Julius Nyerere, at the time chief minister of Tanganyika, declared in a letter to the *Observer* that his country would not want membership in the Commonwealth if South Africa remained a member.[44]

Both South Africa and the Commonwealth were confronted with a grave choice. Prime Minister John G. Diefenbaker of Canada expressed the general attitude of his colleagues when he told his Parliament that they deplored the racial policy of the Union government and the anxiety it was arousing in millions of people throughout the world. They were concerned about "its impact on the relations among the member countries of the Commonwealth and on the cohesion of the Commonwealth itself as a multi-racial association."[45] South Africa could change its racial policy or, as Verwoerd put it, retain the right "to continue in her own way to strive for the preservation of the White man on a basis of coexistence with the non-White,"[46] but in defiance of world opinion. The

[42] Ibid., cols. 4833–36. Verwoerd warned that if rights were going to be reserved he also would reserve the right to attack Ghana if it did not practice democracy, which he regarded as one of the basic principles of the Commonwealth, "if there are in fact basic principles."

[43] As revealed by Minister for External Affairs Louw in the House on 18 April 1961, ibid., col. 4835. There would seem to have been another alternative, that is, withdrawal from the Commonwealth by the other nations.

[44] 21 Mar. 1961.

[45] Mansergh, ed., *Documents and Speeches on British Commonwealth Affairs, 1952–1962*, p. 368.

[46] Minister of Economic Affairs Diedrichs put it bluntly, "The Prime Minister was not faced with the choice of being in or outside the Commonwealth. He had to choose between our continued existence or our doom as a White nation. He had to

South African government refused to change its policy. It chose to stand against the world.

Some of Verwoerd's bitter critics more than insinuated that he had gone to the conference with the secret intention of taking South Africa out of the Commonwealth. There is no evidence to support such a charge[47] and much to the contrary. But to allay the alarm of those who feared that establishing a republic would mean the loss of Commonwealth membership, the Nationalists went far in declaring that there was no danger whatever of the latter. Verwoerd, as well as most white South Africans, was deeply shocked by the expulsion.[48] Probably the best summary of the event is that the prime minister suffered a defeat but the National party scored a victory.

On the rebound, Verwoerd took the line that the new situation which had been created was not necessarily to the detriment of South Africa. On the contrary he believed it would be better for all concerned. An end had come to the background of the fight between English and Afrikaners. "Now there is a chance of standing together in one free country and co-operating on a basis which is *the* basis that the English-speaking people desire above all, namely great friendship with Great Britain." South African whites would grow together as one nation "closing our ranks as White people who will have to defend their future together." He appealed for friendship between Afrikaans- and English-speaking South Africans. He appealed to the nonwhites to believe that the government wanted to be the protector of their rights. Its object was coexistence and not domination.[49] But the two victories for Afrikaner Nationalism caused apprehension among English-speaking South Africans for the future of their culture.

---

choose between the Afro-Asian policy and our traditional policy of separation in South Africa. That and that alone" (*Hansard*, vol. 107, col. 3721).

[47] At a reception given in his honor at Cape Town on his return from London, Verwoerd said, "What happened is nothing less than a miracle, so many nations have had to get their complete freedom by armed struggle" (quoted by *Cape Times*, 21 Mar. 1961). These inane remarks can be accounted for only as an ill-considered response to an embarrassing situation and a momentary yielding to extreme Nationalists.

[48] See Fred Barnard, *13 Jaar in die Skadu van Dr. H. F. Verwoerd* [Thirteen Years in the Shadow of Dr. H. F. Verwoerd] (Johannesburg, 1967). Barnard was the prime minister's personal secretary and accompanied Verwoerd and Louw to the conference.

[49] *Hansard*, vol. 107, cols. 3509–10.

14

Conflict with
the United Nations:
Treatment of Indians

General Smuts was too sensitive a man not to know that new winds were blowing in the world. But of their strength he really did not become aware until he encountered them in the First Session of the United Nations General Assembly. Equal rights, he told Jan H. Hofmeyr in May 1945, would be the cry at the United Nations.[1] That South Africa would be an early target of the drive must have caused him some concern. South Africa was vulnerable on more than one front. In addition to the treatment of Indians there was its policy with respect to the Bantu. Also coming to an untimely head was the Union's South West Africa policy—Smuts wanted to incorporate this mandated territory in the Union.

Indians in South Africa suffer a number of disabilities. They are denied the right to vote or to hold public office; certain jobs are closed to them (reserved for Europeans), and they are forced to confine their trade to certain reserved areas; freedom of movement is restricted (Asians may not move from the province in which they are domiciled without a permit from a magistrate or passport control office); migration to another province is prohibited and in the Orange Free State there is a total ban on their residence; they are subject to segregation and discrimination in the use of public facilities and administration; they are prohibited from occupying new land or premises in many districts, even for commercial purposes; they are compelled to live in separate group areas. The area in which they have been living and carrying on business may be declared "white" and if so, they must move to a new area which may mean severe economic loss.[2]

The treatment of Indians in South Africa, which India had asked be placed on the agenda of the First Session of the General Assembly, was first discussed by the Joint First and Sixth Committees. A resolution, presented by France and Mexico, declaring that the "treatment of Indians in the Union should be in conformity with the international obligations under the agreements concluded between the two Governments and the relevant provisions of the Charter" and requesting that the two governments report at the next session of the General Assembly the measures adopted to this effect, was approved by this joint committee for presentation to the General Assembly.[3] Smuts countered this move by proposing that the General Assembly request the International Court of Justice to give an advisory opinion "on the question whether the matters referred to in the Indian application are, under Article 2, paragraph 7 of the Charter, essentially within the domestic jurisdiction of the Union."[4] In support of this proposed resolution Smuts contended that South Africa had a clear right to ask for an appeal to the Court. India's complaint could only be based on legal obligations which South Africa had failed to observe and the Court had been expressly created to advise on legal questions and adjudicate legal disputes between parties.[5]

Sir Hartley Shawcross, the United Kingdom delegate, made a strong speech in support of Smuts's draft amendment. He asserted that a denial of this appeal for an authoritative legal decision would harm the United Nations far more that it would do good for the Indians in South Africa. A decision passed by the General Assembly having no obligatory force

---

[1] W. K. Hancock, *Smuts*, 2 vols. (Cambridge, 1962, 1968), Vol. 2: *The Fields of Force*, p. 445.

[2] In view of these many restrictions on Indians in South Africa the complaint of J. G. Strauss, at the time the leader of the United party in Parliament, is a bit amusing. He charged that South Africans traveling in India and Pakistan were subjected to humiliating treatment (*Hansard*, vol. 78, col. 4332, 24 April 1952).

[3] United Nations, General Assembly, Official Records (hereafter cited UN-GAOR), 1st Sess. 2d Pt., Plenary Meetings, Verbatim Record, 7 Dec. 1946, p. 1007.

[4] Ibid., pp. 1009–10.

[5] The vote was 24 for, 19 against, and 11 abstentions.

could only exacerbate the present unhappy situation in South Africa. The juridical solution is always more acceptable and easier to apply than the political one.[6] South Africa was supported by the United States, the Netherlands, Denmark, Sweden, and a few Latin American states, but Smuts's proposed substitute amendment was rejected by a vote of thirty-one to twenty-one.[7]

Mrs. Vijaya Lakshmi Pandit of India vigorously attacked the policy and position of South Africa. There were three sets of facts beyond dispute, she said. The first was that the South African government did not deny the practice of racial discrimination and segregation; the second was that the Indian government had over many years "appealed, complained, protested, sought compromises and agreements" to no avail. The third fact was that the Union government was a signatory to the Charter. Mrs. Pandit dealt caustically with Smuts's contention that segregation and discrimination were essential to the maintenance of Western standards of life. If this were true, she said, "then the existence of Indians, other Asiatics, and all non-Europeans is a threat to western civilization." The ghetto had to be legalized as part of the world's stable organization. "In fact, this is what the Union Government has invited us to do." She ended with an appeal "to the conscience of the world, which this Assembly is."[8]

The Franco-Mexican resolution was adopted by the required two-thirds vote.[9] Technically, South Africa had not come off badly, but from the point of view of world opinion its image was severely damaged. For Smuts it was an outrageous anticlimax to his thirty years of service in the cause of international cooperation and world peace. His past and his expressed philosophy made him especially vulnerable. He professed universal ideals but was not ready to put them into practice. In his speech before the joint meeting of the First and Sixth Committees the philosopher-statesman sought to reduce the issue rigidly to legal rights and obligations. He argued that human rights had not yet received an internationally recognized and binding formulation, hence members of the United Nations had no specific obligations under the Charter. Smuts was in a difficult political position. He lived with the ever-present

[6] UNGAOR, 1st Sess., 2d Pt., Plenary Meetings, Verbatim Record, 8 Dec. 1946, pp. 1033–36.

[7] Ibid., p. 1061.

[8] Ibid., pp. 1015–19.

[9] The vote was 32 in favor, 15 against, and 7 abstentions.

danger of being voted out of power in favor of the Nationalists, which he undoubtedly believed would be a calamity for his country.[10] This consideration also argued against his resigning as premier. The only alternative was to adjust his foreign policy to the realities of domestic policies. But this angered the Indians in South Africa, antagonized India, tended to alienate the British, offended liberal opinion throughout the world, and exposed South Africa to bitter attack in the United Nations. He yielded to his domestic political needs, but this in the end could not save him because the white electorate lacked confidence in his commitment to South Africa's traditional racial policy.[11]

Smuts was shaken by his experience at the United Nations. He told Parliament that he had taken the best possible line but he had met a stone wall of ignorance, prejudice, and emotions. "Every consideration was overwhelmed by passions and emotional motives which we could not overcome." Arguments were of no avail, lamented Smuts. "It was as though the minds of the members were fogged and benumbed."[12] He warned against adopting a measure like that of Malan's motion to repeal the act giving Indians representation in Parliament. South Africa had to proceed with the utmost caution, he said, "let us proceed slowly lest we fall headlong down the precipice. . . . There is a wind blowing in the world and our position is not without its dangers. The whole world is being hit by a storm and that storm is hitting us in this country, too, and in these circumstances, with the small European community we have today and the mass of world opinion against us, we must be very cautious."[13]

Smuts expressed disappointment with the United Nations; he even wondered whether it would survive the storm which had hit the world. However, at the conclusion of a radio report to the country something of his old philosophic attitude returned to him. "Mankind," he said, "has set out on a difficult road, a long road stretching far into the distant future. It is the road the United Nations Organization is now travelling away from war, towards peace and understanding." He warned against doubt and discouragement and extravagant expecta-

---

[10] Smuts was especially vulnerable on the Indian question, since the Indians were concentrated in Natal, which was a stronghold of his party.

[11] UNGAOR, 1st Sess., 2d Pt., Plenary Meetings, Verbatim Record, 8 Dec. 1946, p. 1033.

[12] *Hansard*, vol. 59, cols. 10920–22, 21 Jan. 1947.

[13] Ibid., cols. 10925–26.

tions.[14] With some feeling, Smuts said that he did not believe that South Africa should withdraw from the organization which had caused them so much unexpected trouble. He found that the center of power, influence, and leadership, which had been vested in Europe, was shifting in a world where new ideologies were rising and the old leadership was disputed. South Africa happened to be the spearhead of this attack.[15] South Africa was behind the United Nations if it followed the Charter which had been drafted at San Francisco. If it did not, it would go the way of the League of Nations; it would fail because it had been unfaithful to its own principles. The fundamental principle of the Charter was that the organization would not get involved in the domestic affairs of its members. He had asked that the world court determine South Africa's legal obligations toward South West Africa, but this appeal was rejected. To assert one's right in a court of law was a fundamental right of both individuals and states. This fundamental right had been violated by the United Nations.[16]

These arguments of Smuts were substantially the same ones used by the Nationalists during the next two decades. But Smuts and Malan differed on the Indian question and on racial policy in general. Smuts was more sensitive to world opinion and was prepared to yield to it in some degree. He believed it was dangerous to defy world forces in a belligerent fashion. He generally sought to temper his measures with compensations of some sort. The opposition, said Smuts, was exploiting for partisan purposes that "gravest," "most difficult," "most far-reaching," and "dangerous" of South Africa's problems. He wondered how the world would react when it noted that the racial problem was being used as a football between the parties.[17]

A resolution of the General Assembly adopted by the 1946 session prompted an interesting exchange of communications between Jawaharlal Nehru, the interim prime minister of India, and Smuts. Nehru wrote to Smuts on April 24, 1947, that the government of India was earnestly desirous of acting in accordance with the terms of the spirit of the resolution and was ready to enter into any discussion that the govern-

[14] Quoted by G. H. Calpin, *Indians in South Africa* (Pietermaritzburg, 1949), p. 252.

[15] Union of South Africa, *Parliamentary Debates* (Senate), 1946–1947, III, cols. 4110–11, 30 Jan. 1947.

[16] Ibid., cols. 4131–37.

[17] *Hansard*, vol. 59, cols. 10925–26.

ment of the Union saw fit to initiate for its implementation. Smuts replied that his government was prevented from entering into any discussion with the government of India because of the absence of the Indian high commissioner from Pretoria. Nehru rejected Smuts's excuse for not beginning discussions and insisted that effective steps be taken at once to implement the resolution after which representatives could be appointed by the two governments for the purpose of considering means to resolve the problem. As soon as relations beween their two countries improved, his government would be pleased to arrange for the high commissioner's return to Pretoria. Smuts complained of India's un-friendly attitude. It had severed trade relations, which was a hostile act for which the Union government would have been justified in invoking the intervention of the Security Council. He again pleaded with the Indian government to return the high commissioner to his duties in the Union.

To this plea Nehru replied that if the Union government would accept the United Nations' resolution, his government would be prepared to send its high commissioner to initiate these discussions. To this Smuts bluntly replied that his government was not prepared to admit that it had broken agreements between their two governments nor violated the Charter. It was not even sure what agreements and principles were referred to, as its request for an advisory opinion by the International Court of Justice had been refused. Smuts went on to point out that the Cape Town Agreement of 1927 was not rigid and binding, and that the Union minister of the interior had said at the time that his government reserved its right to deal legislatively with the Indian problem. No exception was taken by the government of India to this statement. The land provisions of the Asiatic Land Tenure and Indian Representation Act did not substantially differ from the practices of other members of the United Nations. There was "no reason why such policies to secure internal peace should be specially singled out for condemnation." More-over, there should be special regard for the principle of domestic jurisdiction as laid down in Article 2, clause 7, of the Charter, which governs all its other principles and provisions.[18]

The Indian question was again before the United Nations General Assembly at its 1947 meeting. Smuts did not go as South Africa's chief delegate; he sent his minister of justice, H. G. Lawrence, who as

[18] UNGAOR, 2d Sess., Doc. No. A/307, 15 Sept. 1947.

previous minister of the interior had had considerable experience with the Indian problem. The situation for South Africa was better than the year before. India, just beginning it existence as an independent state, was experiencing great difficulties due to communal conflict. This fact and the Palestine problem, which was looming threateningly, took some of the heat off the Union. The First Committee presented a resolution which reaffirmed the one of the previous year and requested the two governments without delay to enter discussions at a round table conference on the basis of that resolution and to invite Pakistan, which had just come into existence, to take part.[19] A second resolution (offered by Belgium, Brazil, Cuba, Denmark, and Norway) was presented to the plenary session by the delegate from Brazil. It called upon the parties to continue their efforts to reach a settlement of the dispute through a round table conference or other direct means, or by mediation or conciliation, and if they should fail to reach an agreement, to submit the question of the extent of the parties' obligation to the International Court of Justice.[20]

Harry G. Lawrence, the Union representative, made a conciliatory speech. He stated that the repatriation of most of the Indians in South Africa was a basic and essential feature of the Cape Town Agreement, but that the Indians did not take advantage of free passage and the bonus offered by the South African government. The latter had nevertheless continued to honor the uplift clause generously. Now the Indians also were being offered the franchise in parliamentary elections. While his government could not admit for the purposes of the desired discussions that it had broken the Cape Town Agreement nor violated the Charter, it was prepared to go to the conference table without prejudice to the views held by either government.[21] Both draft resolutions were rejected by the plenary session of the General Assembly.

When the new Parliament met in August, the Malan government, almost as an act of defiance, introduced a bill to repeal that part of the act of 1946 which provided for the representation of Indians in Parliament. The Smuts government had not implemented this part of the act, chiefly because of the opposition of the Indian community to the act as a

[19] UNGAOR, 2d Sess., Plenary Meetings, Verbatim Record, 20 Nov. 1947, pp. 1111–13.

[20] UNGAOR, 2d Sess., p. 1616, Doc. A/496, Annex 26a, 19 Nov. 1947.

[21] UNGAOR, 2d Sess., Plenary Meetings, Verbatim Record, 20 Nov. 1947, pp. 1113–22.

whole. Smuts warned the new government against defying or seeming to defy world opinion. More than the Indian question was involved as the Malan government also proposed to take away from the natives the right of indirect representation in Parliament and to remove the colored voters from the common role to a separate role. These measures, warned Smuts, would create a difficult situation for South Africa at the United Nations. The days of isolation for all nations was rapidly disappearing, probably more rapidly for South Africa than for any other country. South Africans may regard these matters as domestic questions, but others viewed them as international questions, and world opinion was hardening on this matter. "Nothing will be more dangerous for us," he warned, "than to see ourselves isolated . . . and the sympathy of friends who have stood by us weakened. . . . We must see that we are in step with world opinion as much as possible and avoid actions which might look like defiance and must look like a challenge to public opinion and the world." Action by the United Nations against South Africa would be a question of life and death for the Union. Getting out of the United Nations would not help; it would only worsen the Union's position.[22]

The discussion of the Indian question was resumed at the Third Session of the General Assembly. The old points were debated again but not at great length in the plenary meeting. There was, of course, a change in the South African representation. Eric Louw, minister of economic affairs, was the chief Union delegate. There was another difference: the Indian government had expanded its complaint to the treatment of other nonwhites as well. The debate, however, was without the bitterness that had marked the 1946 discussion, and Louw was in one of his less irritating moods. He again stressed the position which had been taken by the Smuts government—that the Indians in South Africa were citizens of the Union and hence the question of their treatment was essentially within its domestic jurisdiction. The General Assembly adopted a resolution sponsored by France and Mexico, inviting the governments of India and Pakistan and South Africa "to enter into a discussion at a round-table conference, taking into consideration the purposes and principles of the Charter of the United Nations and the Declaration of Human Rights."[23]

[22] *Hansard*, vol. 64, cols. 1270–75, 31 Aug. 1948.
[23] UNGAOR, 3d Sess., Pt. II, *Resolutions*, Res. No. 265 (III), p. 6. The resolution was adopted by a vote of 47 to 1, with 10 abstentions (UNGAOR, 3d Sess., Pt. II, Plenary Meetings, Verbatim Record, 14 May 1949, p. 453).

In pursuance of the above resolution preliminary talks were held by the two governments to determine the agenda of the conference. Two items were agreed upon: 1) reduction of the Indian population in South Africa and 2) removal of political, social, and economic disabilities of South African nationals of Indian and Pakistani origin, and the provision of opportunities for their fullest development. The first was proposed by the Union and the second jointly by India and Pakistan. In the meanwhile the Union government had resorted to new anti-Indian measures with the passage of the Group Areas Act and by executive action under the Land Tenure Act of 1949. When India received a negative response to its request that these measures be postponed pending the conference, it informed the Union government that it could not participate in the proposed conference and again requested the General Assembly to place the question of the treatment of Indians in South Africa on the agenda of the Fifth Session of the General Assembly. That body, in plenary meeting, without debate, adopted a resolution (December 2, 1950) recommending that the three governments proceed with the holding of the round table conference on the basis of their agreed agenda. In the event of failure to hold the conference before April 1951 or to reach an agreement within a reasonable time a commission of three members would be established to assist the parties in carrying through appropriate negotiations.[24]

The resolution had called upon the parties to refrain from further steps which would prejudice the success of their negotiations and in particular had requested that the provisions of the Group Areas Act not be enforced nor implemented pending the conclusions of the negotiations. The Union government ignored this request; it brought the Act into force on March 31, 1951. Before doing so, it had declared that it could not accept the resolution on the ground that it constituted intervention in a matter essentially within the domestic jurisdiction of South Africa. However, it expressed its willingness to join in a conference on the basis of the agreement reached in 1950.

No progress having been made in negotiations the matter was again before the General Assembly of the United Nations when it met in November 1951.[25] The General Assembly this time adopted a resolution

[24] UNGAOR, 4th Sess., Supp. No. 20 (A/1775), Res. No. 395(V), p. 24, 2 Dec. 1950.
[25] Discussion before the Ad Hoc Political Committee took place 20–21 Dec. 1951 and 2–5 Jan. 1952 (UNGAOR, 6th Sess., Ad Hoc Political Committee, Summary

which was much sharper than preceding ones. It declared that "a policy of 'racial segregation' (*apartheid*) is necessarily based on doctrines of racial discrimination," and also that South Africa had contravened the General Assembly's previous resolution by proclamations enforcing the provisions of the Group Areas Act. It again recommended that a commission of three members be established for the purpose of assisting the parties in carrying through appropriate negotiations. Further, the resolution called upon the Union government to suspend the implementation or enforcement of the provisions of the Group Areas Act pending the conclusion of the negotiations, and included this item on the agenda of the next regular session of the General Assembly.[26]

South Africa refused to cooperate in forming the commission so the General Assembly set up its own Good Offices Commission by resolution adopted in December 1952,[27] but the Union government would have no more to do with this commission than with the previous one. The General Assembly at its next session decided to continue the Good Offices Commission and charged it to report to the Assembly's next regular session on the progress it had achieved, together with its own views on the problem and any proposals which in its opinion might lead to a peaceful settlement of the question.[28] The Good Offices Commission reported to the Ninth Session of the General Assembly that the South African government had refused to recognize it and that it was unable to suggest any new procedure for negotiation between the parties or to submit proposals likely to lead to a settlement of the problem. The Ninth Assembly adopted a resolution suggesting that the three governments seek a solution by direct negotiations.[29]

This conciliatory resolution met with a response from South Africa, within the limits of its basic position. The Union minister for external

Records, pp. 155–74). For debate in General Assembly see UNGAOR, 6th Sess., Plenary Meetings, Verbatim Record, 12 Jan. 1952, pp. 327–31.

[26] UNGAOR, 6th Sess., Supp. No. 20 (A/2119), p. 11, Res. No. 511(VI), 12 Jan. 1952. Adopted by a vote of 44 to 0 with 14 abstentions.

[27] UNGAOR, 7th Sess., Supp. No. 20 (A/2361), p. 8, Res. No. 615(VII), 5 Dec. 1952.

[28] The resolution was adopted by the plenary session without debate by a vote of 42 for, 1 against, and 17 abstentions. However, the question was discussed at ten successive meetings of the Ad Hoc Political Committee (UNGAOR, 8th Sess., Ad Hoc Political Committee, Summary Records, 16–29 Oct. 1953, pp. 63–111).

[29] UNGAOR, 9th Sess., Supp. No. 21 (A/2890), pp. 7–8, Res. No. 816(IX), 4 Nov. 1954.

affairs informed the Indian government that, while his government did not surrender in any way its position that the treatment of Indians was an internal matter solely within its own jurisdiction, South Africa was, as in the past, willing to discuss the problem with India and Pakistan with the object of finding an acceptable solution. With the understanding by India and Pakistan that the Union's willingness to discuss the matter outside the United Nations did not prejudice its juridical position, South Africa was prepared to discuss the problem with them. Karachi and New Delhi in January 1955 separately replied to the Union telegram that they had no desire to interfere in the internal affairs of South Africa, but they wished to restate their position that this problem did not have a purely domestic character. Further, the two governments declared that they could not ignore the purposes and principles of the Charter of the United Nations and the decisions made by the organization from 1946 on, nor the obligations which resulted. But both declared their willingness to pursue negotiations without prejudice to the views held by any of the parties concerned in respect of domestic jurisdiction under Article 2, clause 7, of the Charter. For a moment it looked as if discussion between the parties might begin, but then Prime Minister Nehru made two speeches in which he branded South Africa's racial policy as "naked persecution on the basis of color." South Africa withdrew its offer to enter negotiations.[30]

The South African reaction to Nehru's speeches was rather odd in view of the anti-Indian speeches by Prime Ministers Malan and Strijdom. In a speech in Parliament in 1953 Malan accused Nehru of inciting Indians in Africa against the Europeans.[31] In a statement to the press in 1954, Malan proposed a defense pact embracing the western Indian Ocean and suggested that the NATO powers extend a military guarantee to South Africa. He left no doubt that he regarded India as the strongest threat to his country. Malan asserted that Nehru used the Indian communities abroad to interfere in the internal affairs of other nations and charged that Nehru's policy in regard to the Portuguese colonies in India was openly aggressive. He hoped that Portugal would

[30] Texts of the telegrams exchanged among the three governments are found in Union of South Africa, White Book, *Verrigtings in die Verenigde Nasies Januarie tot December 1955: Behandeling van Indiers in die Unie van Suid Afrika* [Actions in the United Nations January to December 1955: Treatment of Indians in the Union of South Africa] (Pretoria, 1956).

[31] *Hansard*, vol. 82, cols. 1326ff.

be more closely bound to South Africa for the mutual defense of their mutual interests.[32] Prime Minister Strijdom stated that in his opinion Nehru had as his object the ousting of all whites from Africa and using it as a dumping ground for the surplus population of India.[33]

As no agreement was reached, the secretary general in June 1955 designated Luis de Faro, Jr., a Brazilian diplomat, to help the parties negotiate a settlement of the dispute. The governments of India and Pakistan offered full cooperation, but the Union government declined to cooperate. About this time South Africa's racial policy in general came under intense fire. After a heated debate in the General Assembly's Special Political Committee on an anti-apartheid resolution, the Union government in protest on November 10, 1955, recalled its delegation. External Affairs Minister Louw said that the time had come for South Africa to take stock of its position as a member of the United Nations. Apparently the Union government felt that it could not afford to withdraw from the world organization, however much it disliked many of its actions, for it returned to full participation in the Twelfth (1958) Session of the General Assembly. On December 14, 1955, the Assembly again adopted a mild resolution on the subject of South African treatment of Indians. It urged the parties concerned to pursue negotiations with a view to bringing about a settlement of the problem and invited the parties to report as appropriate, jointly or separately, to the next session of the General Assembly. Similar resolutions were adopted by the General Assembly at each of its succeeding sessions until 1962 (Seventeenth Session) when the question of the treatment of Indians was combined with that of race conflict and the policy of apartheid in South Africa, and a strong resolution was adopted. The resolution adopted on November 6, 1962, requested the members of the United Nations to apply a number of sanctions against South Africa.

The assimilation of the question of the treatment of Indians with that of South Africa's racial policy in general was logical. There was some excuse for separate treatment of the Indian question originally when there were still members of the Indian community in South Africa who reasonably could be regarded as nationals of India and Pakistan and as long as the South African government refused to recognize the Indians as more than transients and insisted on their repatriation. But when

---

[32] *New York Times*, 2 Aug. 1954.

[33] *Hansard*, Vol. 88, col. 4024, 18 April 1955.

finally the minister of Indian affairs admitted in Parliament that the repatriation scheme had failed and that the government had decided that there was no choice but to regard the Indians as permanent inhabitants of the Republic,[34] there was little reason for the United Nations to deal with the Indian question separately. It is true that India regarded the Cape Town Agreement of 1927 as a treaty between two states and therefore as creating international legal obligations. South Africa rejected this interpretation, but it was willing to submit this question to the International Court of Justice. Smuts's government held that the Cape Town Agreement was not an international agreement and as evidence pointed to the fact that it had not been registered at the League of Nations as the Covenant required of all treaties. The so-called agreement was merely consultation between governments. It is a pity that this interesting question was not submitted to the Court either as a case or upon request for an advisory opinion. Certainly it would have been highly appropriate for the General Assembly to request an advisory opinion.

South Africa maintained throughout that the treatment of Indians in its territory was an internal matter and therefore fell under Article 2, clause 7, of the Charter. The position taken by South Africa was basically inconsistent. So long as it regarded the Indians as transient aliens it could not logically deny the Indians an appeal to India for protection nor reject India's intervention in their behalf as unwarranted intervention in its internal affairs. This was one reason Smuts gave for opposing the repeal of the measure giving the Indians representation in Parliament. "It gives the Indians," said Smuts, "a platform in South Africa. We do not want people in South Africa to go and make appeals in other countries. If they want to make any appeal let them do so in South Africa. We are now giving them political status. They are given a say in the Parliament of this country and there is no need for them to go elsewhere. That is the correct position."[35]

The Nationalist government, however, adamantly proceeded along its course even after it finally admitted, in 1962, that all efforts at repatriation of the Indians had failed and that the Indians would have to be regarded as permanent inhabitants of the country. It repealed the measure giving the Indians representation in Parliament and tightened

[34] Ibid., Vol. 4, cols. 5814–19, 17 May 1962.
[35] Ibid., Vol. 59, col. 10922, 21 Jan. 1947.

the restrictions that hemmed them in. In compensation, if that is what it can be called, the minister of Indian affairs announced that he was setting up a consultative body to be called the National Indian Council. It was to be composed of twenty-five members, all nominated by the minister of Indian affairs, and would serve as a link between the Indian people and the government. In 1968 the Council was given a statutory basis, with the plan ultimately of allowing the Indians to elect its members, but it was still to have only advisory rights in the field of the special political and social needs of the Indian community. The minister of Indian affairs stated in Parliament that the political rights of Indians would be limited to "a self-government within their own community, but there it will end."[36] Most Indians rejected this meager concession as inadequate in meeting their community's legitimate aspirations and refused to cooperate with the council. They also feared that acceptance of the council would destroy any hopes they still may have had of ever being granted direct representation in Parliament and other legislative bodies.

Prime Minister Malan had strongly supported India's continued membership in the Commonwealth when it became a republic. Obviously he did this to set a precedent which might enable South Africa to remain a member of the Commonwealth if and when it became a republic. India could not bring the question of the treatment of Indians in South Africa before the Prime Ministers' Conferences, so it brought the question to the United Nations. However, in effect, the United Nations was used to undermine the Commonwealth.[37] South Africa's racial policies could not indefinitely be kept out of the Commonwealth conferences and ultimately led to South Africa's expulsion from that association.

[36] Ibid., Vol. 7, col. 6434, 21 May 1963.

[37] The Indian question may also have contributed to the development of republican sentiment. There was the feeling that South African interests had been and would be surrendered by the British to Indian pressure (see A. M. Moll, *The Necessity for Independence* [Cape Town, 1920], preface by D. F. Malan).

15

Conflict with
the United Nations:
South West Africa

South West Africa is a large territory with a sparse population. It has an area of 317,725 square miles but in 1960 its inhabitants numbered only 525,064, of whom 73,154 were whites, 427,980 Bantu, and 23,930 coloreds.[1] Climate and geography account for the sparseness of the population. Much of the territory is desert or semi-arid. The amount of rainfall increases from the southwest to the northeast corner of the territory, but even in the northeast corner the annual rainfall is not much over twenty inches and the soil is so poor and the water table so high that profitable cultivation is impossible. The central plateau area has fairly good pastureland. But if the territory's agricultural possibilities are limited, it is fairly well off in minerals, the most valuable of which are diamonds. There are considerable deposits of copper, lead, zinc, and iron ore, and lesser quantities of other minerals. Rich rock lobster beds off the southern coast have made Luderitz the center of a flourishing canning industry.

It should be noted that Afrikaners constitute a larger percentage of the white population of South West Africa than they do in the Union.[2] The large percentage of Afrikaners gives the National party a potential advantage in the dependency. The nonwhite population is almost exclu-

204   *South Africa and the World*

sively Bantu, divided into a number of tribes, of which the largest is the Ovambo, with 270,900 people or about half of the native population of the territory. The next in order of size is the Damau tribe with only about 50,000 members. Then follow the Herero and Nakua tribes each with about 40,000 members. The remainder of the native population is divided among a number of small tribes.

The Covenant of the League of Nations (Art. 22, p. 6)[3] grouped South West Africa with those former enemy territories "which owing to the sparseness of their population or their small size, or their remoteness from centers of civilization, or their geographical contiguity to the territory of the Mandatory, and other circumstances can be best administered under the laws of the Mandatory as integral portions of its territory, subject to the safeguards above mentioned in the interest of the indigenous populations."[4] An agreement between the Council of the League and South Africa was signed on December 17, 1920. Article Two stated that the Mandatory shall have "full power of administration and legislation subject to the present mandate as an integral portion of the Union of South Africa, and may apply the laws of the Union of South Africa to the territory subject to such local modifications as circumstances may require."[5] While the agreement gave South Africa broad legislative and administrative power over the territory, it did not, even by implication, indicate that annexation was the ultimate goal of the arrangement. The agreement stipulated (Art. 7) that the consent of the Council of the League of Nations was necessary for any modification of its terms.

On occasion the Union government acted as if it had sovereignty over

---

[1] The total population in 1966 was estimated at 610,000.

[2] According to the 1951 census, 66.3 percent spoke Afrikaans; 23.9, German; and only 8.3 percent, English (*State of South Africa:* Yearbook, 1963).

[3] Chapter 3.

[4] The mandated territories were later classified as "A," "B," and "C"—South West Africa was a "C" mandate. In the case of the "C" mandates the administering state was subject to fewer restrictions than in the others.

[5] The agreement stipulated that the Mandatory shall "promote to the utmost the material and moral well-being and social progress" of the inhabitants, prohibit the slave trade, proscribe forced labor except for essential public works and services, control the traffic in arms and munitions, prohibit the supply of intoxicating spirits to the natives, give no military training to natives other than for purposes of internal police and the local defense of the territory, establish no military or naval bases or erect fortifications in the territory, and ensure freedom of conscience and religion.

the territory only to be rebuked by the Mandates Commission and the Council of the League.[6] In 1922 when the Union transferred the narrow Caprivi Zipfel strip which juts eastward from the main body of the territory on the north of what was then Bechuanaland, to the Bechuanaland Administration, the League Council objected. The Union government explained that no cession was intended and that it remained responsible to the Council for the administration of the area.[7] Parliament by an act of 1922 transferred to the Union, in full dominion, the immovable property of the railways and harbors in the territory. The League Council took note of this and suggested the advisability of altering the text. Parliament by an act of 1930 conceded the point. On this occasion Prime Minister Hertzog said, "The previous government held the same view that we have adopted, namely, that we as South Africans, associate ourselves with South-West Africa, but not by annexation."[8]

The Union Parliament in 1925 enacted the South West African Constitutional Act which provided for the establishment of a Legislative Assembly of eighteen members, of whom twelve were elective and six appointive. The Assembly was given limited legislative power. Native affairs were among the large number of subjects reserved to the Union government. It was this white Legislative Assembly which in the early 1930s passed a resolution stating that the time had arrived for the territory to be administered as "a fifth province of the Union subject to the provisions of the Mandate," and that in conformity with this status the territory be represented in the House and Senate of the Union. This move for the virtual incorporation of the territory into the Union caused the members of the League's Permanent Mandates Commission grave concern. The Commission gave considerable attention to the matter in its 1934 and 1935 sessions. The members wanted to know what the attitude of the Union government was to the agitation for incorporation. South Africa's representative, Eric Louw, could give no answer.

At the next session of the Mandates Commission the Union representative was Charles te Water, the high commissioner in London and president of the Assembly of the League of Nations. He assured the

[6] General Smuts had a tendency to speak of the mandate as virtual annexation. See I. Goldblatt, *The Mandated Territory of South West Africa in Relation to the United Nations* (Cape Town, 1962).

[7] Ibid., p. 12.

[8] *Hansard*, vol. 14, col. 66.

Commission that his government had absolutely no intention of presenting it with a *fait accompli.* However, the Union government had been compelled to take note, "in accordance with the tradition of democratic government," of the situation which had developed in South West Africa, and had appointed a commission to inquire into the situation. Members of the Mandates Commission took a critical view of the last statement. William E. Rappard stated that little weight should be given to the views of a small minority in territories where white settlers lived in the midst of a native population. Under these conditions there was always a tendency to reduce the natives to a purely ornamental status. Rappard was very critical of the administration of the territory. After watching developments for the preceding fourteen years he could find no evidence of progress in preparing the natives of South West Africa to support themselves. "Their position was static and static on a very low level."[9] There was some discussion of how a mandate could be terminated. The prevailing view seemed to be that the decision would rest with the League of Nations, and the criterion would be whether the territory had reached such a stage of development that it could stand alone as an independent state.

Te Water had quoted a statement by Prime Minister Hertzog that the future of the territory would be determined by its inhabitants. When he was asked whether Hertzog meant the whole population or only the white inhabitants, he stated that when a South African spoke of self-determination he was not thinking of the natives, for the Bantu was under tutelage of the European. D. F. W. Van Rees, vice-chairman of the Commission for a number of years, noted that the same question had arisen some years earlier and that the Commission had received the impression that South Africa regarded only the Europeans as the population that counted. The Commission had indicated its view that the opinion of the white population would not be the decisive factor in the termination of the mandate or of the political incorporation of the territory in the Union. The important consideration was the stage of development. With respect to South Africa's proposal to administer South West Africa as a province of the Union the Commission confined itself to making all legal reservations on the question.[10]

[9] League of Nations, Permanent Mandates Commission, *Minutes of the Twenty-Sixth Session, 1934* (Geneva, 1934), p. 52.

[10] League of Nations, Permanent Mandates Commission, *Minutes of the Thirty-First Session, 1937* (Geneva, 1937), p. 192. This statement sounds very liberal,

The Permanent Mandates Commission did not function during World War II. If the Union had wanted to annex South West Africa the war seemed to offer a good opportunity. Smuts wanted sovereignty over the territory, but he wanted it with the seal of international recognition.[11] Union with South Africa was probably the best solution of a troublesome problem, but the Union's racial policy made it impossible for the world to acquiesce in annexation of the territory.

General Smuts headed the Union's delegation at the San Francisco Conference which drafted the Charter of the United Nations. He was the chief architect of the mandates system of the League; there is no evidence that he had or tried to exercise any influence in drafting the articles on dependent territories in the Charter. Under the Charter a trusteeship system replaced the League mandates system.

With respect to the controversy that developed between the United Nations and South Africa, the important article of the Charter is Article 77 which stipulated that the trusteeship system "shall apply to such territories in the following categories as may be placed thereunder by means of trusteeship agreements: a. territories now held under mandate." Paragraph 2 of this article states that "it will be a matter for subsequent agreement as to which territories in the foregoing categories will be brought under the trusteeship system and upon what terms." Also relevant is Article 80 which provides that until such individual trusteeship agreements have been concluded nothing "in this Chapter shall be construed in or of itself to alter in any manner the rights whatsoever of any states or any peoples or the terms of existing international instruments to which Members of the United Nations may respectively be parties." Paragraph 2 of this article is highly significant in this particular controversy. It states that this provision "shall not be interpreted as giving grounds for delay or postponement of the negotiation and conclusion of agreements for placing mandated . . . territories under the trusteeship system as provided for in Article 77."

---

except that Hertzog was thinking only of the white population. Moreover, South West Africa was not highly regarded in the 1930s. Its economic condition and financial situation were bad. From 1926 to 1936 it could not balance its budget and the Union government made up the deficits.

[11] W. K. Hancock, *Smuts*, 2 vols. (Cambridge, Eng., 1962, 1968), Vol. 2: *Fields of Force, 1919–1950*, p. 467. Hancock is of the opinion that had the Union simply annexed the territory during the war "Not a dog would have barked," but Smuts's "old fashioned respect for the legal fabric of the Society of Nations restrained."

Though annexation was not specifically mentioned in his speech, Heaton Nicholls, Union high commissioner in London and a member of the Union delegation to the first session of the General Assembly of the United Nations, opened the campaign of the Union for the annexation of South West Africa by his address to that body on January 17, 1946. He stated that South West Africa was unique among mandated territories because of its situation. Its borders were contiguous with those of the mandatory power. The uncertainty of its future had retarded the development of the territory. Doubts about its stability caused capital to hesitate to move in. Its population was too small to make possible a strong independent state. The position of the territory in relation to the Union made South West Africa's case different from that of the other mandates. "This special position should be given full consideration in determining the future status of the territory," concluded Nicholls.[12]

The next step in the move to annex South West Africa was made by Prime Minister Smuts in the second part of the first session of the General Assembly. His government had submitted a statement on the outcome of its consultations with the peoples of that territory as to its future status.[13] At the meeting of the Fourth Committee on November 4, 1946, Smuts declared that South West Africa was essentially a part of the South African territory and people.[14] Because of the physical contiguity of South West Africa to the Union and its anthropological kinship with the rest of South Africa, "the Union of South Africa was legitimately concerned in securing the annexation of that territory." President Woodrow Wilson, said Smuts, understood that the future of the territory lay in its incorporation in the Union. South West Africa had become so thoroughly integrated with the Union, argued Smuts, "that its formal incorporation was mainly required to remove doubts," so as to attract capital and encourage individual initiative and to render unnecessary a separate fiscal system. It would admit the inhabitants to the full benefits enjoyed by the people of the Union.

With the desirability of incorporation in view, the Union government had, according to Smuts, entered a reservation at the San Francisco

[12] United Nations, General Assembly, 1st Sess., Journal, 17 Jan. 1946, pp. 188–93.

[13] UNGAOR, 1st Sess., Pt. II, Fourth Committee, Pt. I, Annex 13, pp. 199–235, 235–44.

[14] No doubt General Smuts sought to have the provisions of the Covenant with respect to the "C" mandates drafted so as to fit especially South West Africa, but there were other "C" mandates.

Conference to ensure that incorporation of the territory in the Union would not be prejudiced by any proposals adopted by the Conference with respect to the future of the mandated territories. South African spokesmen repeatedly referred to this reservation as if it had legal force.[15] Smuts's own statements were guarded. In a statement to Parliament on March 16, 1946, he stated clearly what the nature of his reservation was. He said, "Our reservation was this: that we claimed in the interests of South West Africa that it should be incorporated as part and parcel of the Union territory and that we are going to plead that case. We are not going to act unilaterally. . . . We are going to argue the case."[16] The South African delegation at the first part of the session of the General Assembly had not joined with other mandatory powers in undertaking to place territories under trusteeship because it had felt that the Union government had an obligation to the peoples of South West Africa to consult them first as to its future status. Since then the Union government had consulted the inhabitants and all of them were in favor of incorporation in the Union. The European population unanimously expressed the wish that the territory be made a part of the Union. The wishes of the non-Europeans had been ascertained tribally, with the result of 208,850 for incorporation and 33,250 opposed. Some 57,000 could not be consulted.[17]

South Africa's request for approval of incorporation was not received sympathetically by the members of the General Assembly. In view of the state of development of the native population members found it difficult to believe that the natives had fully understood the consultation, or that they knew of the advantages of the trusteeship system. Sir Maharaja

[15] Louw said in the General Assembly, 26 Nov. 1948, that the then prime minister of South Africa had at a meeting of Committee Four of Commission II "again formally reserved his country's position regarding South West Africa" (UNGAOR, 3d Sess., Pt. I, Plenary Meetings, Summary Records, 1948, p. 588).

[16] *Hansard*, vol. 56, cols. 3677–78. What actually happened is that the South African delegate read a statement in the meeting of Committee Four of Commission II, in which his delegation claimed that "the mandate should be terminated and that the territory should be incorporated as part of the Union of South Africa." The chairman of the committee, Prime Minister Peter Fraser of New Zealand, correctly ruled that reference to specific territories was used only for illustrative purposes. "The task of the Committee was to discuss principles and machinery, not individual territorial issues" (United Nations, *Documents of the United Nations Conference on International Organization* [New York, 1945], 10: 4340).

[17] UNGAOR, 1st Sess., Pt. II, Fourth Committee, Pt. I, Summary Records, 4 Nov. 1946, pp. 62–65.

Singh, the representative of India who had served as high commissioner in South Africa, asked what advantages would accrue to the natives from incorporation of the territory in the Union in view of the policy of segregation and discrimination which the Union practiced against all non-Europeans. He pointed out that the consultation had been conducted by officials and magistrates of the government. Some representatives asserted that annexation was against both the letter and spirit of the Charter. Irrespective of whether the real wishes of the population had been ascertained, annexation was juridically and constitutionally impossible, they contended.

In response to the unfriendly attitudes, Smuts countered that it would be impossible for the Union government as a former mandatory to submit a trusteeship agreement in conflict with the clearly expressed wishes of the inhabitants of the territory. If the General Assembly did not agree that the clear wishes of the inhabitants should be implemented the Union government could take no other course than to abide by the declaration it had made to the last Assembly of the League of Nations that it would continue to administer the territory as heretofore as an integral part of the Union in the spirit of the principles laid down in the mandate.[18]

The General Assembly adopted a resolution recommended by the Fourth Committee which was conciliatory but firm. It declared that the General Assembly was unable to accede to the incorporation of South West Africa in the Union and recommended that the mandated territory be placed under the international trusteeship system and invited the Union government to propose such an agreement for the consideration of the General Assembly. It gave as its reason for rejecting South Africa's request for incorporation that the inhabitants had not yet secured political autonomy or reached a stage of political development which enabled them to express a considered opinion which the General Assembly could recognize on such an important question.[19]

It was not long before there were repercussions in the South African Parliament to the General Assembly's rejection of the Union government's request for approval to annex. Eric Louw, the National party's specialist on foreign affairs, moved that the House request the govern-

[18] Ibid., p. 101.
[19] UNGAOR, 1st Sess., Pt. II, *Resolutions*, Res. No. 65(I), 14 Dec. 1946, pp. 123–24.

ment to introduce the necessary legislation for the integration of South West Africa with the Union.[20] In the debate on his resolution Louw made all the arguments which were to be used by the South African government at the United Nations in the years following the succession to power by the National party in 1948. South West Africa had been accorded to the Union under the mandate of the League of Nations to be administered as an integral part of the Union under the League's authority and supervision. The League had ceased to exist; it had not been empowered to transfer its rights and powers with respect to South West Africa to any other body or organization and in fact had not done so. Hence, the Union was in *de jure* as well as in *de facto* possession of the territory. With the passing of the League of Nations the nine points of the law rising from possession became the ten points of the law. It could therefore administer it without any responsibility to the United Nations or to any other international organization or body. It was not in the interest of South Africa or of South West Africa to conclude a trusteeship agreement as provided in the United Nations Charter. For all practical purposes the territory was a part of South Africa.

Smuts's views were different, but with some strange refinements. As he saw it, Germany had ceded her colonies to the Allied and Associated Powers, who in turn had distributed these territories under mandate to other countries. Thus the Union held South West Africa as a "C" mandate not from the League of Nations but from the Allied and Associated Powers and was accountable to the League for its administration of the territory. As the mandatory the Union acquired full power of legislation and administration over the mandated area as an "integral part of its own territory." The first formula was "as if an integral part" of the territory of the mandatory, but Smuts and Botha objected to the inclusion of "if" and after a serious and prolonged debate with the representatives of the Allied and Associated Powers the word was dropped from the draft (Art. 22, cl. 6, of the Covenant). The Union government had unified the public railway and police services and had exercised the "fullest measure of power" over the territory, but had not annexed it because the Union authority was so wide that it was not necessary. With the United Nations a new situation had been created. There was no derivation of authority from the League of Nations; the

[20] 19 Mar. 1947. See *Hansard*, vol. 60, cols. 1320–71, 2582–2623, for the resolution and debate on it.

Charter dealt with the question anew. By doing so, it avoided legal questions such as the authority of the League of Nations to transfer its authority and functions to the United Nations. The Charter provides that there must be a new agreement between the mandatory powers and the states directly concerned (Art. 79). Until a new agreement has been made the status quo under the old mandate agreement shall be maintained. When asked whether the mandatory powers were under obligations to enter into a new agreement, Smuts said that they were not, but they must take steps to enter into an agreement; they must be serious about it but there was no compulsion to accept the terms. Mandatory powers were prevented by Article 80, clause 2, from saying, "The League of Nations is dead: I do not want to come under the U.N.O. at all and I do not want to come under the trusteeship council at all."[21] He was doubtful whether in terms of the mandate South Africa had from the principal Allied and Associated Powers it could annex the territory. Smuts thought it would be wise, at least for the present, to continue on the old lines and render reports to the United Nations, not as an obligation, but as a way of easing the tension. Instead of incorporating the territory he proposed that it should be represented in the Parliament of the Union "as an integral portion thereof."

The Nationalist leaders were concerned about the effect which the dispute with the United Nations was having and would have increasingly on the attitude of the non-Europeans in both the Union and South West Africa. Malan spoke of this frequently. On March 15, 1946, he said in Parliament, "We don't want South West Africa under control of a foreign power which does not understand our problems of colour here, and which can make enormous difficulties for us by following a different policy in South-West Africa."[22] The United Nations intervention in the Union's policy in South West Africa and the treatment of Indians was having serious repercussions among the non-Europeans in South Africa and was aggravating the color problem, he declared on January 21, 1947.[23] Louw declared the Smuts defeat on South West Africa in the United Nations had "repercussions on the native population in this country," and he concluded his speech in support of his proposed resolution with the statement that "the position of the white race . . .

---

[21] Ibid., vol. 56, cols. 3672–76, 15 Mar. 1946.
[22] Ibid., col. 3688.
[23] Ibid., vol. 59, col. 10899.

[and] the maintenance of white civilization in this country is at stake."[24]

In a letter of July 23, 1947, South Africa informed the United Nations that it had decided not to proceed with the incorporation of South West Africa and that it would continue to administer the territory in the spirit of the existing mandate and would submit reports on its administration for the information of the United Nations and that consideration was being given to granting representation to the territory in the Union Parliament. Smuts's view was that the status of South West Africa was that of a non-self-governing territory to which Articles 73 and 74 of the Charter applied and not Articles 75–85 which deal with the trusteeship system.[25]

The response of the General Assembly to this communication was a resolution in which it firmly maintained its recommendation that the territory be placed under the trusteeship system and urged the Union government to propose a trusteeship agreement for its consideration at the next session and authorized the Trusteeship Council in the meantime to examine the report on South West Africa submitted by the government of the Union and to submit its observations on the report to the General Assembly.[26]

The Trusteeship Council was critical of South Africa's administration of the territory. It questioned the following: the lack of representation by natives in the governing bodies or in the administration; the system of reserves and urban segregation; the failure to restore the traditional lands of the natives; the small percentage of the budget (slightly more than 10 percent) which went for native welfare; the use of prison labor; and the disparity in educational facilities for natives and Europeans.[27] The Union government, now controlled by the National party, was bitter about the procedure and the Trusteeship Council's report. It declared that since South West Africa was not a trust territory, the assignment of South Africa's report to the Trusteeship Council was

[24] Ibid., vol. 60, col. 1347.

[25] Smuts apparently never seriously considered the status of a strategic trust territory under Articles 82 and 83. "To my mind," he said, "the strategic idea applies rather to other areas, not so much to South Africa" (ibid., vol. 55, col. 1171, 6 Feb. 1946).

[26] UNGAOR, 2d Sess., Res. No. 141(II), 1 Nov. 1947, p. 47.

[27] United Nations, Trusteeship Records, 3d Sess., Supp. (T/175), Dec. 1948, pp. 51–52.

illegal. By letter of July 11, 1949, the Union government notified the United Nations that it would furnish no further reports on the territory. This decision brought into sharp focus the issue of the status of South West Africa and South Africa's rights and obligations with respect to it. The Union government maintained that it had submitted its report under Article 73 (e) of the Charter while the General Assembly assumed that the status of South West Africa was essentially that of a trust territory. The position of neither party was wholly correct. South West Africa was not an ordinary dependency, as it had an international status and therefore did not properly fall under Article 73 (e) but it is also clear that the territory was not in the Trusteeship system.[28] United States Secretary of State John Foster Dulles recognized the problem and had suggested that the Fourth Committee (Trusteeship) of the General Assembly be authorized to consider the reports on South West Africa.[29]

For aid in resolving this legal dilemma the General Assembly turned to the International Court of Justice for an advisory opinion. The Court, on July 11, 1950, stated that the General Assembly of the United Nations was legally qualified to exercise the supervisory functions previously exercised by the League of Nations with regard to the administration of the territory, and that the Union was obliged to submit to supervision and control of the General Assembly and render annual reports to it, but the degree of supervision by this body should not exceed that which had previously applied and should conform as far as possible to the procedure followed by the Council of the League. The Court was of the opinion that there was no legal obligation for mandatory states to negotiate and conclude trusteeship agreements, but also that the Union had no competence unilaterally to modify the international status of the territory. The Court implied that the territory's status could be changed by the Union with the consent of the General Assembly.[30]

[28] See Faye Carroll, *South West Africa and the United Nations* (Lexington, Ky., 1967), for an excellent analysis of the controversy.

[29] UNGAOR, 2d Sess., Fourth Committee, Summary Records, 1947, pp. 5–6.

[30] "International Status of South West Africa, Advisory Opinion," International Court of Justice (hereafter I.C.J.) *Reports,* 1950, pp. 128ff. The General Assembly submitted the following particular questions to the Court: "a) Does the Union of South Africa continue to have international obligations under the mandate for South West Africa, and if so, what are those obligations, b) Are the provisions of Chapter XI of the Charter applicable and, if so, in what manner, to the Ter-

In the next decade the General Assembly vainly sought to reach an agreement by negotiation with the Union for the implementation of the Court's advisory opinion.[31] The Union government did not accept the Court's advisory opinion, refused to place the territory under the trusteeship system or to make reports or to accept any form of United Nations supervision over its administration of the territory. The most the Union government would concede was a new agreement with the remaining Allied and Associated Powers, namely France, the United Kingdom, and the United States. Prime Minister Malan did acknowledge that South Africa acquired control of the territory as the result of a treaty. Hence, South Africa must have an international instrument; the status of the territory could not be kept suspended in midair. Malan said his government wanted that agreement with the three remaining Allied and Associated Powers of World War I "to put this matter in order formally." But this agreement was not to give these powers any check on South Africa's administration of the territory. South Africa would not agree to submit reports to them. Clearly what Malan's government wanted was a treaty which would give the Union sovereignty over South West Africa, subject only to the vague undertaking to govern it in the spirit of the mandates system.[32]

Not only would South Africa not enter into any agreement with the United Nations in regard to the territory, it also protested all measures of the United Nations which it contended went beyond the degree and manner of supervision which South Africa had assumed under the mandates system. The only form of supervision which the Union was prepared to accept was judicial supervision by the International Court of Justice. Malan believed that the object of the attack on South Africa was "directly and indirectly to force on to South West Africa, and also on the Union, an ideology which would simply mean the undoing of the white population in the country, namely, the surrender of power into the hands of the non-European population."[33]

---

ritory of South West Africa, and c) Has the Union of South Africa the competence to modify the international status of the Territory of South West Africa, or in the event of a negative reply, where does competence rest to determine and modify the international status of the Territory" (UNGAOR, 4th Sess., Res. No. 338 [IV], 6 Dec. 1949, p. 45).

[31] UNGAOR, 5th Sess., Supp. No. 20 (A/1775), Res. No. 449(V), 13 Dec. 1950, pp. 55–56.

[32] *Hansard*, vol. 85, cols. 4486–87, 4 May 1954.

[33] Ibid., vol. 74, col. 186, 25 Jan. 1951.

In spite of almost yearly resolutions, an enlarged Committee on South West Africa created in 1953 (to be replaced by a Special Committee in 1961) and the establishment of a Good Offices Committee in 1957,[34] the General Assembly made no progress in reaching an agreement with South Africa on the status and administration of the territory. When the General Assembly failed to get any cooperation from South Africa, it proceeded independently to perform the functions of the League under the mandates system. This provoked the bitter charge by the Union government that the General Assembly, in violation of the advisory opinion of the International Court of Justice, had exceeded the degree of supervision and control which had been exercised by the League of Nations. This led the General Assembly to ask the Court for two supplementary opinions, which were rendered in 1955 and 1956, dealing with the method of voting in the Assembly and the hearing of petitioners.

If the reason for the South African government's refusal to cooperate or negotiate with the United Nations about the status and administration of South West Africa was the fear that its racial policy would be discussed in the world forum, its tactics were a complete failure. On December 6, 1955, the General Assembly adopted a resolution which emphasized racial policy in the territory as the chief issue. It reminded the Union government "of the faith it had re-affirmed in signing the Charter, in fundamental human rights and in the dignity and worth of the human person," and called on it to observe Article 56 of the Charter.[35] This resolution so offended the South African delegation that it withdrew from the General Assembly.

As a result of the impasse the General Assembly began to consider what legal action was open to ensure that the Union government fulfill the obligations it had assumed under the mandates system of the League

---

[34] The Good Offices Committee, after discussions with the Union government, proposed that the General Assembly encourage the Union government to make an investigation of the practicability of partition and advise the General Assembly of the result. The suggested plan envisaged the annexation of the southern part of the territory, which is predominantly white, by South Africa and placing the northern half, which is almost exclusively native, under a United Nations trusteeship. The Union government was interested in the proposal, but it was rejected by the 1958 General Assembly.

[35] UNGAOR, 10th Sess., Supp. No. 19 (A/3116), Res. No. 917(X), 6 Dec. 1955, p. 8.

of Nations.[36] In 1957 it requested the Committee on South West Africa to study the matter. The Committee advised the General Assembly that there was little doubt that those former members of the League at the date of its dissolution which were now members of the United Nations had the right to invoke Article 7 of the mandate agreement.

In 1960 the governments of Ethiopia and Liberia filed concurrent applications with the International Court of Justice instituting contentious proceedings against the Union of South Africa, contending that South Africa had violated its obligations under the mandate, chiefly by introducing apartheid.[37] The International Court of Justice rejected the preliminary objections which the South African government had filed as to the jurisdiction of the Court and decided by a vote of eight to seven that it did have jurisdiction.[38] Four years later, after ninety-nine public sittings devoted to oral hearings on the merits of the dispute, and six months of private deliberations, the Court startled the world by its pronouncement that the "applicants cannot be considered to have established any legal right or interest appertaining to them in the subject-matter of the present claims, and that, accordingly, the Court must decline to give effect to them."[39] It was thought that the Court in its 1962 decision had affirmed the right of the applicants to bring the suit,

[36] Article 2, clause 2, of the agreement between the League of Nations and South Africa states "the Mandatory shall promote to the utmost the material and moral well-being and the social progress of the inhabitants of the territory subject to the present Mandate."

[37] Article 7 of the Mandate for South West Africa provided that "if any dispute whatever should arise between the Mandatory and another member of the League of Nations relating to the interpretation or the application of the provisions of the mandate, such dispute if it cannot be settled by negotiation, shall be submitted to the Permanent Court of International Justice provided for by Article 14 of the Covenant of the League of Nations." The necessary link with the International Court of Justice, an organ of the United Nations, was provided by Article 37 of its Statute, which states that "whenever a treaty or convention in force provides for reference of a matter to a tribunal to have been instituted by the League of Nations, or to the Permanent Court of International Justice, the matter shall, as between parties to the present Statute, be referred to the International Court of Justice."

[38] International Court of Justice, South West Africa Cases (*Ethiopia* v. *South Africa; Liberia* v. *South Africa*) *Preliminary Objections, Judgment of,* 21 Dec. 1962, I.C.J. *Reports,* 1962, pp. 321ff.

[39] International Court of Justice, South West Africa Cases (*Ethiopia* v. *South Africa; Liberia* v. *South Africa*), *Second Phase,* I.C.J. *Reports,* 1966, pp. 6ff. Also reported in American Journal of International Law, vol. 61, no. 1 (Jan. 1967), 116–210.

but the Court in the second decision declared that with respect to those clauses of the mandate which referred to the conduct or carrying out duties of the mandatory League members could have recourse to the Court only if they could show some special national interest. The Court ruled that neither Ethiopia nor Liberia had such special interests, and therefore adjudication on the merits of the case was not required. In view of the fact that all the pleadings, hearings, and evidence related solely to the merits of the dispute and that numerous questions addressed by the judges to counsel and the witnesses were all directed to the merits of the dispute, the Court's decision was indeed astonishing. The vote of the sitting judges was a tie (seven to seven), which enabled the president of the Court to cast a second vote and thus produce an eight to seven decision.[40]

Instead of transforming the advisory opinion of 1950 into an enforceable judgment, the Court's decision produced uncertainty and confusion. South African spokesmen often talk as if the Court had confirmed Pretoria's position, but this is not so. About the only thing the decision settled was that no individual state can arraign South Africa before the International Court of Justice on charges of having failed to live up to its obligations undertaken in the mandate agreement. Only the Assembly or the Council of the League could do this, and they no longer were in existence. If the Court had not found this technicality, it presumably would have had to make a pronouncement on the substantive question of whether apartheid was compatible with Article 2 of the mandate agreement. It does not seem possible that the Court could have come to any other conclusion than that South Africa had failed to live up to its obligations.[41] Had the Court so decided, South Africa would have found itself in an embarrassing position, as it had repeatedly called for a judicial determination of the question of its racial policy and the domestic jurisdiction clause of the Charter. The position of the General Assembly would have been greatly strengthened. In case of South African noncompliance it could have called on the Security Council for enforcement measures.

A legal approach was still open to the General Assembly; it could ask

[40] This method of breaking an equality of votes is in accordance with Article 55 of the Statute of the International Court of Justice.

[41] See Ernest A. Gross, Chief Counsel to Liberia and Ethiopia, "The South West Africa Case: What Happened?" *Foreign Affairs,* 45 (Oct. 1966), pp. 36–48.

the International Court of Justice for more advisory opinions centering on the question of the compatibility of apartheid with the principles of the mandate system in the administration of South West Africa. It could bluntly ask for an opinion whether the introduction of the policy of apartheid constituted a violation of the mandate principles and agreements. But so intense was the antagonism to the Court for its decision that the United Nations turned to drastic nonjudicial measures. The mood of the General Assembly had begun to change notably several years before the Court's paralyzing decision. In 1960 it moved from a policy of conciliation to one of action; its policy of pacific pressure, followed over a dozen years, had failed.[42]

At this session the General Assembly also adopted the Declaration on the Granting of Independence to Colonial Countries and Peoples, which called for a speedy and unconditional end to colonialism in all its forms and manifestations.[43] Also the Committee on South West Africa made its very critical report on the administration of the territory. The committee concluded that the mandatory power had continued to administer South West Africa on the "basis of apartheid and White supremacy," which was contrary to the mandate, the Charter of the United Nations, the Universal Declaration of Human Rights, the advisory opinions of the International Court of Justice, and the resolutions of the General Assembly. The trend of the administration, it averred, was to subordinate the well-being and paramount interests of the native and colored sections of the population to those of Europeans. The former had little, "if any, share in the profits derived from the exploitation of the natural resources of the territory"; even their training and education seemed directed "merely to preparing the 'Natives' as a source of cheap labor for the benefit of the Europeans."[44] The General Assembly, by resolution, invited the committee "to investigate the situation prevailing in the territory and to ascertain and make proposals" on "the steps which would enable the indigenous inhabitants of South West Africa to achieve a wide measure of internal self-government designed to lead them to complete independence as soon as possible."[45]

[42] UNGAOR, 15th Sess., Supp. No. 16 (A/4684), Res. No. 1565(XV), Dec. 1960.
[43] UNGAOR, 15th Sess., Supp. No. 16 (A/4484), Res. No. 1514(XV), 14 Dec. 1960.
[44] UNGAOR, 15th Sess., Supp. No. 12 (A/4464), Dec. 1960.
[45] UNGAOR, 15th Sess., Supp. No. 16 (A/4684), Res. No. 1568(XV), 18 Dec. 1960, p. 33.

South Africa refused to offer the committee facilities or cooperation on the ground that the dispute was *sub judice,* that is, before the International Court of Justice. In its report to the General Assembly the committee declared that South Africa was the only state in the world today to practice racism as an official policy, not only within its boundaries, but throughout the Mandated Territory of South West Africa, and that this policy was the most pervasive feature of the administration of the territory, extending to all aspects of the life of the natives. The committee judged the South African government unfit further to administer the territory and recommended that the General Assembly undertake a study of ways and means by which to terminate its administration.[46]

The mounting pressure may have caused the South African government real concern as it made a conciliatory move. The racial disorders at Sharpeville resulting in the death of some seventy people produced worldwide reaction and put South Africa on the defensive. By letter of May 10, 1961, it offered to invite an independent person of international standing, to be mutually agreed upon by the president of the General Assembly and the South African government, to conduct an impartial inquiry to determine whether international peace and security were threatened in South West Africa. A General Assembly resolution of 1961 had declared the situation in the territory constituted a threat or potential threat to international peace and security. When this offer received no response the South African government decided to invite three past presidents of the General Assembly to visit South West Africa to determine whether there existed any threat to international peace and security, or whether there was any truth in the allegations that South Africa was militarizing the territory, or whether there existed an explosive situation or a planned extermination of the non-European inhabitants. The South African government would undertake to publish their report in full.[47] This move was no better received than the first. The offer came too late and was too restricted. The General Assembly replaced the Committee on South West Africa with a Special Committee on South West Africa to prepare the territory for independence.

Only the chairman and the vice chairman visited South Africa and

[46] UNGAOR, 16th Sess., Supp. No. 12A (A/4926), 1961, pp. 3–22.
[47] UNGAOR, 17th Sess., Plenary Meetings, Verbatim Record, 24 Sept. 1964, p. 64.

South West Africa as Pretoria would not admit the whole committee. After the two had made a ten-day tour of South West Africa and had long discussions with Prime Minister Verwoerd and Foreign Minister Louw, a joint communique was issued in which the chairman and vice chairman of the committee stated that "in the places visited they had found no evidence and heard no allegations that there was a threat to international peace and security within South West Africa, or that there were signs of military action in the territory or that the indigenous population was being exterminated" and no case of detention of political prisoners had been brought to their attention during their visit. Ten days later the chairman, Ambassador Victorio D. Carpio of the Philippines, denied association with the statement. The committee, however, reported that the policy of apartheid had been intensified and made "more systematic in recent years." It concluded that the complete implementation of the General Assembly's resolutions would require the establishment of a United Nations presence in the territory. It considered that the time had come for firm and decisive action.[48]

The General Assembly in 1962 dissolved the Special Committee on South West Africa and transferred its functions to its special committee on the situation with regard to the implementation of the Declaration on the Granting of Independence to Colonial Countries and Peoples, known as the Special Committee of Twenty-Four. In order to prepare South West Africa for independence the General Assembly requested the secretary-general to establish a special educational and training program for the natives of the territory and to appoint a United Nations Technical Assistance Resident Representative for South West Africa for the task of establishing an effective United Nations presence in the territory.[49] South Africa bluntly informed the secretary-general that outside help in administering the territory was neither necessary nor desirable, and that the establishment of a United Nations presence in the territory was the issue in dispute in the long controversy between South Africa and the United Nations and was now before the International Court of Justice. In 1963 the General Assembly declared that any attempt to annex South West Africa would be an act of aggression,

[48] UNGAOR, 17th Sess., Supp. No. 12 (A/5212), 1962. Louw gave an account of the strange affair of the joint communique in the General Assembly (UNGAOR, 17th Sess., Plenary Meeting, Verbatim Record, 24 Sept. 1962, p. 64).
[49] UNGAOR, 17th Sess., Supp. No. 17 (A/5217), 1962, p. 39.

urged members to impose an embargo on the shipping of arms and oil to South Africa, and requested the Security Council to consider the situation in South West Africa.[50]

In September 1962 the South African government appointed a commission of experts to draft a five-year plan for promoting the material and moral welfare and social progress of the inhabitants of South West Africa. The plan should be designed particularly for the nonwhites whose background, traditions, and habits should be taken into consideration. Frans H. Odendaal, administrator of the Transvaal, served as chairman. In its report, made in 1964, the Odendaal commission in effect recommended the extension of the "homelands" or Bantustans policy to the territory. It proposed the creation of homelands for each of the nonwhite groups—ten in all—and a white area. These homelands would be prepared gradually for political independence, but the existing economic interdependence of the parts of the territory would be continued. As in South Africa, the coloreds present a difficult problem because they have no homeland. No provision was made for a "coloredstan," but a council to deal with colored affairs would be established. To carry out the plan about 28 percent of the nonwhites would have to be moved. Their areas would be enlarged to embrace about 40 percent of the territory and the white area would be reduced to about 44 percent. To make available the water and power necessary for the economic development of the territory the commission proposed a large hydroelectric scheme on the Kunene River to be undertaken in cooperation with the Portuguese, since the river forms part of the boundary between South West Africa and Angola. The South African government accepted the recommendations of the report in principle but indicated it would delay action on it until the International Court of Justice had rendered its decision in the case brought by Ethiopia and Liberia. The United Nations Committee of Twenty-Four called on South Africa not to implement the recommendations.

The astonishing decision of the International Court of Justice in 1966 evoked a sharp reaction from the General Assembly. It declared that South Africa had failed "to insure the moral and material well-being and security of the indigenous inhabitants of South West Africa" and had "in fact disavowed the mandate." It decided that the mandate was

---

[50] UNGAOR, 18th Sess., Supp. No. 15 (A/5515), Res. Nos. 899(XVIII), 1900(XVIII), 1901(XVIII), 13 Nov., 1963, pp. 46–48.

terminated and that henceforth South West Africa came "under the direct responsibility of the United Nations." It set up an Ad Hoc Committee for South West Africa to recommend practical means by which the territory should be administered so as to enable its inhabitants "to exercise the right of self-determination and to achieve independence."[51] The Ad Hoc Committee could not agree on a line of action when it reported to the special session of the General Assembly which met from April 21 to June 13, 1967, and the latter itself could only agree on a compromise resolution, with thirty members abstaining. By this resolution the General Assembly created a council of eleven members to govern the territory, assisted by a United Nations commission nominated by the secretary-general and appointed by the Assembly. The council was to call upon Pretoria to cooperate in the transfer of administration; the Security Council and all members were asked to take appropriate measures to effect implementation of the resolution. June 1968 was the goal set for the independence of the territory.[52]

The South African government was no more inclined to implement this resolution than the earlier ones, but it did make some countermoves. In February 1967 it declared that all of the twenty diplomatic missions in South Africa were free to visit South West Africa and in March it announced the offer of self-determination to the Ovambos with the prospect of either complete independence or "some other relationship with other nations."[53] By this offer of preparation for independence to the tribe which accounts for nearly half of the population of the territory the South African government undoubtedly hoped to undercut the United Nations.[54] The scheme was essentially the extension of separate development (of creating Bantustans) to the mandate. It also involved the partition of the territory into white and black areas, with the practical annexation of the white area by South Africa. Prime Minister Vorster stated in September 1967 that his government would ask Parliament for legislation to increase Pretoria's powers with respect to certain functions of the South West African administration. As for the United Nations plan to take over the administration of South West

[51] UNGAOR, 21st Sess., Supp. No. 16 (A/6316), Res. No. 2145(XXI), 27 Oct. 1966, pp. 2–3.

[52] UNGAOR, 5th Special Sess., Supp. No. 1 (A/6651), Res. No. 2248(XXI), 19 May 1967, p. 1.

[53] *New York Times*, 22 Mar. 1967.

[54] *The Star* (Johannesburg), Weekly Air Edition, 25 Mar. 1967.

Africa, Vorster declared that no United Nations representative would be allowed to enter the territory. "We shall adopt a strong attitude," he declared, "because I am convinced that if we show the slightest sign of weakness, they will chase us till we can run no more, and this the people of South Africa will never do."[55] Sir de Villiers Graaf, leader of the opposition United party, wholeheartedly supported the government's position—"to hand over the territory was unthinkable!"[56]

While the United Nations vainly tried to take over the administration of South West Africa, an event occurred exacerbating the situation. Thirty-five Africans (Ovambos) were tried for violation of the draconian Terrorist Act of South Africa passed after the alleged acts were committed. The Security Council of the United Nations called for the release of the accused, but the South African court (the accused were tried in Pretoria) sentenced thirty to prison terms—nineteen for life.[57] The United Nations Security Council on January 25, 1968, declared the trial illegal and called for release of the accused. On March 14 it adopted a resolution censuring South Africa for its failure to comply with its resolutions of January 25 and warned South Africa that it would take "effective steps or measures if South Africa failed to comply."[58] The General Assembly by resolution of June 12, 1968, proclaimed that South West Africa should henceforth be known as Namibia in accordance with the desire of its people.[59]

The South West Africa problem is a phase of the decolonization process, complicated by racial ideology. The many fragments of the former great colonial empires are not easily fitted into the pattern of the contemporary world structure. The strongly anti-colonial sentiment of the postwar world, which found such fervent and sweeping expression in the Declaration on the Granting of Independence to Colonial Countries and Peoples, brooks no delays and no excuses or exceptions to the demand for political independence, regardless of the social and economic conditions which may obtain in these remnants of empire. However, effective modern government requires a nation to sustain it. With the exception of New Guinea, the situation in South West Africa

---

[55] Ibid., 30 Mar. 1968.

[56] Ibid., 28 Oct. 1967.

[57] Ibid., 27 Jan. 1968; *New York Times*, 10 Feb. 1968.

[58] The *New York Times* editorially characterized the trial as a "burlesque of justice" (11 Feb. 1968).

[59] A/Res/2372(XXII), *United Nations Monthly Chronicle*, July 1968, pp. 30–32.

was probably the most difficult in the world from the point of view of nation-building. Numerous tribes, some with a membership of only a few thousand and all primitive, occupying a vast, physically hostile territory, would have made nation-building very difficult, even if South Africa seriously had made that aim its policy. To complicate matters, the South African government induced its white nationals to settle in the territory by selling them large farms and giving them generous financial assistance. Besides the obvious purpose of creating enduring bonds between the territory and the Union, there was the pressing problem of developing the economy. The territory was bankrupt; the skills, initiative, and entrepreneurship of the whites were necessary to stimulate the economy. As a result of this immigration the whites now constitute the second largest ethnic group, and the most powerful.

Integration of the various peoples into a nation was never a goal of South Africa's administration of the territory and now the policy is in the other direction. The new policy is clearly related to the policy of separate development which was adopted a decade earlier for South Africa. Just as this policy called for a reverse of South Africa's attitude to the Protectorates, so the policy of self-determination for the peoples of South West Africa followed logically. It is part of the same pattern. As the South African whites see it, this policy offers the best chance for complete white control of the heartland of southern Africa, and indirect control of the surrounding Bantustans by means of economic dominance and overwhelming military power.

South Africa maintains that its policy is wholly within the spirit of the mandate agreement. It asserts that South West Africa has a separate and international identity and character and that it honors the trust which it accepted "in a spirit of guardianship and of responsibility, with equal care for all the population groups." Self-government would not be furthered, it contends, by "one mixed central authority for the whole territory." A policy of welding South West Africa into an integrated whole would lead to unhappy results. It would produce tensions among the various groups and a struggle for supremacy, with the prospect of the domination of one of the indigenous groups over the others. This was the problem that had developed in many African states. The South African government had, therefore, resolved upon the broad approach of separate development as the best means of hastening emancipation. When the various groups reach the stage at which they are able to control their own destiny they may negotiate with others on a basis of equality concerning economic and political cooperation.[60] It may be added that since these tribes are too small to be politically or economically viable they inevitably would have to find a place in South Africa's orbit.

A number of questions may be raised about the action of the General Assembly in terminating the mandate. Was this one-sided revocation of the mandate legal? The International Court of Justice in its advisory opinion of 1950 stated that competence to change or modify the mandate rests with the Union of South Africa acting with the consent of the United Nations. It may be argued that the General Assembly terminated the mandate on the ground of the adverse breach of a treaty, namely, the mandate agreement. However, there is no judicial pronouncement on the breach of the agreement. The General Assembly almost certainly could obtain what would be nearly the equivalent of such a pronouncement by asking the International Court of Justice for an advisory opinion on the matter. But their faith in the rule of law and judicial settlement was so badly shaken that the Afro-Asian states have no inclination to go to the Court again.

It is questionable whether the United Nations' attempt to set up its own administration in the territory can lead to any good results. Obviously, the United Nations' writ can be enforced in South West Africa only with the active support of Great Britain and the United States, and they have made it known that they are not going to join in any movement to "liberate" South West Africa by force. But even if that difficulty were overcome it is uncertain whether the United Nations could succeed in politicially integrating South West Africa and prepare it for early independence or extricate the territory and its peoples from economic dependence on the markets of South Africa. It would be tragic indeed if the United Nations were compelled to maintain a long rule and to resort to repressive measures to keep the territory from falling into chaos. Lord Caradon, the British representative, warned the General Assembly against arousing false hopes and promises that could not be fulfilled. "If such proposals are made," he said, "they not only raise hopes amongst the people of the territory which we cannot satisfy . . .

---

[60] See statement by Foreign Minister Muller, 19 April 1967, *Hansard*, vol. 20, cols. 4524–28, and Department of Foreign Affairs, *South West Africa Survey* (Pretoria, 1967).

they also by their ineffectiveness give encouragement to the South African government in pursuing the oppressive and objectionable measures which we all condemn."[61]

Both South Africa and the United Nations have started on a hazardous road. The point of no return has been reached. South Africa will yield to the United Nations only when confronted with irresistible force which the international organization is unlikely soon to command. The world organization is floundering in a frustrating and humiliating experience. South Africa also may have opened a Pandora's box by its new policy. Pretoria may not be able to control developments.

[61] Quoted in *The Star*, Weekly Air Edition, 21 Dec. 1968. George Ignatieff, the Canadian representative declared. "We should acknowledge that often the approaches adopted in the United Nations have shown little recognition of the realities."

16

Conflict with
the United Nations:
Apartheid

At the heart of the difficulties between South Africa and the United Nations and the world is the racial policy relentlessly pursued by the Republic. The controversy over the treatment of Indians and the dispute with respect to South West Africa are basically conflicts over apartheid. The triumph of the Nationalists in 1948 represents a watershed in South African political history. This was the first time in the history of the Union that a ministry composed solely of Afrikaners governed the country. While the practice of racial segregation goes back almost to the first years of the planting of the colony at the Cape, it now has become a philosophy of life, thoroughly rationalized and elevated to a moral principle and sometimes to a religious dogma.[1] During the Nationalist rule a mass of repressive and discriminatory—discriminatory in fact if not always on its face—legislation was enacted. The philosophy of apartheid was applied with a rigid consistency to every phase of life. Everything is in a logical pattern with rarely a deviation from principle. With the rise to power of the Naionalists there came also a change in the attitude of the South African whites, but especially of the Afrikaners, toward the centralization of governmental power. Traditionally they opposed strong government, but the policy of apartheid could be carried out only by a highly centralized political authority. Their complete commitment to apartheid prepared the South African whites for a drastic extension and centralization of governmental power. Few peoples in the world have accepted such detailed regulation of their lives.[2]

Long before he became prime minister, D. F. Malan had urged the necessity for a policy of racial segregation. In 1940 he introduced a resolution in Parliament that such a policy "immediately be put into effect for residential, industrial and political purposes." He also demanded a law to prevent miscegenation. He declared that in this motion Parliament confronted "South Africa's greatest and most urgent problem." War was a passing matter but the racial problem was ever present. It was met daily "in our streets, in our political and economic life, a problem which we meet in our homes, which affects the future of our children and grandchildren. That problem will decide the future of the White race and also of the non-White races in South Africa."[3] The Nationalist government lost little time in introducing and enacting a broad and intensive program of racial legislation.

Only the most important racial laws put on the statute books since 1948 can be mentioned here, as the amount of such legislation is massive. Obviously, a first requirement of a system of racial segregation as all-embracing as that practiced in South Africa is a registration of the population by race. This was provided for by an act of 1950 in accordance with which persons were classified as white, native, colored, or Asian.[4] Great difficulty has been experienced in arriving at an exact definition of a colored person. Appearance and acceptance by the community are the tests applied.[5] The racial classification required by the Population Registration Act caused many persons hardship and humiliation. Their racial status was sometimes uncertain for a long period. In some cases families were broken up because of diverse classification of members. An Immorality Act of 1927 penalized extramarital relations between Europeans and Africans; in 1949 the Nation-

[1] Chapter 2.
[2] See the Introduction in Edgar H. Brookes, ed., *Apartheid: A Documentary Study of Modern South Africa* (London, 1968).
[3] *Hansard*, vol. 41, col. 594, 30 Jan. 1940.
[4] Technically the Asians constituted a subgroup of the coloreds.
[5] South African Institute of Race Relations, *A Survey of Race Relations in South Africa, 1962* (Johannesburg, 1963), pp. 70–72.

alist government passed a law prohibiting mixed marriages and in 1950 amended the Immorality Act to extend its provisions to relations between Europeans and coloreds.

Parliament in 1950 enacted the Group Areas Act which authorizes the government to proclaim an area reserved for occupation or ownership by members of a specified racial group. Families that have lived in an area for decades may be ejected from their old homes. Whole communities may be uprooted and relocated. Some of the new areas are a considerable distance from the heart of the city and thus impose a severe hardship on their inhabitants. Indian traders have experienced not only hardship but frequently also economic loss. While whites are sometimes requested to move out of an area, this occurs rarely in comparison with the numbers of the other racial groups who are compulsorily displaced.[6] Elementary education had always been on a segregated basis in South Africa, but when Africans became ready for higher education they were admitted to some of the established universities.[7] By an act of 1959 the government adopted the policy of complete segregation also in higher education, and separate universities for nonwhites were established.

Under the Nationalists, the nonwhites' political participation has declined. Until 1936 the Bantu and the coloreds in Cape Colony had the right to vote for members of Parliament. In that year the Bantu were taken off the common voters' roll and placed on a separate roll with the right to elect three white members of the House of Assembly and four senators. In 1960 this indirect native representation was abolished. The coloreds of the Cape were represented in the Cape Provincial Council and in Parliament by four whites in the House, but this token representation was abolished in 1968. This deprivation of political representation was justified on the ground of the new policy of separate development. The Bantu ultimately would have citizenship in one or other of

[6] This is not a study of the policy of apartheid in its internal aspects. Suffice it to note that "petty" apartheid (the regulations which govern social relations between Europeans and non-Europeans) forbids intercourse between the races by innumerable laws and regulations. See Neville Rubin, *This Is Apartheid*, new ed. (London, 1966).

[7] Cape Town and Witwatersrand did so and were known as "open universities." On the subject of South African racial policy and education, see an interesting and excellent UNESCO publication: *Apartheid: Its Effects on Education, Science, Culture and Information* (Paris, 1967).

the Bantustans. But this scarcely plausible justification cannot be used in the case of the coloreds and Indians as no separate territorial political unit is planned for them. They must find their compensation in representation in the councils of limited functions.[8]

South Africa also has a network of drastic, repressive laws which are not racially discriminatory but which evidently are thought necessary to enforce the policy of apartheid. In 1950 there was enacted the Suppression of Communism Act, under which persons and organizations may be banned for furthering the aims of Communism. Banning may involve what amounts to internment in a specified place or area and even house arrest. A person banned may be prohibited from being or becoming a member of specified organizations and from attending gatherings of any kind. To record, publish, or disseminate any speech, utterance, or writing of a banned person is an offense under the law. Banned persons may not work as teachers, lawyers, or journalists.[9]

In the General Law Amendment Act, 1963, there was the ninety-day detention clause which was withdrawn in 1965 to be replaced by the 180-day detention measure of the Criminal Procedure Amendment Act of 1965, under which the minister of justice may authorize the arrest and detention for a maximum of six months of any person who is likely to give evidence for the state with respect to certain offenses, as long as that detention is deemed to be in the interest of such a person or of the administration of justice.[10] At every session of Parliament the ministry asks for additional drastic legislation to control threatened disorders and terrorism. Under the Terrorism Act of 1967 the government was granted the power to detain persons indefinitely for interrogation. The

[8] The Colored Peoples Representative Council and the South African Indian Council.

[9] The number of banned persons was 102 in 1962, 303 in 1964, 664 in 1967, 498 in 1968, and 355 in 1969 (*The Star*, Weekly Air Edition, 2 Aug. 1969). Banishment has been called civil death.

[10] The International Commission of Jurists characterized the Act as giving "the most extraordinary powers that have ever been granted outside a period of emergency" (International Commission of Jurists, *Bulletin* [Geneva, 1966]). Six years earlier the International Commission of Jurists in a report on *South Africa and the Law* (Geneva, 1960), p. 91, concluded: "In pursuit of this objective [apartheid] the Government has established a rigid and all embracing network of legislation which denies to a vast majority of the population those opportunities without which the legitimate aspirations and dignity of a human being cannot be realized."

act defined terrorism so broadly as to include "embarrassing the administration of the affairs of the state." The act was made retroactive five years. In 1969 the so-called BOSS Act made communicating anything about what the Bureau for State Security is doing an offense punishable with a maximum of seven years of confinement in jail. The law authorizes the prime minister to stop taking evidence in any court if he decides it is contrary to state security or interest. Thus it gives the government —and deprives the courts—of the power to decide what is prejudicial to safety and what is in the state's interest.[11]

Apartheid was used as a slogan in the 1948 election campaign; it was not presented as a program. The opposition, after the election, sought to obtain from the government clearer statements as to what it meant. A Nationalist leader declared that his party had proclaimed total separation as a policy but that no ill-considered steps would be taken and that it might take fifty or even a hundred years to achieve.[12] Prime Minister Malan said that total territorial separation was "impractical under present circumstances in South Africa, where our whole economic structure is to a large extent based on Native labour."[13] General Smuts stated that only one conclusion was possible, that it meant more than the traditional policy of social and residential separation—it meant total separation. "But what does that mean," he asked, "if *apartheid* can only be carried out by complete separation? It means a Bantu state on the one side and a European state on the other side."[14] It took the Nationalists nearly a decade to acknowledge that this was the only logical conclusion to their basic premise.

The racial policy of South Africa in the form of the treatment of Indians had been before the General Assembly from the beginning of the United Nations, but it was not until 1952 that the policy of apartheid appeared on its agenda. As early as 1946 the General Assembly had unanimously adopted an anti-racial resolution, but only in general terms and naming no state.[15] The General Assembly proceeded

---

[11] Professor Edgar Brookes, the former senator, in commenting on the bill when it was still before Parliament said that South Africa had virtually become a police state. "As far as the Africans are concerned, it is a kind of Gestapo," he said of the police force (*The Star*, Weekly Air Edition, 21 June 1969).

[12] Michael D. C. de W. Nel. *Hansard*, vol. 71, col. 4097.

[13] Ibid., col. 4113.

[14] Ibid., col. 4074.

[15] UNGAOR, 1st Sess., Plenary Meetings, Verbatim Record, 19 Nov. 1946, p. 975.

cautiously in considering a resolution directed at the policies of a specific member state and acted only after the constitutionality of such action had been thoroughly discussed. The request for placing the question on the agenda came from a number of Asian and Middle East states. The General Assembly adopted two resolutions: one declaring a policy of racial segregation as necessarily based on doctrines of racial discrimination, established a commission of three members to study the racial situation in the Union of South Africa in the light of the purposes and principles of the Charter and to report its conclusions to the General Assembly at its next session; the other called on member states "to bring their policies into conformity with their obligation under the Charter to promote the observance of human rights and fundamental freedoms."[16]

The South African delegate fought valiantly both in the committee and in the plenary session stages to obtain a decision on the competence of the General Assembly to deal with his country's racial policies. He introduced a resolution declaring that the General Assembly lacked competence to consider apartheid, arguing that Article 2, paragraph 7, of the Charter prohibited United Nations intervention in the domestic affairs of member states and barred even discussion of apartheid in the General Assembly.[17] The domestic jurisdiction clause of the Charter, he contended, represented for the small states what the veto represented for the great powers. It gave the former protection of their inherent right to manage their own affairs without outside interference. Without this protection the small states would not have become members of the United Nations any more than the great powers would have joined without the veto. The problem had been discussed fully at the San Francisco Conference which drafted the Charter, and the agreed interpretation was that the reservation extended even to discussion. The argument that Article 2, paragraph 7, did not apply in cases alleged to involve human rights, he declared, is erroneous. Articles 55 and 56 of the Charter left each member state with exclusive jurisdiction over its

[16] UNGAOR, 7th Sess., Supp. No. 20 (A/2361), Res. No. 616A(VII) and Res. No. 616B(VII), pp. 8–9, 5 Dec. 1952.

[17] The debates on the draft resolution took place in the Ad Hoc Political Committee and in the plenary meetings of the General Assembly. UNGAOR, 7th Sess., Ad Hoc Political Committee, Summary Records, 12 Nov. 1952, pp. 65–125; UNGAOR, 7th Sess., Plenary Meetings, Verbatim Record, 17 Oct. and 5 Dec. 1952, pp. 53–69, 331–36.

own affairs until by international agreement provision was made for action.

Neither in the Charter nor in any binding international agreement was there a definition of human rights against which the actions of governments could be tested. That was why a covenant of human rights was regarded as necessary. The charge that South Africa's racial policy was a threat to peace, the Union delegate branded as "unrealistic and mischievous." His government was not threatening any state with hostile action. If South Africa's racial laws, which all dealt with purely domestic concerns, constituted a threat to the peace of the world, what about tariffs, immigration, and fiscal policies which certainly affect relations between states? It should be obvious that if intervention in the internal affairs of member states was justified on the ground that state action on matters of purely domestic concern constituted a threat to international peace, no small state could ever hope to conduct its own affairs without fear of external interference. But the United Nations had been established to protect all states, and especially the small ones.

South Africa received significant support for its position. The British delegate declared the matter outside the competence of the United Nations and refused to identify his government in any way with the discussion of the substance of the matter or the draft resolution arising from it. If a real threat to peace did exist the Security Council could consider the question and take measures under Chapter VII. He stated that it should be noted that Articles 55 and 56 dealt not only with human rights but also with economic, social, and cultural activities; thus if interference was permissible for a state's failure to promote human rights then no aspect of a state's internal affairs would be free from interference by the United Nations. The United Kingdom delegate issued a warning: most states had problems to solve that were related to purposes set out in the Charter. Debate on them in the international organization was not likely to further a solution. The French delegate asserted rather bluntly that the first draft resolution was a clear case of intervention in the internal affairs of a member state in contravention of Article 2, paragraph 7, of the Charter. The Mexican representative declared that nonintervention was "a fundamental principle which could not be ignored," that Article 2, paragraph 7, of the Charter was "a powerful instrument in defence of small states." But here it came in conflict with another principle, namely, respect for human rights. Reconciling these two principles was a very thorny problem for the United Nations.

The Netherlands delegation took a position which was shared by a number of member states. It did not doubt the General Assembly's right to discuss the question of South Africa's racial policies under Article 55 of the Charter, but it did question that body's right to make recommendations. Only an advisory opinion of the International Court of Justice could decide that.[18] Norway and Sweden took a different line. The repercussions which the race conflicts and the racial policy of South Africa had had on world opinion and on the relations between states had removed the matter beyond the realm of purely domestic affairs, but this in itself did not make the United Nations competent to deal with the question. The United Nations had never been intended to serve as an instrument for the elimination of all disturbing factors in the world. However, the situation was different if states had assumed obligations. If they had, their policies in such matters were no longer exclusively their own concern. Under Articles 55 and 56 of the Charter the member states had assumed the obligation to promote a greater degree of human liberty and equality. When a state disregarded this obligation and placed new restrictions on the exercise of human liberties and equalities, the matter at once became the concern of the United Nations. By the Group Areas Act and other laws and regulations South Africa had legalized actions which all members had pledged themselves to abandon.[19]

In the debate the United States took a middle position, wishing, according to its spokesman, to avoid "both excess of zeal and timid legalism" in dealing with the question. The United States questioned the wisdom of the South African racial policy as being incompatible with the generally accepted interpretation of the obligations of the Charter; in the long run its repercussions might be adverse to the South African government itself and harmful to the development of racial harmony in the world. But the role of the United Nations was limited; it could not intervene in matters essentially within the domestic jurisdiction of states. "It had no power to impose standards but only to proclaim them.

[18] New Zealand, the United Kingdom, Norway, and Sweden also favored asking the court for an advisory opinion.

[19] The proper action in this case would seem to be expulsion under Article 6 of the Charter.

It could reaffirm the principles of respect for human rights and call upon Member States to orient national policy towards embodying those principles in law and custom as rapidly as local conditions permitted. Such an appeal, in general terms, would avoid the vexing issue of competence and obviate the danger to the stability of the Organization inherent in singling out for direct action special legislation of a Member State. Moreover, it might be more effective than any recommendation which might injure national pride."

Most of the delegations probably shared the views expressed by the representative of India, who held that Article 2, paragraph 7, did not bar discussion by the organs of the United Nations. Article 1, paragraph 3, of the Charter proclaimed promotion of respect for human rights as one of the purposes of the United Nations and Article 10 authorized the General Assembly to discuss any question within the scope of the Charter and to make recommendations to the members of the United Nations on the matter. Moreover, Article 13 required the General Assembly to initiate studies and make recommendations for the purpose of assisting in the realization of human rights and fundamental freedoms for all. This is what the proposed resolution sought to do. Maintenance of international peace was one of the primary purposes of the United Nations and the situation in South Africa clearly constituted a threat to international peace. The Pakistani delegation took an even broader position. The United Nations could not prevent war by closing its eyes to the perpetuation of circumstances which must lead to war. The situation in South Africa was linked with colonialism—the "enforcement of white supremacy in the colonial parts of the world."

It is interesting to examine the vote on the three resolutions before the General Assembly. The South African resolution, which would have declared that the General Assembly lacked competence to deal with the Union's racial policy, was rejected by a vote of forty-five to six, with eight abstentions. Only Australia, Belgium, France, Luxembourg, and Portugal voted with South Africa in favor of it. The United States abstained. By this vote the General Assembly decided at least negatively that the question was within its competence. Resolution "A," which called for the establishment of a three-man commission to study the racial situation, was adopted by a vote of thirty-five to one, with thirty-four abstentions, while Resolution "B," which called all member states to bring their policies into conformity with their obligations under the Charter to promote the observance of human rights and fundamental freedoms, was adopted by a vote of twenty-four to one, with thirty-four abstentions. Striking is the number of abstentions in each of the last two votes. Resolution "B" received the vote of less than half of the members present. Do these figures justify the conclusion that many member states were more interested in putting pressure on a particular country to observe humanitarian standards which they were not prepared to accept for themselves?

The Commission on the Racial Situation in the Union of South Africa reported in each of three successive years. The South African government refused to give the commission any cooperation or to allow its members to enter South African territory. The commission's first, rather lengthy report was based on an examination of the declarations of Union politicians, the study of the principal racial laws of South Africa, and memoranda submitted to it and the hearing of witnesses. The commission concluded that "these facts and figures constitute obvious racial discrimination. Four-fifths of the population are thereby reduced to a humiliating level of inferiority which is injurious to human dignity and makes the full development of personality impossible or very difficult"; and it considered that "the doctrine of racial differentiation and superiority on which the apartheid policy is based is scientifically false, extremely dangerous to international peace and international relations, as is proved by the tragic experience of the world in the past twenty years, and contrary to the dignity and worth of the human person."[20] The commission was, however, conciliatory in its attitude. It was convinced that "if the South African government merely indicated its wish to review its racial policy and to accept spontaneously, in complete sovereignty and independence, the fraternal collaboration of the community of nations in solving that problem, a simple gesture of that kind might even now clear the air and open a new path of justice and peace to the development of the Union of South Africa within the United Nations."[21]

The attitude of the General Assembly as well as of the commission remained conciliatory throughout the 1950s, regardless of the adamantly noncooperative position of South Africa. In 1953 the General

[20] UNGAOR, 8th Sess., "Report of the Commission on the Racial Situation in South Africa," Supp. No. 16 (A/2505) and (A/2505/Add 1), 1953, p. 116.
[21] Ibid., p. 119.

Assembly requested the commission to continue its study and to suggest measures which would help to alleviate the situation and promote a peaceful settlement.[22]

In its second and third reports the commission suggested that the United Nations should offer "the intellectual and material resources which the United Nations specialized agencies can command," for the purpose of promoting a peaceful settlement.[23] At every session the General Assembly adopted a resolution deploring South Africa's refusal to cooperate, affirming its conviction that perseverance in such disciminatory policies is inconsistent with the Charter and the forces of progress and international cooperation in implementing the ideals of equality, freedom, and justice, and calling upon the government of South Africa to reconsider its position and revise its policies in the light of its obligations and responsibilities under the Charter.[24] In spite of the mild mood of the General Assembly as a whole, the government of South Africa became irritated and offended to such a degree that in the general debate in the 1955 General Assembly the South African representative declared that his delegation would not participate further in the discussions of his country's racial policies. In justification of this decision he said that for nine successive years the Union government had been attacked because of its domestic policies and for nine years had replied with "patience and forbearance." His government was no longer prepared to continue replying to these attacks.[25] When the First Committee accepted the report of the Commission on the Racial Situation in the Union of South Africa, External Affairs Minister Louw, who headed the Union's delegation, upon authorization of his government withdrew the South African delegation from the meetings of the United

[22] UNGAOR, 8th Sess., Supp. No. 17 (A/2630), Res. No. 721(VIII), p. 6, 8 Dec. 1953.

[23] UNGAOR, 10th Sess., "Third Report of the Commission on the Racial Situation in South Africa," Supp. No. 14 (A/2931), p. 96, 1955.

[24] UNGAOR, 9th Sess., Supp. No. 21 (A/2890), Res. No. 820(IX), p. 9, 14 Dec. 1954; 10th Sess., Supp. No. 19 (A/3116), Res. No. 917(X), p. 8, 6 Dec. 1955; 11th Sess., Supp. No. 17 (A/3572), Res. No. 1016 (XI), p. 5, 30 Jan. 1957; 12th Sess., Supp. No. 18 (A/3805), Res. No. 1178(XII), p. 7, 26 Nov. 1957; 13th Sess., Supp. No. 18 (A/4090), Res. No. 1248(XIII), p. 7, 30 Oct. 1958; 14th Sess., Supp. No. 16 (A/4354), Res. No. 1375(XIV), p. 7, 17 Nov. 1959.

[25] UNGAOR, 10th Sess., Plenary Meetings, Verbatim Record, 29 Sept. 1955, p. 160.

Nations.[26] When the General Assembly in 1956 again voted to place the question of South Africa's racial policies on its agenda, the Union delegation announced the decision of its government that South Africa would remain a member of the United Nations but that until the United Nations decided to conform to the provisions of its own Charter, specifically Article 2, paragraph 7, South Africa would maintain only a token representation in the General Assembly.[27] Louw claimed that the partial withdrawal had a salutary effect. There was a more friendly tone in the 1957 session, and South Africa's friends had urged her to return.[28] She then resumed full participation in the General Assembly.

The South African government seemed to believe that the prime minister's announcement in 1959 of the policy of separate development would modify the attitude of foreign governments and peoples toward the Union. In the foreign policy debate in the House in 1959 the external affairs minister complained bitterly that the prejudice against South Africa had increased, but a leading spokesman for the National party expressed gratification that the "outside world is prepared more and more to appreciate South Africa's standpoint."[29] If there was a trend toward a friendlier attitude toward South Africa and a more sympathetic understanding of its problems, a sharp turn in the opposite direction occurred in 1960, which was a bad year for the Union. In that year sixteen new African states were admitted to membership in the United Nations and in 1961 four more. At the end of 1963, African states—excluding South Africa but including Egypt—numbered thirty-seven or about a third of the total membership of the United Nations. It was in February 1960 that Prime Minister Harold Macmillan made his famous "wind of change" speech to the members of the Union Parliament. He tried to make them aware of the rapidly changing conditions in the world. He emphasized the importance of keeping the African states from joining the Communist bloc, but he dissociated the United Kingdom from South Africa's policies and stated that his government intended to move rapidly in granting the colonies independence. The

---

[26] Louw's statement in the House of Assembly, *Hansard*, vol. 91, cols. 4434–35, 26 April 1956.

[27] External Affairs Minister Louw made a statement justifying the decision in the House on 10 June 1957 (*Hansard*, vol. 95, cols. 7595–7611).

[28] Ibid., vol. 101, col. 5563, 11 May 1959.

[29] Ibid., cols. 5521 and 5577 (Carel de Wet).

British sought to create a society which respected the rights of individuals and gave men the opportunity to have an increasing share in political power. In countries inhabited by different races "it has been our aim to find the means by which community can become more of a community, and fellowship can be fostered between its various parts." He also gave warning that Britain's policy might run counter to that of South Africa. "It may well be that in trying to do our duty as we see it, we shall sometimes make difficulties for you. It this proves to be so we shall regret it. But I know that even so, you would not ask us to flinch from doing our duty. You, too, will do your duty as you see it."[30]

Macmillan's speech did nothing to diminish the difference in outlook between the British and white South Africans. It may have increased the determination of the Nationalists to accelerate their policy of separate development and emboldened the Africans to resist government policies. However that may be, not many weeks after the British prime minister's challenging speech the tragedy at Sharpeville occurred. In quelling demonstrations against the pass laws the police killed sixty-nine Africans and wounded 178. In a disturbance at Langa near Cape Town on the same day (March 21) two Africans were killed and forty-seven were wounded or injured. Reaction to these events was immediate and worldwide. The Pan-African Federation conference decided to employ commercial, diplomatic, and political sanctions against South Africa. The Netherlands prime minister declared that the sad events in South Africa were a consequence of its racial policy.[31]

Within ten days after the Sharpeville riots the Security Council of the United Nations met to consider the situation—convened at the request of twenty-nine Afro-Asian states. Though not a member of the Council, South Africa was permitted to state its case. The Union delegate questioned the competence of the Security Council to consider the matter. Articles 34 and 35 of the Charter, on which the proponents for Security Council action relied, gave that body power to consider only disturbances and situations arising directly between states and not situations within states. There were disturbances and riots in many countries, he observed. Were the members of the Council willing to

---

[30] Nicholas Mansergh, ed., *Documents and Speeches on Commonwealth Affairs, 1952–1962* (London, 1963), pp. 347–51.

[31] South African Institute of Race Relations, *A Survey of Race Relations in South Africa, 1959–1960* (Johannesburg, 1961), pp. 274–86.

submit to the consideration of the Council their efforts to maintain law and order in their own countries? It was his government's belief that the annual discussion of South Africa's racial problem in the General Assembly had helped to inflame the situation. It would be even more serious if the discussion in the Security Council were to embolden the agitators or serve as incitement to further demonstrations and rioting with subsequent attacks on police and civilians trying to carry on a normal life. If this were to be the result the blame would rest squarely on the shoulders of the Council.[32]

The United Kingdom and France adhered to their position that the matter fell under Article 2, paragraph 7, of the Charter. Italy did likewise, but with a reservation. It was troubled by what appeared to be an internal contradiction within the Charter itself. There was the need "to give practical expression to the provisions of the Charter concerning human rights and fundamental freedoms and those aimed at protecting States from interference in their internal affairs. Both provisions are of fundamental importance in the present structure of the United Nations." How to steer a proper course between the two basic requirements was the problem. In the present unusual situation considerations of legality would not weigh as much as "the special political purport of the recent tragic developments which appear to justify within limits, some kind of exceptional procedure on our part."[33] The delegate of Ceylon bluntly answered the question of jurisdiction pressed by South Africa. It was true that there were disturbances in many countries, but they were due to sudden emotional eruptions or to misguided actions on the part of the authorities or to other factors, but the disorders in South Africa were connected with a "consistent, deliberate and persistent" attempt "almost to safeguard the interests of a small minority, of a certain racial group, and for that purpose not only to disregard but completely to extinguish the ordinary human rights of a majority."[34] The delegate of Tunisia made the same point. By its policy South Africa had created a dangerous situation not only within its own territory but also for the peace and security of its continent, and consequently, of the whole world.[35]

---

[32] United Nations, Security Council, Official Records (hereafter cited as UNSCOR), 851st Meeting, 30 Mar. 1960, pp. 8–15.

[33] Ibid., pp. 3–4.

[34] Ibid., p. 6.

[35] Ibid., p. 23.

On April 1, the Security Council adopted a resolution in which it recognized that the situation in South Africa, if continued, might endanger international peace and security, deplored the policies and actions of the government of South Africa which gave rise to the situation, and called upon the Union government "to initiate measures aimed at bringing about racial harmony based on equality in order to ensure that the present situation does not continue or recur and to abandon its policies of *apartheid* and racial discrimination." It also requested the secretary-general, in consultation with the government of the Union of South Africa, to make such arrangements as would adequately help in upholding the purposes and principles of the Charter and to report to the Security Council whenever necessary and appropriate.[36]

Secretary-General Dag Hammarskjold visited South Africa in January 1961. In extending the invitation to the secretary-general the South African government stated that no infringement on the sovereign independence of the Union, or intervention in its domestic affairs, or any action implying accountability to the United Nations for its policies or their implementation could be implied or countenanced. The government found the talks with the secretary-general useful and constructive and invited him to visit the Union again.[37] The secretary-general in his report to the Security Council said he had had six meetings with the prime minister and had had unofficial contacts with various sections of the South African community but that no mutually acceptable arrangement had been found. However, he did not regard this lack of agreement as conclusive. The exchange of views in general had served a most useful purpose; he looked forward to a continuation of the consultations.[38]

The South African government was undoubtedly frightened by the disturbances of 1960. Several hundred million dollars of private capital had been withdrawn from the country; emigration exceeded immigration; and the world had reacted to the tragic events with stronger

[36] UNSCOR, 856th Meeting, 1 April 1960. Resolution S/4300; for text see *Yearbook of the United Nations, 1960,* p. 147.

[37] Statement of Prime Minister Verwoerd to the House of Assembly, 23 Jan. 1961, *Hansard,* vol. 106, col. 15.

[38] *Yearbook of the United Nations, 1960,* pp. 146–47. Also see UNGAOR, 16th Sess., "Annual Report of the Secretary-General on the Work of the Organization, 16 June 1960–15 June 1961," Supp. No. 1 (A/4800), p. 81.

aversion to South Africa's racial policy, which almost universally was believed to be the root cause of Bantu demonstrations. But Verwoerd's policy of "granite" won against flesh and blood. Order was restored and the government recovered its confidence. Also the Nationalists won the popular referendum in October on the republic issue, even if only by a 2 percent margin. In the no-confidence debate in the House in the following January, the prime minister was undaunted and unyielding. He declared there would be no wavering in the government's determination to move forward with its separate development policy. When the question of the treatment of the coloreds was raised, he declared that they would never be given direct representation in Parliament. Nor would the Asians. The government had to choose between "international popularity and the destruction of the White nation in South Africa."[39]

The United Nations and South Africa were both moving steadily to positions from which there was no retreat. The latter's partial withdrawal from the General Assembly had had little, or at best only a temporary, effect on the former's attitude. The speeches of the delegates of South Africa became more combative. In his main policy speech in the General Assembly, External Affairs Minister Louw asserted that South Africans regarded with apprehension the signs of growing Communist influence in Africa south of the Sahara. Well-known Communists had been the leaders of the African National Congress, a subversive organization which had contributed to the Sharpeville riots. Communists were busy stirring up trouble in South West Africa. He charged that "the bulk of the 41 States that are this year again preferring charges against South Africa have not come to this Assembly with clean hands." Riots in India were a regular occurrence and they had been "ruthlessly suppressed by the police," with frequent loss of life. The critics of South Africa frequently had attacked the conditions under which the Bantu were living, yet shocking conditions prevailed in India, as well as discrimination. He referred to the treatment and condition of the Lapps in Sweden and Norway. A system of slavery existed in Arabia, in certain other countries of the Near East, and in Western African countries. Racial discrimination was practised in Liberia and democracy had all but disappeared in Ghana. "The unsavory history of oppression and the denial of human rights and freedoms in

[39] *Hansard*, vol. 103, col. 98. The no-confidence debate took place on 23–27 Jan. 1961, ibid., cols. 17–322.

Soviet Russia and her colonies—and in other Communist countries—
are so well known that further information or comment from me would
be superfluous."[40]

A speech of the same tenor a year later provoked the Liberian
delegate to move that the whole speech be deleted from the official
records. He declared that the speech was an "insult to every African
here, and not only to every African, but to every man of intelligence."
He was supported by the Ethiopian delegate. The delegate of Australia
objected. The proposed action would become a precedent so that a
statement by a sovereign government in the United Nations could be
expunged because other members were opposed to it. Statements were
needed in order to rebut them, and a statement could not be answered if
it did not appear in the records.[41] The motion to expunge Louw's speech
was withdrawn, but a motion of censure was adopted by a vote of
sixty-seven in favor, one against, twenty abstentions, and nine not
participating in the vote.[42]

As the South African representative became less temperate in his
objections and protests, the delegates of other member states became
more direct and blunt in their statements. The United Kingdom, which
had supported South Africa's contention that its racial policies fell
under the reservation of Article 2, paragraph 7, began to show signs of
wavering. Its delegate declared in 1961 that his government feared that
the continued pursuit of the policy of apartheid would disastrously
affect "not only the peoples of South Africa but also reach far beyond
its borders."[43] Another member which South Africa liked to regard as
its friend—the United States—began to take a hard line. Its delegate
declared that "deliberate deprivation of human rights had always been
and must continue to be the legitimate concern of the United Nations."
South Africa had broken the pledge undertaken under the Charter, but

[40] UNGAOR, 15th Sess., 905th Plenary Meeting, Verbatim Record, I, 723–30, 14
Oct. 1960.
[41] To this argument the Liberian delegate made the interesting reply that if a
statement was not part of the record, "we need not answer it. There is nothing to
answer."
[42] UNGAOR, 16th Sess., Plenary Meetings, Verbatim Record, I, 387–95, 11 Oct.
1961 (Louw's speech), and I, 395–406 (discussion of motions to expunge and to
censure). France, the United Kingdom, and the United States were among the
members not participating in the voting.
[43] UNGAOR, 16th Sess., Special Political Committee, Summary Records, p. 69,
31 Oct. 1961.

even if there had been no Charter and South Africa had not been a member of the United Nations, the United States would have condemned apartheid; the provisions of the Charter reinforced his country's disapproval. A "mental barrier" seemed to separate the government of South Africa from all other governments, which made it insensible to the depth of unanimity of the world community's opposition to apartheid. The American delegate declared that his government was not convinced by attempts to justify apartheid as benefiting the disenfranchised millions of nonwhite South Africans. It did not seem likely that the South African government would ever grant full independence to the so-called Bantu states. "Its intention seemed rather to be to keep the non-white population in a subordinate status in enclaves within its territory, for ever, and exploit them as a source of labour."[44]

The Indian delegate again answered South Africa's charge that many of the members which were condemning South Africa were themselves guilty of discrimination and the denial of human rights, and that the United Nations had a double standard. He admitted that there were few countries in which there was not some form of discrimination. "South Africa was criticized chiefly not on account of the enormity of its discrimination, but because of its insistence on pursuing racial discrimination as a State policy sanctioned by law. It went so far as to advocate 'apartheid' as the only sensible policy and an ideal for all other multi-racial countries, even adducing religious arguments in support of its claim."[45]

The Sixteenth (1961) General Assembly rejected a thirty-one-power draft resolution relating to possible expulsion of South Africa from the United Nations and recommending sanctions, but it adopted a resolution which took a slight step beyond its earlier ones. It called the attention of the Security Council to Article 11, paragraph 3, which authorizes the General Assembly to call the attention of the Council to "situations which are likely to endanger international peace and security" and it urged all states "to take such separate and collective action as is open to them in conformity with the Charter to bring about an abandonment of those policies."[46]

[44] Ibid., pp. 41–42.
[45] Ibid., p. 95.
[46] UNGAOR, 16th Sess., Res. No. 1663(XVI), Annexes, III, Agenda Item 76, Doc. A/4968, pp. 9–10, 28 Nov. 1961. Of significance was the vote for the

As the world's disapproval of South Africa's racial policy intensified, Foreign Minister Louw's utterances became more provocative. In his speech in the general debate at the Seventeenth Session of the General Assembly he painted a dismal picture of conditions in much of the world in contrast with an idyllic situation in his country.[47] This was scarcely a way to make friends or to influence delegates, except adversely. The General Assembly adopted a strong resolution—one that went considerably beyond regretting, deploring, deprecating, and reaffirming. It requested the member states separately or collectively, a) to break off diplomatic relations with South Africa or to refrain from establishing them; b) to close their ports to vessels flying the South African flag; c) to enact legislation prohibiting their ships from entering South African ports; d) to boycott South African goods and to refrain from exporting goods, including arms and munitions, to South Africa; and e) to refuse landing and passage facilities to South African aircraft. The resolution also called for the establishment of a special committee to keep under review the racial policies of the government of South Africa during the period when the Assembly was not in session. Since the General Assembly can only recommend, it requested the Security Council "to take appropriate measures, including sanctions, to secure South Africa's compliance with the resolutions of the General Assembly and of the Security Council on this subject and, if necessary, to consider action under Article 6 [expulsion from the organization] of the Charter."[48] South Africa could take little comfort from the number of members voting against the adoption of the resolution. It included states such as the Netherlands whose friendship and goodwill meant much to white South Africans, and in this particular case to the Afrikaners. The Dutch delegation in explaining its vote declared that although it recognized that many countries are guilty of some form of

---

resolution by the United Kingdom, whose delegate declared that his government was "glad to be able to give further expression to its abhorrence of *apartheid*" by voting for it. He sincerely hoped that the overwhelming vote cast in favor of the resolution would really have effect (UNGAOR, 16th Sess., Plenary Meetings, Verbatim Record, II, 889, 28 Nov. 1961). The vote was 97 in favor, 2 (South Africa and Portugal) against, and only 1 abstention.

[47] UNGAOR, 17th Sess., Plenary Meetings, Verbatim Record, I, p. 59, 24 Sept. 1962.

[48] The resolution was adopted by a vote of 67 for, 16 against, and 23 abstentions. UNGAOR, 17th Sess., Plenary Meetings, Verbatim Record, II, 679; Res. No. 1761(XVII), Supp. No. 17 (A/5217), p. 9, 6 Nov. 1962.

discrimination, it could "hardly find a formula severe enough to express our abhorrence of the systematic infringements of human rights suffered by the non-white population of South Africa as a result of the deliberate policy of that country." The hearts and minds of the South African government needed to be changed, but this could not be achieved by placing it in a position of "national 'apartheid' among the nations of the world." Moreover the Netherlands delegation doubted the efficacy of punishment meted out to a country as a whole. It would prove harmful to "precisely that majority of the South African people which we are morally bound to defend and assist in their struggle for freedom."[49]

The African states then turned to the Security Council for action.[50] They wanted to secure that body's backing for the General Assembly resolution adopted in 1962, that is, to make the recommendations of the resolution obligatory on all members of the United Nations. In July 1963 thirty-two African members requested a meeting of the Security Council "to consider the explosive situation in the Republic of South Africa, which constitutes a serious threat to international peace and security." They were convinced that some of the big powers were giving aid and comfort to South Africa. By bringing the matter before the Security Council they hoped to force these states to take a more positive position. The Council adopted a resolution calling upon South Africa to abandon the policies of apartheid and to liberate all persons inprisoned or interned for opposing apartheid, called upon all states to cease forthwith the sale and shipment of arms, ammunition of all types and military vehicles to South Africa, and requested the secretary-general to keep the situation in South Africa under observation and to report to the Security Council by October 30, 1963. There were no votes against the resolution, but France and the United Kingdom again abstained.[51]

[49] UNGAOR, 17th Sess., Plenary Meetings, Verbatim Record, II, 680, 6 Nov. 1962. Members voting against the resolution were France, Greece, Ireland, Japan, Luxembourg, Netherlands, New Zealand, Portugal, South Africa, Spain, Turkey, United Kingdom, United States, Australia, Belgium, and Canada.

[50] The African drive against South Africa took on momentum after a conference of African heads of state which met at Addis Ababa in June 1963. Apparently the strategy adopted was to hold up to contempt the racial policies of South Africa and to seek the application of sanctions as well as to press for South Africa's expulsion from international organizations.

[51] Resolution S/5386, adopted 7 Aug. 1963, UNSCOR, 1056th Meeting. For text of resolution see *Yearbook of the United Nations, 1963*, p. 20.

The special committee set up in conformity with the 1962 General Assembly's resolution reported in September 1963 that the extreme gravity of the situation in South Africa called for new measures. It proposed the expulsion of the Republic from the United Nations and its specialized agencies. The committee suggested that a study should be made of how to ensure an effective embargo on arms and oil destined for South Africa, and recommended the discouragement of investments in South Africa and loans to the government or private companies and emigration to the Republic. Neighboring states should provide asylum, and relief to political refugees and assistance to victims of apartheid should be given through appropriate international agencies.[52] When the South African delegate rose in the General Assembly to reply to the committee's report, Algeria moved that the proceedings be suspended for twenty minutes as a symbolic demonstration of abhorrence of racial discrimination. The motion was adopted by a vote of sixty-eight to seventeen, with twenty-two abstentions. As the South African delegate mounted the rostrum after the suspension a large number of delegates —African, Communist, some Asian and Latin American—walked out.[53]

The Scandinavian countries came to the Eighteenth Session of the General Assembly with a constructive proposal for an alternative to apartheid. Their leading spokesman, Per Haekkerup, foreign minister of Denmark, noted that apartheid must be abolished as contrary to the principles of the United Nations' Charter and that if persuasion was not sufficient to induce South Africa to change its policy, graduated pressure would have to be used. Haekkerup feared that a policy of sanctions alone might well "defeat its own ends, aggravate the present state of tension in the area and bring the possibility of tragic events closer." It was now necessary to formulate a supplementary policy. The European population of South Africa feared that the abandonment of white supremacy meant abandonment of their own existence. It was the duty of the United Nations to prove to them that this was not so, that there was an alternative to catastrophe. "Changing a society so deeply rooted in *apartheid* and dominated by a minority into a free, democratic, multiracial society may well prove to be a task which cannot be solved by the people of South Africa alone," he concluded. "I feel convinced

[52] UNGAOR, 18th Sess., Plenary Meetings, Annexes, II, Agenda Item 30, Doc. A/5497, 1963.
[53] *New York Times*, 21 Sept. 1963.

that in such a process of development the United Nations will have to play a major role if we are to avoid a tragic disaster. We must consider how, if necessary, we can, in a transitional period, contribute to the maintenance of law and order and the protection of life and civil rights of all individuals."[54]

The General Assembly on October 11, 1963, adopted a resolution requesting the government to release all political prisoners and calling on all member states to induce the South African government to carry out this demand. A new factor was the nearly unanimous vote (106 to 1) in favor of the resolution. Members that had previously voted against the anti-apartheid resolutions or abstained, voted for it. Their attitude was probably expressed by the Netherlands delegate. The trials in South Africa were the consequence of the policy of apartheid. "Elementary human rights are at stake, and the necessity of intervening for humanitarian reasons seems to my delegation in this case to overrule Article 2, paragraph 7."[55] Two years earlier the British government had arrived at similar views. Its delegate declared his government regarded apartheid as being now so exceptional that his delegation was able to consider the draft resolution under discussion on its merits.[56] This shift was significant; it had become increasingly embarrassing for these members to vote against the anti-apartheid resolutions, even on important constitutional grounds.

The Afro-Asian states wanted the Security Council to deal with the South African question under Chapter VII, which is concerned with action with respect to threats to the peace, breaches of the peace, and acts of aggression, rather than under Chapter VI, which is concerned with the pacific settlement of disputes and which does not authorize the Council to resort to sanctions. France, the United Kingdom, and the United States were not prepared to support action under Chapter VII. However repugnant the racial policy of South Africa, its government was not threatening the territorial integrity or the political independence of another state. The United States government supported the August 7 resolution of the Council only after the wording "is seriously

[54] UNGAOR, 18th Sess., Plenary Meetings, Verbatim Record, 1215th Meeting, pp. 5–7, 25 Sept. 1963.

[55] UNGAOR, 18th Sess., Plenary Meetings, Verbatim Record, 1238th Meeting, p. 7, 11 Oct. 1963; Res. No. 1881 (XVIII), Supp. No. 15 (A/5515), p. 19.

[56] UNGAOR, 16th Sess., Pt. II, Special Political Committee, Summary Records, p. 77, 5 April 1961.

endangering international peace and security" was changed to "is seriously disturbing international peace and security," which clearly brought the resolution under Chapter VI, for Chapter VII does not speak "in terms of disturbances of the peace, even serious ones, but only of actual threats to the peace or breaches of the peace, or acts of aggression."[57] In a lengthy resolution adopted by the Security Council on December 4, 1963, the phrase "disturbing international peace and security" was again used. A new element in this resolution was a request made of the secretary-general to establish "under his direction and reporting to him a small group of recognized experts to examine methods of resolving the present situation in South Africa through full, peaceful and orderly application of human rights and fundamental freedoms to all inhabitants of the territory as a whole, regardless of race, colour or creed, and to consider what part the United Nations might play in the achievement of that end."[58] The resolution, sponsored by Norway, embodied the ideas of the Scandinavian governments.

Two more resolutions dealing with the situation in South Africa were adopted by the General Assembly in December 1963. One appealed to all members to intensify their efforts to dissuade the government of South Africa from pursuing its policy of apartheid and called upon the Special Committee to continue its work. The second requested the secretary-general to seek ways of providing relief and assistance to the families of persons persecuted by the government of South Africa and inviting member states and organizations to contribute generously to such relief.[59]

The group of experts appointed by the secretary-general[60] submitted its report the following April. It observed that while world condemnation of apartheid was mounting, South Africa was intensifying its racial policies. The government was increasing its expenditures on armaments, having quadrupled its defense budget. The group expressed the conviction that a continuation of the present policies must lead to violent conflict and tragedy. The future of the country should be settled by all the people of South Africa. All efforts should be directed to the convening of a national convention which would be fully representative of the

[57] UNSCOR, 1056th Meeting, 7 Aug. 1963, p. 6.
[58] Resolution S/5471. UNSCOR, Supp. for Oct., Nov., Dec. 1963, Doc. S/5471.
[59] UNGAOR, 18th Sess., Supp. No. 15 (A/5515), Resolutions 1978(XVIII)A and 1978(XVIII)B.
[60] Mrs. Karl Gunnar Myrdal of Sweden was named chairman.

whole population, would consider the views and proposals of its members, and would set a new course for the country. The United Nations could help make the transition by offering services such as helping to organize and supervise elections, to maintain law and order and training South Africans for leadership in the new environment. If within a stipulated period the South African government had not replied to an invitation to discuss the calling of a national convention, the Security Council should apply economic sanctions, which the group believed would be effective if universally applied. It recommended that the Council sponsor a "practical and technical study of the 'logistics' of sanctions by experts in the economic and strategic field."[61]

The Security Council met in June 1964 to consider the group's report. The Afro-Asian states pressed for the application of economic sanctions against South Africa, but three of the permanent members of the Council —France, the United Kingdom, and the United States—gave the idea a cool reception. The Council adopted a lengthy resolution repeating the points of the earlier resolutions of the General Assembly and itself, but also embodying important recommendations of the group of experts. The resolution requested the secretary-general to consider what assistance the United Nations could offer to facilitate consultations among representatives of all the population groups in South Africa, to establish an expert committee to undertake "a technical and practical study . . . as to the feasibility, effectiveness and implications of measures" which could be undertaken by the Security Council, and invited the secretary-general to establish an educational and training program abroad for South Africans. The United Kingdom and France stated that their vote for the resolution did not imply a commitment to accept the recommendations which the committee of experts might make.[62]

The General Assembly's Special Committee on Apartheid in June 1964 had recommended the application without further delay of decisive, mandatory measures. The Security Council's committee of experts, which made its report in February 1965, was unable to reach full agreement on its conclusions. France even refused to participate in the

[61] UNSCOR, 19th Year, Supp. for April, May, June 1964, pp. 23–43, "Report of the Group of Experts."

[62] Resolution S/5773, UNSCOR Supp. for April, May, June 1964. The resolution was adopted by a vote of eight to zero, with the Soviet Union, Czechoslovakia, and France abstaining. The resolution was too strong for France and too weak for the Communist states.

work of the committee on the grounds of nonintervention in the internal affairs of member states.[63] A majority of the committee concluded that many economic sanctions against South Africa were feasible and would be effective if the trade embargoes were total and applied universally. There also should be a cessation of emigration of technicians and skilled manpower to South Africa and a prohibition of communications with the republic.[64]

At its Twentieth Session, the General Assembly reviewed the situation as it had developed and adopted a wide-ranging resolution to deal with it. By implication the committee laid much of the blame for the failure of its efforts to dissuade South Africa from its course on the United Kingdom, the United States, France, and West Germany as it urgently appealed to the major trading partners of South Africa "to cease their increasing economic collaboration with the Government of South Africa, which encourages that Government to defy world opinion and to accelerate the implementation of the policies of *apartheid*." The General Assembly decided to enlarge the Special Committee on Apartheid by six members to be appointed by the president of the General Assembly on the basis of three criteria, namely, primary responsibility with regard to world trade, primary responsibility under the Charter for maintenance of international peace and security, and equitable geographical distribution. This provision was obviously included to put pressure on states such as the United Kingdom, the United States, and France to support sanctions against South Africa, but these states refused to accept membership on the committee.

In a separate article the resolution "deplored the action of those States, which, through political, economic and military collaboration with the Government of South Africa, are encouraging it to persist in its racial policies." The General Assembly also called for the use of the whole apparatus of the Secretariat in a propaganda war against apartheid. The secretary-general was requested "to take appropriate measures for the widest possible dissemination of information on the policies of *apartheid*" and on United Nations efforts to deal with the situation and requested all members, specialized agencies, and nongovernmental organizations to cooperate with the secretary-general and the Special

[63] The committee was composed of representatives of each member of the Security Council.

[64] *Yearbook of the United Nations, 1965*, pp. 102–103.

Committee in this regard, and invited the specialized agencies "to take active measures, within their fields of competence, to compel the Government of South Africa to abandon its racial policies." In this resolution the General Assembly tried again to induce the Security Council to take more drastic measures against South Africa by alleging as a fact that the situation in South Africa constituted a threat to international peace and security and stating that universally applied economic sanctions were the only means to achieve a peaceful solution.[65] In a companion resolution the General Assembly requested the secretary-general to set up a trust fund, made up of voluntary contributions from states, organizations, and individuals to be used for legal assistance to persons charged under "discriminatory and repressive legislation" in South Africa, for relief of persons persecuted for acts arising from opposition to the policies of apartheid, for the education of prisoners and their dependents, and for relief for refugees from South Africa.[66]

The General Assembly in 1966 and 1967 adopted similar resolutions. The resolution of December 16, 1966, condemned the policies of apartheid practiced by the government of South Africa as "a crime against humanity," reaffirmed that the "explosive" situation in southern Africa posed a grave threat to international peace and security, again deplored the attitude of the main trading partners of South Africa and urged them to take urgent steps toward disengagement from South Africa and to facilitate effective action to secure the elimination of apartheid and requested the secretary-general to take further steps in the international publicity campaign against apartheid. It appealed to all states to consider effective political, moral, and material assistance to all who combat the policies of apartheid.[67] The 1967 resolution requested the secretary-general to intensify the dissemination of information on the evils of apartheid.[68] The General Assembly in November, 1969, adopted a reso-

[65] Resolution A/2054(XX). UNGAOR, 20th Sess., Supp. No. 14 (A/6014), pp. 16–17, 15 Dec. 1965.

[66] Resolution B/2054(XX). UNGAOR, 20th Sess., Supp. No. 14 (A/6014), pp. 17–18, 15 Dec. 1965.

[67] Resolution 2202(XXI). UNGAOR, 21st Sess., Supp. No. 16 (A/6316), pp. 20–21, 16 Dec. 1966.

[68] Resolution 2307(XXII). UNGAOR, 22d Sess., vol. I. Supp. No. 16 (A/6716), 13 Dec. 1967. Seminars on apartheid were held at Brasilia, Brazil, in 1966, and at Kitwa, Zambia, in 1967. In accordance with a 1966 resolution of the General Assembly a special section was set up in the Secretariat to deal with apartheid policies. In September 1969 the United Nations Secretariat issued the first number

lution urging members to give aid to the "national movement of the oppressed people" and to stop air and sea traffic to South Africa and to deny facilities to lines serving it.[69]

The government of South Africa throughout the controversy with the General Assembly of the United Nations has adamantly maintained that the question of its racial policies was a domestic matter and hence outside of the organization's jurisdiction, in accordance with Article 2, paragraph 7, of the Charter. A number of member states sided with South Africa on this issue, but as time passed their number decreased. Even the United Kingdom finally abandoned this position in fact if not in theory. The question may be asked whether an unfortunate precedent has been set. Many states have situations which they would not like to have discussed by the United Nations. It is an evidence of the deep repugnance with which racial discrimination enforced by law is universally regarded that the barrier set up by Article 2, paragraph 7, to safeguard members against intervention in domestic matters was overridden. But the precedent set may be an embarrassment in the future. The question of discrimination based on ideology may be raised.

In the matter of the treatment of Indians it could be argued that some of the Indians had a foreign nationality and that some sort of international agreement was involved, thus making it an international question. The same argument could have been invoked with reference to apartheid as applied to Africans, and with greater logic. There are over 600,000 alien Africans in South Africa, all of whom are subject to apartheid regulations. But these alien Africans come from the former Protectorates, Mozambique, Malawi, and Rhodesia, whose governments are not at all inclined to raise the issue of the treatment of their nationals. Britain, as the protector of Bechunaland, Basutoland, and

---

of a magazine, *Objective: Justice: A Periodical Review of the United Nations Activity against Apartheid, Racial Discrimination and Colonialism.* UNESCO published a report: *Apartheid: Its Effects on Education, Science, Culture and Information* (Paris, 1967). The Commission on Human Rights in 1967 appointed Manoucher Ganji of Iran to survey United Nations actions on apartheid and to recommend further measures that should be taken.

[69] *New York Times*, 22 Nov. 1969. The vote was 80 to 5, but there were many abstentions. The United States as well as Britain voted against the resolution. This was the first time in many years that the United States voted against a resolution on apartheid. It did so on the ground that South Africa's racial policies did not constitute a threat to international peace, hence the sanctions called for in the resolution were not warranted.

Swaziland, had ample reasons for not raising the issue. However, it is strange that this point was not raised in the numerous and lengthy debates on United Nations competence to deal with South Africa's racial policy.

South Africa considerably weakened its position when it embraced the policy of separate development and the creation of Bantustans. Since under the policy proclaimed, the Africans were never to have South African citizenship but were assumed to have the nationality of their "homelands" and the Bantustans were not to have independence at least for a considerable number of years, the Republic of South Africa had clearly become a colonial power and placed itself, with respect to them, subject to the provisions of Articles 73 and 74 of the Charter, which lay down the obligations of members with respect to non-self-governing territories. This was not used by the leaders of the anti-apartheid movement, probably because they regarded racial discrimination as more offensive than even colonialism. Rarely ever in the debates was the distinction made between social segregation and discrimination on the one hand and territorial separation of the races on the other.

Quite obviously the Western great powers were right in maintaining that Chapter VII of the Charter did not apply to the situation. South Africa was not threatening any foreign state or government with hostile action. President Nyerere of Tanzania is reported to have said that "if our pressures do not succeed, then we fight. We have no other alternative."[70] If this threat became serious, the question would then clearly fall under Chapter VII, with Tanzania as the immediate aggressor.

Expulsion of South Africa from the United Nations was never seriously considered by the anti-apartheid leaders, though this would seem to be the appropriate action. South Africa is charged with persistently violating the principles contained in the Charter and for this, Article 6 provides expulsion. A legal difficulty is that the General Assembly may expel a member only upon the recommendation of the Security Council, where the great powers sit ensconced with the veto, as well as with power to make decisions which bind all members of the organization. A second reason probably was that they felt that they could exert more pressure on the South African government inside than outside the United Nations.

The tension that developed between the General Assembly and the

[70] *Washington Post*, 25 July 1963.

Security Council on the approach to the problem reflects the peculiar structure of the United Nations. Political power is located in the Assembly, in which each member regardless of its population or economic and social development has a vote, while economic and military power is concentrated in the Council, which because of the veto can become operative only if there is unanimity among the five permanent members.[71] However this may be, the General Assembly, in spite of lack of agreement on the best means of opposing apartheid, has committed the United Nations to a contest with South Africa from which there is no retreat without serious loss of prestige to the world organization.[72]

[71] It is not surprising that the United States in 1969 came forward with a proposal to halt the influx of little states (in many cases the fragments of empire) to membership in the United Nations.

[72] That the United Nations is often ineffective is a general complaint. The late Emilio Arenales of Guatemala, who served as the president of the Twenty-third Session of the General Assembly, observed that the approach of most delegates is "unrealistic and emotional, and I might even say demagogic" (*New York Times* editorial, 16 Sept. 1969).

17

Siege and
Counteroffensive

Few states have been so isolated morally and diplomatically as is the Republic of South Africa today. The growing isolation of the country in the United Nations was due in part to the large increase in African and Asian members, but also to the desertion of its old friends. South Africa has been suspended or expelled or has withdrawn from the following public international organizations: UNESCO, the Commonwealth, the Committee for Technical Cooperation in Africa, the Scientific Council for Africa, the Economic Commission for Africa, the International Civil Aviation Organization, the International Telecommunications Union, the International Labor Organization, the Food and Agriculture Organization, and from the Congress of the Universal Postal Union, but not the Union itself. The question of South Africa's participation and membership is raised at nearly every international conference South African delegates attend.[1]

South Africa has further isolated herself by denying passports to many of its own nationals who wish to go abroad or visas to foreigners wishing to visit the country. Its political isolation in Africa is almost complete—it has diplomatic relations with four African states—Malawi and the three former Protectorates, and semidiplomatic relations with Rhodesia and counselor posts in Angola and Mozambique. The situation with respect to Asia is not much better.[2]

For the Nationalists, relations with the Netherlands have special meaning: hence they react more sharply to criticism from the Dutch than from others. Though the political ties between South Africa and the Netherlands were severed in 1815, cultural and ecclesiastical ties remained very much alive. Relations between the two peoples have deteriorated under the Nationalist regime. With strange insensitivity the Malan government in 1948 proposed sending as minister to The Hague a person who had been a leader in the pro-German movement during the war. The Hague refused to receive him. The Reformed churches in the Netherlands, with which the Reformed churches in South Africa had close relations, officially rejected apartheid as unchristian and were sharply critical of their sister churches in South Africa for supporting it.[3] The Free University of Amsterdam, the Calvinist university, conferred an honorary doctor's degree on Martin Luther King, Jr., in 1965, an act that deeply offended the Afrikaners, especially since Queen Juliana and members of the cabinet honored the occasion with their presence.

The South African government has protested at The Hague the position taken by the Netherlands at the United Nations in the debates on apartheid.[4] A semiofficial visit to South Africa of a delegation of five members of the Netherlands Parliament was arranged by the two

[1] *New York Times*, 10 Oct. 1969. The story is much the same with respect to nongovernmental and private international organizations. In the field of sports South Africa has met with increasing difficulty, chiefly because it does not permit mixed sports within the country or even mixed attendance.

[2] In 1965 South Africa had diplomatic and consular posts only in Lebanon and Japan; in South America, only in the Argentine and Brazil.

[3] As evidence of the unusual relations between the Afrikaners and the Dutch, mention should be made of an interesting journalistic exchange between *Die Burger*, the Nationalist daily of Cape Town, and *Trouw*, the Calvinist daily of Amsterdam. Each was given a page in the other. The editors of *Die Burger* described and defended the government's racial policy, while several writers for *Trouw* set forth their objections—factual, moral, and religious—to apartheid. The exchange, which took place on 26 Nov. 1963, was followed by another a year later. Subsequently the editor of *Die Burger* visited the Netherlands as the guest of its government to continue the dialogue in person. Dr. J. A. H. J. S. Bruins Slot, editor of *Trouw*, was a member of the United Nations anti-apartheid seminar at Brasilia in 1966.

[4] Such a protest was made on 11 Jan. 1960 (*Het Algemeen Handelsblad*, 10 Feb. 1960).

governments in 1964, when suddenly it was called off by Pretoria. The explanation given by the South African foreign minister was that members of the Dutch delegation wanted to talk with Chief Luthuli but his government would not allow it.[5] The explanation from the Dutch side was more fundamental. C. L. Patijn, who was to have been a member of the mission, declared that he and his associates were under the impression that the government of South Africa really did not want a Dutch parliamentary mission to visit the country because of the publicity which would attend it. This means, he said, "that at the moment an attempt at dialogue between the Netherlands and South Africa on the basis of the old kinship and the old bonds is no longer possible and thus the old ties no longer have any function in the present political tensions. I regret it. It means that one of the few contacts which still in this world remained open for South Africa can no longer be utilized."[6] Not long after the parliamentary mission was canceled by Pretoria the Dutch government again deeply offended the South African government by making a donation of 100,000 guilders ($28,000) to the Defense and Aid Fund which provides legal counsel for Africans arrested on political charges and assistance for their families while in jail.[7] The South African foreign minister made a formal protest.[8]

The moral loneliness of the South African whites is emphasized by the dissociation of Portugal from any policy of racial discrimination. The Portuguese delegate declared to the General Assembly of the United Nations that his country's policy was based on the equality of races and opposition to any kind of racial segregation. Portuguese policy is aimed at an integrated multiracial society. In keeping with Articles 55 and 56 of the Charter "all persons were equal, all had the same civil and political rights, all enjoyed the same political representation, and all had access to the same opportunities for education and social advancement."[9]

[5] *Hansard*, vol. 15, cols. 7692–93, 10 June 1965.

[6] *Handelingen*, der Staten Generaal, *Begrootingscommissie voor Buitenlandsche Zaken*, Zitting 1965–1966, Tweede Kamer, col. 641, 1 Dec. 1965.

[7] Ibid., cols. 647–49.

[8] In reprisal for the "insult" the South African government canceled negotiations with the Royal Dutch Airlines over additional landing rights on its territory and canceled a planned visit of the South African naval chief of staff to Dutch shipyards (*New York Times*, 17 June 1965).

[9] UNGAOR, 21st Sess., Special Political Committee, Summary Records, p. 254, 12 Dec. 1966.

The World Council of Churches in many ways has expressed its concern about the racial policy of South Africa. After the Council arranged for a consultation of the eight South African denominations that were Council members to discuss the racial situation in South Africa, the three largest Dutch Reformed Churches withdrew their membership.[10] The Vatican also has declared publicly its disapproval of South Africa's racialism. Pope Paul VI in his address to African heads of states at Kampala, Uganda, undoubtedly was referring to South Africa when he stated that he deplored "the fact, that in certain parts of the world, there persist situations based upon racial discrimination, and often willed and sustained by systems of thought; such situations constitute a manifest and inadmissable affront to the fundamental rights of the human person, and to the laws of civilized living."[11]

If external pressure is unlikely to cause white South Africans to change their racial policy there is little chance of change as the result of an upheaval of the non-European majority, or a shift of political control among the whites, or a shift of policy in the present dominant party. How much ferment there is among Africans is almost impossible to ascertain. The African National Congress and the Pan-African Congress were banned in 1960 and as no new political parties have emerged, Africans have no political organization through which they can express their views. Many of the former political leaders are in prison or in exile or subject to banning orders. Public disturbances and sabotage caused the government much concern for a few years after Sharpeville but now have all but ceased.

It may well be that, as government spokesmen boast, there is less racial tension in South Africa than in the United States, but if this is so, why are there yearly additions to the mass of repressive legislation? Since interracial contact is now practically confined to the economic sphere and political movements among Africans have been driven underground, only the secret police can know the real situation.[12] And

---

[10] The consultation was held at Johannesburg in Dec. 1960. See *Cottesloe Consultation: The Report of the Consultation among South African Member Churches of the World Council of Churches* (Johannesburg, 1961).

[11] *New York Times*, 2 Aug. 1969.

[12] South Africa probably has the highest rate of death sentences and executions in the world. During the two-year period 1963–1965, South Africa accounted for about 47 percent of the world's executions (*A Survey of Race Relations in South Africa, 1968* [Johannesburg, 1969], p. 51). This statement is based on a survey

as the Africans receive more education they will undoubtedly resent apartheid increasingly, but there is no indication yet of violent reaction. Nor does there seem to be any likelihood of early trouble of a grave nature from the coloreds or the Indians. Government spokesmen have claimed that most Bantu, coloreds, and Indians have come to accept separate development, or parallel development as they prefer to call it, as a solution to the race problem, but the first election of members of the Colored Peoples Representative Council, held in September 1969, proved that they were wrong. The Labor party, which opposes the government's racial policy, won twenty-six of the forty elective seats. Moreover, some of the pro-apartheid candidates support the policy on the grounds of expediency, hoping that cooperation with the government will win concessions for the coloreds. To make sure of a majority in the Council favorable to the government, the law provides for twenty appointive seats. To fill these seats the government appointed supporters of apartheid, including thirteen candidates defeated in the election.[13]

As for a change in political control, the possibilities of this for a number of years seem small. In spite of inconsistencies, inner contradictions, and heavy outside pressure, apartheid has proved a very successful slogan for winning elections. In 1948 the Nationalist party received less than 40 percent of the total popular votes cast; in 1953, 49 percent; and in 1958, 58 percent. The Nationalist vote in the 1961 elections fell sharply as a result of the Sharpeville and other disturbances, the consequent flight of foreign capital, and economic stagnation. In that election the party won only 46 percent of the vote but because the opposition was badly divided it retained control of Parliament. By 1966 the country had recovered from the shock of Sharpeville and its aftermath and in the election of that year the National party bounced back to 58 percent of the total vote.

The United party has groped for an effective alternative policy to apartheid. It opposed the fragmentation of the country which the policy of separate development would bring, but it retained the principle of white supremacy under such slogans as "leadership with justice" and "leadership based on merit." If returned to power, the United party

---

made by B. van D. van Niekerk, senior lecturer in law at the Witwatersrand University and published in *Africa Digest*, Dec. 1968.

[13] *New York Times*, 12 Oct. 1969. But apparently the pro-government candidates won a majority of the popular votes.

would set up a federation of races, with each racial group eventually represented in Parliament in accordance with the standard of civilization it had reached. Social and residential separation would be retained, but the petty restrictions and discriminations would be abolished. Africans should be given the right to own property. The Progressive party, which has only one representative in Parliament,[14] rejects racial discrimination and separate development, and favors a qualified nonracial franchise based on educational achievements and/or economic attainment. To protect the rights of minority groups, the party advocates a rigid constitution with an entrenched bill of rights. The Liberal party, headed by Alan Paton and former Senator Edgar H. Brookes, advocated a nonqualified adult franchise. It ran no candidates in the 1966 general election because most of its leading members were immobilized by banning orders, and in 1968 the party dissolved, since the Prohibition of Political Interference Act of that year made the existence of multiracial political parties illegal.[15]

After Sharpeville, the expulsion from the Commonwealth, and the establishment of the Republic in 1961, Verwoerd pleaded for unity among South African whites. He urged the Europeans to submerge their old differences and form a united front against an increasingly antagonistic world. He began to emphasize white rather than Afrikaner nationalism. He gave cabinet posts to two English-speaking South Africans.[16] Vorster has followed the same policy. The National party has had its greatest success in drawing English-speaking support in Natal. Probably the most uncritical support of the government comes from that province.[17]

The English-speaking element has been rather apathetic toward politics. The United party, where most of them are found, has put up a rather feeble opposition to the National government's policy, which

[14] But a very effective one—Mrs. Helen Suzman.

[15] At its dissolution Alan Paton declared that the great advantage of this law was that "it will only allow the Nationalist party to interfere in the politics of other races in the future" (*New York Times*, 9 May 1968).

[16] F. W. Waring, minister of information; A. E. Trollip, minister of labor and information. Both were appointed after the parliamentary election of 1961.

[17] The fact that the whites constitute a lower percentage of the total population in Natal than in any other province helps to account for this fact. In early 1969, Harry Lewis, United party member of Parliament, crossed the floor of the House to join the government party. A few months later, Professor Owen Horwood, principal of the University of Natal, resigned his post and joined the National party. He is a brother-in-law of Prime Minister Ian Smith of Rhodesia.

probably reflects the attitude of its members. The country has been prosperous and the English-speaking community is more interested in business than in politics. The turmoil in other African countries and the bitter campaign these new but influential members of the United Nations were waging against South Africa drove the English-speaking South Africans to give the government qualified and reluctant support. Their churches might condemn apartheid in clear-cut terms, but statements by the ecclesiastical courts or officials do not accurately reflect their views. The English dislike the crudities of the Nationalist methods, but if they are necessary to preserve the white man's gains and Western civilization in southern Africa, it is better that these things be done by Afrikaners than by the English. Edgar Brookes has branded the English-speaking South Africans as the villains of the piece. "It is the bulk of the English-speaking population which has thus put itself into a position where it can only earn contempt." But not all are like that, he said, "Some, with even more heroic Afrikaans-speaking South Africans, are fighting for justice. They take their careers and reputations in their hands, but their fellow-citizens do not care."[18] Practically all the English newspapers are opposed to the Nationalist government, and they still have by far the largest number of readers, though the circulation of Afrikaans journals is rapidly increasing.[19] The English-speaking people may feel that they have no choice but to support the racial policies of the government, however much they may regret some of its practices, and they resent the more violent foreign criticism, but they are not yet prepared to move into the Afrikaner Nationalist camp.[20]

HESITANT REAPPRAISAL

Disappointment and disillusionment have set in with respect to apartheid. The National party has been in power more than two decades but

[18] From an article in *Reality*, a journal of liberal opinion, quoted by *The Star*, (Johannesburg), Weekly Air Edition, 17 May 1969.

[19] After the conviction in July 1969 of Lawrence Gandar, editor of the *Rand Daily Mail*, and Benjamin Pogrund, a reporter for the same paper, for violating the Prisons Act, newspapers may be more cautious in expressing their views about government policy and practices. Both got off with light sentences—Gandar a fine of $280 and Pogrund a suspended sentence of three months—but the costs of their defense, estimated at $280,000, may have an inhibiting influence.

[20] In reply to an appeal for white unity by the Nationalist administration of Natal, *The Star* asked a number of pointed questions about which political party had consistently preached white separatism (editorial, 23 Sept. 1967).

almost no progress has been made in making apartheid a reality. Indeed, there is strong evidence to indicate that ground has been lost. Pressed by the opposition on this point, Prime Minister Verwoerd made statements which must have caused many of his supporters to lose heart and some to develop gnawing doubts. He declared that total racial segregation was the ideal, the objective of his party and government, but because of the economic and social structure which had been allowed to develop before 1948, this objective could not be achieved quickly, as that would disrupt the economy and arrest industrial development. The objective would be reached in stages. Political separation would be achieved first, and then economic and social separation, but the process of physical separation would be carried out gradually over a long period. He himself years before had used the year 1978 as the turning point. The number of Bantu in the white areas would increase relatively to the Europeans until that year and then begin to decline, and by the year 2000 "we would probably again reach the stage when the number of Bantu in the White area of the country would be equal to the figures for 1950, which was when I said this."[21]

South Africa is enjoying great economic prosperity and so long as this continues the cities will strongly attract the Africans. Eighty percent of the Republic's total labor force consists of nonwhites. About 40 percent of South Africa's thirteen million Africans live in the homelands and more than 40 percent of their economically active men are absent at any given time, employed in the white areas. There is also a steady movement of both whites and Africans from the rural to the urban areas, but the increase in the number of Africans in the cities outstrips that of the whites. G. M. E. Leistner, chief economist of the Africa Institute of South Africa, has predicted on the basis of present trends that there will be twenty-five Africans for every ten whites in urban areas by the end of the century.[22] Merely to absorb the homelands

[21] *Hansard*, vol. 14, cols. 4176–89. He admitted there could be no homelands for the coloreds or Indians; they would be permitted "to develop their own potential, without a ceiling, in regard to the posts they may occupy and *inter alia* also self-government in regard to their own affairs" (ibid., cols. 4180–81). An exciting prospect for the two groups which in a couple of decades may outnumber the whites!

[22] *The Star*, Weekly Air Edition, 16 Aug. 1969. A report of the Department of Labor indicates that in the two years from 1963 to 1964 inclusive, the number of white workers in registered factories increased by 57,000 to a total of 289,000, but the number of nonwhites increased by 166,000 to almost 850,000 (see article by Marais Steyn, M. P., in *The Star*, Weekly Air Edition, 15 June 1968).

natural increase requires an estimated 39,000 new jobs annually, but the industrial development in the homelands has hardly begun while the industries in the white areas on the border of the reserves are at present absorbing less than 10,000 Africans a year. Moreover, the development of border industries is retarding the industrial development of the homelands.[23]

In view of the meager natural resources of the homelands, it is extremely doubtful that they can absorb more than a fraction of the eight million and more Africans now in the rest of South Africa. Nor would the whites want this to happen, as their prosperity is dependent on these workers. It is doubtful that a people can believe for very long in the morality and stability of a political system in which Europeans, who alone have full political and civil rights, are greatly outnumbered by migratory workers and a body of coloreds and Indians who though they are permanent residents and approach the Europeans in numbers are denied the essentials of citizenship. "What is wrong," concludes the Johannesburg *Star*, reflecting the growing uneasiness about the situation, "is that apartheid should ever have been regarded as anything more than a fluid instrument of White convenience."[24]

The Nationalists also face a dilemma with respect to the economy and immigration. They are not eager to encourage immigration, white any more than black, as they fear that it will weaken the Afrikaner's position in the country relative to other groups. In justifying the government's immigration policy to his fellow party members, C. P. Mulder, the minister of immigration, declared that the only alternatives to a vigorous immigration were economic stagnation or an ending to separate development. To maintain the current economic growth rate of 5.5 percent, 12,000 to 13,000 additional skilled white workers were needed each year. This required an average of 30,000 to 35,000 immigrants annually. As an alternative to an active immigration policy the country would have to accept a lower growth rate with consequent economic retrogression, devaluation, and unemployment. Another alternative was to elevate 12,000 to 13,000 nonwhites to the status of skilled workers. This would involve relaxing the industrial color-bar (job reservation and the like). This would mean the eventual ending of separate development. The government had rejected both of these

[23] This is the analysis of the problem by Dr. P. Smit, head of the geography department of Africa Institute (ibid., 12 July 1969).

[24] Editorial, 26 July 1969.

courses and decided to bring in white skilled labor from the outside, but it gave the assurance that it would select immigrants so as not to disturb the present numerical relationship between English-speaking and Afrikaans-speaking South Africans, and between Protestants and Catholics.[25] These are unpleasant alternatives for the whites, and many Afrikaners are unhappy about the situation.

There are some developments which strongly suggest that political conditions are changing. The long tenure of the National party may not be over but cracks are developing in the "wall of granite." There have been cracks before but they were plastered over. Can this be done again? Or will there be a realignment of political forces with possible modification of policies?

The chief reason for belief in the possibility of political change is the bitter division which has developed in the National party between the *verkramptes* (cramped, narrow-minded) and the *verligtes* (enlightened). The first group is very critical of Vorster's outward-policy, while the latter supports it and some would liberalize it somewhat. The division came to a head with the speech in Parliament on April 15, 1969, by Albert Hertzog, son of the Boer general who was prime minister from 1924 to 1939. Hertzog, who had been dropped from the cabinet in 1968, in a sensational speech declared in essence that only Calvinists have the toughness required to maintain white, Christian civilization in South Africa, and that only Afrikaners are Calvinists. "Our English-speaking Afrikaners have wonderful virtues," he said, but "basically they are not Calvinists; basically they differ from the Afrikaners, basically the English Afrikaner is liberal. . . . That is why our English speaking-people fall victim to the onslaughts of the Communists."[26] By virtually making Calvinism a condition for membership in the National party, he was driving a wedge between Afrikaners and English-speaking whites. The prime minister indicted Hertzog as dis-

[25] *The Star*, Weekly Air Edition, 20 Sept. 1969. A leading industrialist, B. A. B. Watson, declared that the job reservation laws were impeding the growth of South Africa's economy. At this stage the concept of job reservation would not be abandoned but steps should be taken to open up some jobs from which nonwhites are presently barred. White workers would earn more (*New York Times*, 19 Nov. 1969).

[26] Quoted, ibid., 9 Aug. 1969. Eben Cuyler, Nationalist member of the Johannesburg City Council, went even further. During a council debate, he declared that "there is only one culture in South Africa. That culture is the Afrikaans culture" (ibid., 9 Aug. 1969).

loyal, but he did not read him out of the party. It was left to Minister B. J. Schoeman to repudiate Hertzog's speech. He did so in Parliament after relentless prodding by the leader of the opposition. Schoeman declared that "not one member of the National Party subscribes to the reflections and insults, as we regard them, which the member for Ermelo [Hertzog] made on the English-speaking people of South Africa. . . . I want to put it very clearly . . . that the Prime Minister and I, as leader of the National Party in the Transvaal, of which the member of Ermelo is a member, reject the imputations he has made against English-speaking South Africans without reserve."[27]

That Vorster and his cabinet were concerned about the dissidence of the right wing of the party is obvious from the heroic measures they took to meet it. In September 1969 they called for a surprise general election to be held in April 1970, instead of 1971 when the five-year term of Parliament would have expired. They gave as reasons for the early election, (1) to get the election out of the way so that the government could deal with important problems and (2) to remove the impression of division which the turmoil in the party had created. Unresolved tensions in the party would weaken the government within and outside of the country. Vorster stated that he also wished to test the electorate's reaction to his policies and leadership.[28] The opposition leaders saw other reasons for calling a "snap" election. Vorster, they said, was uncertain of his strength. By calling an early election he hoped to mobilize the massive power of the National political machine to destroy the Hertzog group and to consolidate his own position.[29]

Many Afrikaners are worried about Vorster's policy of white unity. They fear such slogans as "a broader South Africanism." As they see it, it was under this phrase that Afrikanerdom once was nearly ploughed under. In spite of all the gains under two decades of Nationalist rule, they feel that Afrikaner identity is still in danger. Their fears were revealed in a speech by D. P. Goosen, the director of the *Suid-Afrikaanse Akademie Vir Wetenschap en Kuns* (South African Academy for Science and Arts), in January 1967. Afrikaans-English integration, he said, had led to the complete Anglicization of nearly 200,000 Afrikaners, and this process was increasing. Afrikaner association forms,

[27] *News-Check*, 2 May/15 May 1969.
[28] *The Star*, Weekly Air Edition, 27 Sept. 1969.
[29] Ibid., 20 Sept. 1969.

behavior patterns, and living style all bore the English stamp. Afrikaners were still poor, the hewers of wood and the bearers of water in their own fatherland. Their share in trade was only 28 percent; in industry, 10; in finance, 14; and in mining, 10. Moreover, the English community was being strengthened in all modes of life by the stream of immigrants, while Afrikaners were being subtly assimilated by the reading of English newspapers, magazines, and books and by being exposed to English sources of entertainment. These were all carriers of liberal thought. "We are integrating," concluded Goosen, "and the result will be an Afrikaans-English culture, but a culture with predominantly English contents and forms."[30]

Right-wing Nationalists do not like the policy of separate development. They reject the idea of independent Bantustans. They want to keep South Africa united and with continued white domination. Some desire a return to the constitutional system of the Boer republics—a state president with all the powers of the prime minister as well. They are concerned about the immigration policy, contending that too many Roman Catholics and others who will not become a part of the Afrikaner community are being admitted.[31] They oppose diplomatic relations with African states because it will involve black diplomats staying at white hotels, living in white residential areas, and their children attending white schools. The *verkramptes* complain that the government is spending too much money on the blacks. They dislike the movement of the government toward multiracial sports by allowing the visit of a New Zealand rugby team which includes Maoris.[32]

The National party also has trouble with its left wing, though it is not

[30] Ibid., 18 Mar. 1967. Similar sentiments have been expressed by persons in high government circles. Dr. P. Koornhof, deputy minister of Bantu administration, is reported to have said, "We desire no integration between Afrikaners and English-speakers, because it will lead to the downfall of Afrikanerdom and White civilization in South Africa" (*Die Transvaler*, 6 Oct. 1966).

[31] In a report of a committee of the Nederduitse Gereformeerde Kerk, it is stated that about a third of the immigrants are "potential Afrikaners" but only 7 percent eventually found themselves in the Afrikaner cultural community. The church was urged to work among non-Afrikaners (*The Star*, Weekly Air Edition, 18 Oct. 1969).

[32] Hertzog made much of the sports issue at the National party convention at Transvaal in September 1969. He is reported to have said of the visit of the New Zealand team, "They will do more than play rugby against our boys. They will sit at the table with our sons and daughters and they will dance with our daughters" (*New York Times*, 14 Sept. 1969).

yet acute. A certain disillusionment with the policy of apartheid has set in. Little progress has been made toward the ideal of territorially separated but friendly races, while petty apartheid, the worst phase of the policy, has been intensified. Statements by government spokesmen have thrown doubts on independence as a goal of separate development. Prime Minister Vorster declared in 1967 that no strings were attached to the independence promised to the Bantustans, but that independence may still be a long time off. When the Transkei Legislative Assembly in June 1968 asked the South African government for assistance in training for independence they were given no encouragement. The minister of Bantu administration and development told the Parliament at Cape Town that there was no "short course" in independence. There were too many unfortunate examples of countries in Africa which had been granted independence before they were ready for it. He listed as conditions necessary for self-government: administrative experience, reliability and responsibility in financial matters, public honesty, a democratic approach, and the desire and the ability to live in peace with neighbors.[33] If this formidable list of conditions has to be met, the Transkei will have to wait a long time for independence, while freedom for the other proposed Bantustans is hardly within the foreseeable future. In the meanwhile petty apartheid grinds on without the least indication of relaxation.

This situation is arousing the Christian conscience of Afrikaners. The presence of several million migratory laborers as a permanent institution in South Africa profoundly disturbs Afrikaner Christians as well as other Christians. The system is destructive of family life, as the father works in a white industrial area while the family lives hundreds of miles away in a reserve or Bantustan. The Reformed churces have repeatedly warned against the dangers and evils of the system. In October 1968 the official organ, *Woord en Daad* (Word and Deed), of the Afrikaanse Calvinistise Beweging (Calvinist Movement) stated that petty apartheid was morally acceptable as a transitional measure to achieve a just and positive form of territorial separation, but if it were to become a permanent feature of the policy of

---

[33] *The Star*, Weekly Air Edition, 8 June 1968. Theodore Gerdener, the administrator of Natal declared in June 1969 that "there are still differences of opinion with respect to the ultimate constitutional independence of the Bantu homelands" (*News-Check*, 27 June/10 July 1969).

separate development it would no longer be morally supportable.[34] The intellectuals centered around the Calvinist university at Potchefstrom also expressed concern about the political rights to be accorded the coloreds. Prime Minister Vorster had declared that the ultimate solution of the colored problem would be left to the next generation. The Potchefstrom group demands clarity about the fate of the coloreds.[35]

Other manifestations of ferment in Afrikaner circles were the launching in 1962 of a Christian monthly journal, *Pro Veritate*, with an interracial board and a Dutch Reformed pastor as its editor, and the establishment the following year of the Christian Institute, an interracial institution with the aim of uniting Christians on an individual basis. The editor of *Pro Veritate*, the Rev. C. F. Beyers Naudé, also serves as the director of the Institute. Another evidence of a loosening of closely knit Afrikanerdom is the participation by some Dutch Reformed churches in a statement entitled "Message to the People of South Africa," issued by the South African Council of Churches, in which racial segregation was attacked as "a false offer of salvation being made in the name of Christianity" and which called on South Africans to "live in accordance with the Christian understanding of man and of community even if this be contrary to some of the customs and laws of this country."[36] Prime Minister Vorster castigated the ministers for making "a political platform of the pulpit" and warned them to stop it immediately. "The cloth you carry will not protect you."[37] In reply the ministers addressed an open letter to the prime minister in which they said they would not allow themselves to be silenced, even in the face of threats. The church was bound to testify when "criteria of God's word" are violated. "In God's name, and even if you do not agree with it, you ought not to seek to silence the Church's

---

[34] *News-Check*, 16 May/29 May 1969. A committee of the Synod of the Nederduitse Gereformeerde Kerk stated in a report that the system of migratory labor had caused a cancer in the life of the African population. "To argue that the migratory labour system is a temporary measure is a case of wishful thinking which could have disastrous results for the Church in the Republic. The Church may never become indifferent to the disintegration of the family life of the non-Whites" (*The Star*, Weekly Air Edition, 14 Sept. 1968).

[35] Vorster's statement marked a shift from the position of Verwoerd who maintained that the coloreds' status had been definitely fixed as a minority group with very limited political rights.

[36] *New York Times*, 22 Sept. 1968.

[37] *The Star*, Weekly Air Edition, 26 Oct. 1968.

testimony that apartheid is contrary to the plain sense of Scripture and to the teaching and faith of almost the whole Christian church."[38]

Foreign reaction to apartheid has hit South Africans in a vulnerable spot. They are sports enthusiasts. Rugby is a form of mania and cricket nearly so. South Africans want their teams to play against the best in the world. South Africa has some outstanding athletes such as Karen Muir, the swimmer, and Paul Nash, the sprinter, who have equaled or broken world records. But because of the application of apartheid to sports as well as to nearly everything else, South Africa was denied participation in the Olympic games in Mexico City in 1968 and has been suspended by the International Football (soccer) Federation. Foreign teams and athletes have refused to play in South Africa. A British cricket team was to have visited South Africa for a series of contests in 1969, but because it included a colored player—a South African who had gone to England because of apartheid in sports in his own country—the government intervened. The colored cricketeer, Basil D'Oliveira, one of the greatest of all times, was subsequently knighted by the queen. The South African government finds this pressure hard to resist. Love of sports and national pride may be causing an erosion of apartheid which with other influences may finally bring about changes in racial policy.[39]

There is increasing recognition among Nationalists that progress in separate development is lagging. The *Transvaler* ascribes the slow pace to the unwillingness of the whites to make the contributions necessary for its success. It has called for a peoples congress for the purpose of enlisting the broadest possible support for the implementation of the policy, but others are joining in the call for such a congress to consider broader aspects of the racial policy.[40] The result might be a reexamination of both the possibility and desirability of separate development. The South African Council of Churches and the Christian Institute have

[38] *New York Times*, 29 Oct. 1968. Another indication of changing attitudes was revealed by the moral support given by white doctors to the colored and Indian physicians employed in state hospitals when the latter threatened to strike because of salary discriminations based on race. (*The Star*, Weekly Air Edition, 26 April 1969).

[39] South Africans are so disturbed about the exclusion of their country from international sports events that they are raising a fund for sending delegates overseas to defend South Africa in international sports congresses (*New York Times*, 22 Oct. 1969).

[40] *The Star*, Weekly Air Edition, 9 Nov. 1968.

launched a two-year study project on Christianity in apartheid society. The director of the project, which has enlisted 132 prominent South Africans, said, "We hope that this project will make a meaningful contribution toward a better social order in South Africa."[41] Dr. Christiaan Barnard, the famous Cape Town heart surgeon, reflects the uneasiness among Afrikaner intellectuals. He is reported to have said in an interview over Danish television that apartheid was not the right answer to South Africa's problem, but nobody had come up with a better solution.[42]

These new attitudes are undoubtedly a reflection of the social changes taking place among Afrikaners. Urbanization, more education, greater participation in the professional, industrial, financial, and intellectual life of the country has brought about an erosion of old values and attitudes and produced more sophistication and greater sensitivity to world opinion. On the other hand, the Afrikaners who have left the farms to join the ranks of labor in the industrial centers will be strongly attracted by the *verkramptes'* position. It was with the support of labor that the Nationalists first came to power—in 1924 and maneuvered by Albert Hertzog's father.

THE OUTWARD-LOOKING POLICY

With the announcement by Prime Minister Verwoerd in 1959 of the policy of developing the Bantu reserves with the aim of granting them ultimate independence, South Africa was faced with the problem of reorienting its external policy. The withdrawal from the Commonwealth in 1961 and the rapid decolonization of Africa increased the necessity for a new approach. The old drive for expansion had to be abandoned or given another form. The policy of separate development and separate freedom, if sincere, is a policy of decolonization. Certainly, after the

---

[41] *New York Times*, 27 July 1969.

[42] *The Star*, Weekly Air Edition, 9 Aug. 1969. *Hoofstad* (Pretoria), the *verkrampte* newspaper, expressed the disappointment of right wing Nationalists in Dr. Barnard, "in reality he is in the opposition and he is just another well-known South African who has let us down abroad" (ibid.). Because of this statement and others made in South Africa the renowned surgeon, who had been acclaimed a national hero and ambassador extraordinary to the world, was quickly denounced as a traitor by extreme Nationalists (*New York Times*, 4 Nov. 1969; *The Star*, Weekly Air Edition, 15 Nov. 1969).

adoption of this policy it no longer made any sense to put pressure on Great Britain to cede the Protectorates to South Africa. Verwoerd recognized that a policy with respect to the new Africa had to be developed.[43] The policy of rigid confrontation with black Africa had become utterly futile, but it was left to his successor, B. J. Vorster, to formulate a more positive policy.

When Vorster became prime minister in 1966 the situation in Africa had become more favorable for South Africa. Pan-Africanism had lost much of its force. The militant Nkrumah had been removed from power in his own country and there had been military takeovers in several other states. East Africa was disunited; Kenya and its neighbors were putting pressure on their Indian minorities in a manner to make their moral condemnation of South Africa's racial policies a bit less convincing; Nigeria was divided and on the brink of a bitter civil war; the Horn of Africa and the Congo remain chronically unstable. The unilateral declaration of independence by the white minority government of Rhodesia deeply offended Africans throughout the continent but it soon became evident that the likelihood of the Smith regime being overthrown or brought to terms was very small. The obvious agencies to check the Rhodesian government—Great Britain, the United Nations, and the Organization of African Unity—either would not or could not take effective action. The paralyzing decision of the International Court of Justice in the South West Africa case heightened the Africans' frustration and feeling of impotence. Big talk of a crusade against South Africa had come to sound rather flat. By contrast, South Africa was daily becoming economically and militarily stronger and its leaders seemingly confident in spite of nearly universal hostility to their racial policy.

Vorster and his government began to give full recognition to the fact that the Republic was an African state, that nearly all the African states were black, and that South Africa had to make some kind of accommodation with them. They also felt that economically and militarily South Africa is the strongest state in Africa and this gives it the opportunity and responsibility to exercise leadership on the continent, at least south of the Sahara. In a rather exuberant speech to his constituents Vorster outlined his policy toward the continent. "We are of Africa," he

[43] See Chapter 10.

declared, "we understand Africa . . . and nothing is going to prevent us from becoming the leaders of Africa in every field." Development had to come to Africa, and it would be led by South Africa. The black states would accept South Africa's leadership for the simple reason "that we are prepared to play our part to develop Africa because like them, we are part of Africa." Vorster admitted that South Africa was motivated in part by self-interest. Its own prosperity was to a certain extent tied to the prosperity of the rest of the continent. But South Africa had a much bigger interest in Africa, said Vorster, and that was the possibility that the Communists would take advantage of the British withdrawal east of Suez to extend their influence from the east to the west coasts. "That is why I found it necessary to establish diplomatic relations with Malawi," he concluded.[44]

An important motive in adopting the outward-looking policy is undoubtedly the fear of Communist infiltration in African countries south of the Sahara. Government spokesmen frequently mention this in justifying the policy to their fellow countrymen. For national security it is necessary to build an anti-Communist bloc in southern Africa, and beyond if possible, they explained. Pretoria seeks to construct an anti-Communist cordon across the continent from Angola through Botswana, Rhodesia, and Malawi to Mozambique. The state president's address to Parliament at its opening in January 1967 declared that the danger of Communist infiltration into the continent of Africa could not be overestimated. By its struggle against the penetration of Communism in southern Africa it also hopes to win Western acceptance and support. The 1967 state president's address comes near pleading for this support. "As a Western nation with our roots firmly in the West," he said, "we have always ranged ourselves on the side of the Free World in their struggle to counter the spread of Communism not only in Africa, but also elsewhere. It is to be hoped that there will be increasing realization of the extremely important role which a strong and resolute South Africa can play in this regard on the continent of Africa."[45]

Frequently this policy is put in terms of creating a southern African coprosperity sphere, with South Africa as its core and generator. The

[44] *The Star*, Weekly Air Edition, 9 Nov. 1968. H. Muller, the foreign minister, stated that South Africa's ability to live in peace with its neighbors in Africa and to fulfill its role as the leading economic state of the African continent would be of conclusive importance for the country's future. (ibid., 29 June 1968).

[45] *Hansard*, vol. 19, cols. 2–3.

chief instruments for building the coprosperity sphere would be economic aid, trade agreements, a common market, joint hydroelectric and irrigation projects, and military understandings. Already South Africa, Botswana, Lesotho, and Swaziland are partners in a customs union. South Africa and Lesotho have agreed in principle to construct a massive hydroelectric project in the Lesotho highlands. The project would provide the Rand with 100 million gallons of water a day and 550 million kilowatt hours of electricity annually. The project would cost over $40 million, which obviously would have to be furnished by South Africa. In September 1969 agreements were signed at Lisbon for the construction of a huge hydroelectric plant at Cabora Bassa on the Zambesi in Mozambique. When completed it will have a capacity almost double that of the Aswan High Dam and will be the fifth largest hydroelectric scheme in the world. The dam will make the 250 miles of the Zambesi to the sea navigable for barges and small vessels and will open up thousands of acres of land for agriculture. South Africa has guaranteed to buy nearly all the scheme's electric power. The project will cost some $500 million. Work has begun on a third scheme on the Kunene River on the border between South West Africa and Angola. Besides producing electric power, the scheme will provide water for irrigation and the consumption needs of the main towns of South West Africa.

Vorster states that the only conditions his government attaches to its offer of friendship and aid are that the recipient accept South Africa just as it is and as part of Africa. By the former he apparently means that they are, by implication at least, to accept apartheid as a South African internal institution. On the other hand, Vorster seems to imply that South Africa will no longer carry apartheid into external relations and is even prepared to relax the rules of petty apartheid in the case of African and non-European visitors to his country, and in international sports. As a solution to the problem of receiving African diplomats, a special residence area in the suburbs of Pretoria has been set aside for diplomats.[46] A Malawian was the first African member of the diplomatic corps at Pretoria. But Vorster makes it plain that his government will not modify its basic racial policy.

Vorster and his government received unexpected help from an influ-

---

[46] Foreign governments and their representatives may well regard this as an application of the Group Areas Act and refuse to accept it.

ential figure in the African world, Robert K. Gardiner, executive secretary of the United Nations Economic Commission for Africa. He
warned African leaders that survival is their problem and that African
states can ill afford to provoke stronger countries. Nearly all African
countries are in a desperate economic situation. The majority of them
are microstates, and all face grave handicaps: a very low per capita
income; high death rates; extremely low levels of school enrollment;
low levels of agricultural production; and little industrial development.
Realism demands that the African states swallow their pride and seek
help wherever they can get it, including South Africa, which is the most
highly developed state on the continent.[47] He suggested that South
Africa resume its place on the United Nations Commission for Africa.[48]
However pleasant statements like those of Dr. Gardiner may be to white
South African ears, they do not constitute the kind of gain that counts
—the cooperation of African states. In the 1969 foreign policy debate in
Parliament, Foreign Minister Muller stated that South Africa was
dealing increasingly with African governments even though it had no
official links with them. "We are in direct contact with more African
Governments than we are now able to, or prepared to disclose," he said.
"There are almost continual discussions in different capitals with Government members and officials." A large number of South African
specialists were being made available for a specific task for a specific
period.[49] However gratifying this may be to the South African government, it is significant that the public and collective attitude of the
African governments remains hostile.

The outward success registered so far for the new policy is not great.
It is limited to the former British Protectorates and Malawi, and in a
sense Rhodesia and the Portuguese territories, but they are white
controlled and complicate the problem. Under the circumstances in
which they find themselves it is not surprising that the small, weak,
economically dependent states of southern Africa should respond to
South African advances. They are in South Africa's sphere of influence
and might as well make the best of it. They would be foolish to reject

[47] Address to African-American Labor Center Congress, Addis Ababa, *The Star,*
Weekly Air Edition, 14 Oct. 1967.

[48] To a press conference at Addis Ababa. Noel Mostert, "Africa: New Nations
and New Alignments," *The Reporter,* 29 June 1967.

[49] *The Star,* Weekly Air Edition, 10 June 1969.

South Africa's offer of badly needed assistance to modernize their economies. To win other African states for friendship and cooperation will not be easy. In pursuing the outward-looking policy, South Africa confronts a number of handicaps and problems. Among these the Rhodesian problem looms large. South African-Rhodesian ties are becoming closer with the continuance of the United Nations-imposed sanctions against Rhodesia. The unilateral declaration by the white minority government of that country enrages all Africans, especially the national leaders. Even Hastings K. Banda, president of Malawi, finds it impossible to say anything good about the Smith regime. Without South Africa's economic support, the rebel government probably would not have lasted very long. South Africa's support of Rhodesia and the development of closer relations with Rhodesia alienate Africans and necessarily constitute an obstacle to Pretoria's advances to other African states.

There are other problems and difficulties. There is a question of the amount of aid South Africa can extend. To maintain the high rate of economic growth it has enjoyed for several years requires considerable capital. The reserves—the future Bantustans—will require great sums, and there are South West Africa, Lesotho, Botswana, and Swaziland which all have claims to priority over more distant countries. Individuals will be cautious about investing funds in African countries in view of the disposition of underdeveloped countries to nationalize business enterprises, especially if they are foreign owned.[50] Nor are the prospects for a rapid development of trade in the would-be coprosperity sphere as bright as it is sometimes pictured, since the various countries produce much the same commodities. The trade most likely to grow rapidly will be that between South Africa—the only industrialized state in the region—and the other states, but this great dependence on South Africa by the smaller, weaker states will scarcely further friendly relations.

The basic problem is the creation of a prosperous economic community of southern African states "within the context of their political differences."[51] Though all except South Africa, Rhodesia, and Swaziland

---

[50] This cautious attitude is not limited to private investors. The South African government hesitated about proceeding with the Lesotho Oxbow hydroelectric scheme on this account (editorial, *The Star*, Weekly Air Edition, 4 Mar. 1967).

[51] Prime Minister Leabua Jonathan of Lesotho. Quoted by *New York Times*, 16 Dec. 1967.

are now desperately poor, most of them are rich in mineral resources and potential hydroelectric power, and thus have considerable possibilities. The nine territories have a combined area of over 2 million square miles and a population of over 36 million. But of this total population only 4 million are white. The ratio of whites to nonwhites is highest in South Africa, where it is one to four, but in Lesotho it is only one to 425. With the whites in control of South Africa, the dominant industrial, financial, and military power of the region, and in Rhodesia and the two Portuguese territories, the economic integration of southern Africa may easily appear to the blacks as a device for white control over the whole region. Given these circumstances, the understanding that politics will be subordinated to economics will be severely tested. Vorster proclaims that South Africa will tolerate no outside interference in its internal affairs or policies, but the leaders of the African states assert just as strongly that they disapprove of apartheid. Even the prime minister of Portugal, Marcello Caetano, coupled the confirmation of the Cabora Bassa hydroelectric scheme with a strong statement that Portugal would not change its multiracial policy.[52] Prime Minister Chief Leabua Jonathan of Lesotho openly asserts that the Basuto abhor apartheid but because of their economic dependence on South Africa they have to retain good relations with South Africa.[53] President Banda of Malawi holds that the war against apartheid can be won only from the inside of South Africa, not from the outside. The only sensible policy open to African leaders, he asserts, is to initiate and maintain a dialogue with South African leaders as Malawi has done. Due to Malawi's policy of good neighborliness and cooperation changes were taking place in South Africa and the administration of Mozambique had become more liberal.[54] Seretse Khama of Botswana used the forum of the United Nations General Assembly to assert his country's independence of South Africa. He declared that his government would not depart from its policy of noninterference in the affairs of neighboring states, but a prosperous nonracial democracy in Botswana could influence the South African government to change its racial policy by presenting a challenge to the credibility of the Bantustan policy. He appealed for aid from other states to reduce Botswana's dependence on neighboring

[52] *The Star*, Weekly Air Edition, 19 April 1969.

[53] Ibid., 7 Oct. 1967.

[54] Ibid., 26 April 1969.

white minority-ruled territories. "We did not win our independence from Britain to lose it to a new form of colonialism," he declared. He appealed to United Nations members to help make sanctions against Rhodesia more effective and he criticized Portugal's refusal to concede that its territories in Africa could ever become independent.[55] This forthright speech by President Khama can hardly be hailed by South Africa as evidence of the progress being made by its outward-looking policy. As a further assertion of freedom from South African control, Botswana in March 1970 established diplomatic relations with the Soviet Union. This announcement caused consternation in Pretoria, as Vorster's government fears Russian influence among its own Africans.

The seizure of power in Lesotho by the prime minister, Chief Jonathan, indicates the dangerous pitfalls which beset South Africa in its relations with neighboring black states. In the election campaign of January 1970, Ntsu Mokhele, the leader of the opposition party, took a strongly anti-South African position. He declared that if his Congress party won the election it would dismiss many of the South Africans in key positions in the administration and judiciary and would look northward to black Africa for support. Before the official report of the election could be made, Chief Jonathan, alleging Communist infiltration, declared a state of emergency, removed the king for meddling in the election, arrested Mokhele, and announced that a new "suitable and workable" constitution was being drafted. This created a delicate situation for South Africa, since Lesotho is completely surrounded by South African territory and so many of the people earn their livelihood there. Situations may arise which will strongly tempt South Africa to intervene, but any move in this direction would draw upon it the heightened enmity of Africa and the world.

Over white-controlled southern Africa hangs the menace of guerrilla terrorism by African nationalists. The guerrilla activities in Angola, Mozambique, and Rhodesia, whose ultimate target is South Africa, will surely tend to draw these states closer together. South Africa has already sent aid to Rhodesia to combat the terrorists—to defend the frontier of white Africa. South Africans fear guerrilla penetration. This fear has been frankly voiced in Parliament: "If anything can ruin what we are achieving and what we are seeking to achieve in Africa," said a member of the House in 1967, "it is that sort of armed subversion

[55] Ibid., 27 Sept. 1969.

which will force not only us but our neighbors as well to divest the resources which are today applied to positive development to the negative means of repression which this kind of subversion brings in its train."[56] He urged the building up of a defensive alliance in southern Africa. Portugal, a poor underdeveloped country, has been fighting the guerrillas since 1960. The war absorbs nearly half of her budget and involves an army of 130,000 men. Portugal undoubtedly needs South African help, but close ties with the racialist neighbor is not going to help win the hearts and minds of her African subjects. Botswana, Lesotho, and Swaziland are preventing political refugees from South Africa from using their territories as a base of operations against their powerful neighbor, but a stepped-up guerrilla warfare between African nationalists and white-controlled territories may put a strain on their policy of neutrality.

Zambia is the chief base from which the terrorist infiltrators operate.[57] President Kaunda of Zambia and President Nyerere of Tanzania are two African leaders bitterly hostile to South Africa. Prime Minister Vorster has warned Kaunda that if he ever tried "to use violence against South Africa we will hit him so hard that he will never forget it."[58] P. W. Botha, minister of defense, made the threat broader. He declared that countries which aided and incited terrorism and guerrilla warfare against South Africa could provoke South Africa into hitting back hard.[59] The situation creates the danger of an escalation of hostilities. Portugal has made air raids on border towns in Zambia, and President Kaunda has sought missiles and anti-aircraft missiles from England. Portugal has warned Zambia against aiding nationalist guerrillas in their attacks along the borders of Angola and Mozambique.[60]

With all these handicaps the outward-looking policy is not likely to make rapid progress. So far it has won only Malawi for the coprosperity bloc, but Malawi is a small and very poor country. If South Africa plans

[56] W. M. Sutton, *Hansard*, vol. 20, cols. 4562–63.

[57] They also operate from Tanzania and the Congo. The guerrilla rebels receive support from many sources. Sweden, for example, makes an annual grant of $140,000 to the Mozambique Liberation movement (*New York Times*, 18 Oct. 1969).

[58] Ibid., 27 July 1968.

[59] *The Star*, Weekly Air Edition, 6 April 1968.

[60] *New York Times*, 8 Aug. 1969. The warning was given a few days after the United Nations Security Council had condemned Portugal for "unprovoked raids against Zambia."

to make Malawi its show window in Africa it will have to be prepared to extend it large sums for economic aid.[61] Because of some remarks made by the foreign minister of Malagasy, South Africa hopes that the African island state may join the South African bloc. The foreign minister called for a more realistic attitude toward South Africa and accused the Organization of African Unity of setting one race against the other.[62] The support of Malagasy may give the South African whites some psychological satisfaction but it is difficult to see how the addition of another weak country some distance from the continent can do much to strengthen the coprosperity sphere.

DILEMMA

The world sharply condemns South Africa for its racial policy and ever since World War II has sought through the United Nations to change it.[63] A small state—actually only a few million whites—is not only rejecting the moral judgment of practically the whole world but is also defying the organization through which the peoples of the world express their collective judgment.[64]

The quick, easy answer is for the United Nations to meet this defiance by applying positive military sanctions. The arguments for the application of all-out sanctions in the situation are persuasive. The moral issue is clear. Apartheid has become a byword throughout the world; the system based on it is abhorrent and evil. It involves endless cruelties. In the interest of the whites themselves and the preservation of European civilization in southern Africa, the small ruling class should be brought to its senses by the display and if necessary the use of external force as it cannot and will not change the policy of its own accord. If the policy

[61] South Africa in 1968 made a loan of $15,400,000 for the construction of a railway line to the east border to connect with a Portuguese railway which runs to the port of Nocale in Mozambique, and a loan of $11,200,000 for the construction of a new capital (ibid., 25 May 1968).

[62] *The Star*, Weekly Air Edition, editorial, 5 July 1969.

[63] The issue with respect to South West Africa is colonialism aggravated by racialism, while with respect to apartheid it is racialism which in essence is a form of colonialism. Racialism is the dominant factor in both.

[64] The Organization of African Unity has, of course, been hostile toward South Africa and has practically declared war against it. The Organization operates through a Liberation Committee with headquarters in Dar es Salaam which plans and directs guerrilla activities against Rhodesia, the Portuguese territories, and South Africa.

is not abandoned soon it will end in a destructive internal upheaval or a bitter racial war. Moreover, the prestige of the United Nations is at stake. The League of Nations after feebly dealing with the situation created by Mussolini's aggression against Abyssinia, abdicated and withered. By not going all the way against South Africa the United Nations is courting the same fate. So runs the argument.

The first objection that may be raised against the application of sanctions against South Africa is the doubtful legality of coercive measures by the United Nations. There can be little doubt that South Africa has failed to live up to the obligations laid down in Articles 55 and 56, but the appropriate action for this failure is expulsion under Article 6. The resort to coercive measures is regulated in Chapter VII. Article 39 envisages, and by implication authorizes, such measures only in cases of a threat to the peace, breach of the peace, or act of aggression. The authority to determine the existence of the situation which calls for the application of sanctions is vested in the Security Council. The language of Article 39 would have to be stretched far indeed to bring the situation in South Africa within its terms. Not only South Africa but also France, the United Kingdom, and the United States have unequivocally and repeatedly voiced their doubts about the legality of the application of sanctions against South Africa. Their delegates have also expressed doubt about the wisdom of employing sanctions. Outside interference only hardens the support of all whites for the government and its policies. Contact with South Africa should not be cut off but increased in the hope that influence can be exerted for change in white South African attitudes.

The United Kingdom has other and very practical reasons for opposing sanctions against South Africa. British investment in the Republic comes to about three billion dollars. The annual return of $200 million on this investment constitutes a contribution to Britain's balance of payments which in its economic difficulties Britain cannot afford to lose or see diminished. British trade with South Africa is likewise important for Britain's economy. About 5 percent of the United Kingdom's exports go to South Africa and about 2.5 percent of its imports come from the Republic.[65] The United States' interest is much less but not unimpor-

[65] Conversely, about 26 percent of South Africa's imports come from the United Kingdom and about 30 percent of its exports, excluding gold, go to Britain.

tant. American investments in South Africa total about $700 million or about 1 percent of the total United States foreign investment, while its trade with South Africa constitutes only about 0.5 percent of its foreign trade.[66] Britain and the United States have a security interest in South Africa because of its geographic position at the lower tip of the African continent. With the closing of the Suez Canal and the use of large tankers to transport oil from the Middle East to Europe, which could not go through the Canal even if it were open, has again made the Cape strategically important. This has enhanced the importance of the Simonstown naval base. The control of South Africa by a friendly and stable government is a matter of no small interest to Britain and the West. The long historical connection and ties of kinship also play a role in British attitudes.

In the United Nations great pressure is being exerted for extreme sanctions by members which lack the means of making them effective and are unlikely to experience any hardship from them, while the members which do have the means are unwilling to support such measures. Naturally the latter fear damage to their particular national interests but also they doubt the wisdom of applying military force. The situation after military action might not be better and could well be much worse. If there is any hope of a change in South African racial policies being brought about by the operation of internal forces, even if it takes a long time, this would be far better than to force change from the outside.

The vast majority of whites in South Africa, and not only the Afrikaners, would support the government in resisting external military force. Outside pressure—interference as they call it—has united the whites behind the Nationalist regime. The South African economy is strong and is growing rapidly.[67] South Africa has strengthened its defenses. In 1969 about 17 percent of its budget was going for defense compared with less than 7 percent in 1961. In spite of the arms embargo, South Africa is not having much difficulty in getting military supplies. It is rapidly developing its own armament and munitions

---

[66] The United States investment in the rest of Africa is nearly three times as great and is growing more rapidly (statement by G. Mennen Williams, assistant secretary of state, before Subcommittee on Africa of House Committee on Foreign Affairs, 1 Mar. 1966, Department of State, *Bulletin*, 21 Mar. 1966, pp. 430–40).

[67] The rate of growth is nearly 7 percent annually.

industries and claims that it has reached the point where it can export certain arms and ammunition.[68] It is clear that none of the African states nor any combination of them could mount a military campaign against South Africa which would really threaten it. The result of large-scale Western military action against South Africa would mean destruction, great bitterness, and chaos for a long time. The Western powers who would have to provide the forces to reduce South Africa to compliance are wise in rejecting the insistent call for comprehensive, mandatory sanctions.

If external military power cannot or will not be mustered to bring about an end to apartheid, only the internal forces operating in South African society can engender a change. Economically South Africa is a multiracial country and will have to remain so unless the whites are prepared to return to a largely agrarian society. The rapid industrialization of the country requires more rather than fewer Bantu laborers and also using them in skilled jobs. Better educated Bantus in more skilled jobs will not docilely accept racial discrimination and the denial of basic civil and political rights. Large numbers of white immigrants, who are nearly all skilled, will accelerate expansion of the economy and the necessity for an ever larger labor force, which will have to be black or colored. To reduce immigration or to freeze the black laborers in unskilled jobs will restrict the economy and might bring on a recession. So little progress has been made in setting up Bantustans and making them viable that many persons are wondering whether separate development is anything more than an election slogan. Few whites are willing to bear the costs which a serious effort to implement the policy would entail, nor do they really want to see the country fragmented.

If all this were not enough there is the insurmountable problem of how to fit the coloreds and the Indians into the scheme. This problem alone could be fatal to the success of the policy. There is no logical or acceptable place for these two groups in the scheme. If they are assimilated the logic of the system is destroyed; if left out they will form centers of such grave discontent as to make it unworkable and endanger internal security. There seems to be no way of removing this huge rock in the road; on it the policy in time will break.

Looking outward the situation is also bleak. Every possible road

[68] Statement by Minister of Defense P. W. Botha, *The Star*, Weekly Air Edition, 10 May 1969.

seems to run into a dead end. Though the United Nations is the chief instrument of attack on apartheid, South Africa cannot afford to withdraw from it. In its forum South Africa must listen to constant bitter attacks on its racial policy. As a member South Africa contributes to the support of an institution which operates as a propaganda machine against its basic domestic policy and practices. For protection against actual and prospective assaults from the north and the infiltration of black nationalists and Communists, South Africa is attempting to form a southern Africa bloc, chiefly in cooperation with Portugal whose ideology is completely different. Portugal will have nothing of territorial separation or racial discrimination. Angola and Mozambique are constitutionally integral parts of a multiracial or, probably better, nonracial state. Indeed, Portugal's policy radically challenges the basic ideas for which South Africa is prepared to battle to the death. Close association with Portugal will jar South African whites and tend to undermine their ideological certainties. Even Rhodesian policy is quite different from that of South Africa, though it is moving in that direction.

There have been many tragedies in the history of Afrikanerdom and South Africa; they may be experiencing their greatest tragedy in the present situation. White South Africans regard themselves and their country as part of the West, and they are passionately on the side of the West in opposing Communism. But because of their racial ideology the West finds South Africa an embarrassment and treats her distantly— even England and Holland, which historically and culturally have the closest ties with them. This near-rejection is a very painful experience.

South Africa believes that Communism threatens not only Africa, but now also the Indian Ocean because of the withdrawal of British forces from the region. Pretoria seems to have approached the countries of the region about defense understandings, but apparently has been cooly received or even rebuffed. So long as South Africa clings to its present racial policy these countries are not likely to enter into any kind of defense agreements with it as these countries have spearheaded the attack against apartheid. South Africa is learning that national security and apartheid are incompatible. It will have to choose one or the other. South Africans overrate the importance of sub-Sahara Africa, and especially South Africa, for the West. They assume that their country's strategic position is so important to the West that it will overlook South

Africa's racial policy and seek the Republic's cooperation. The great Western powers may conclude exactly the reverse—that South Africa with its 2,000 miles of coastline on an important sea lane is so vulnerable that it must have the protection of the Western naval powers and that as soon as the Cape and its hinterland are actually threatened Pretoria will ask the West for aid. In that event the West would be faced with a dilemma. How much would support of South Africa cost it in its relations with the rest of Africa and Asia and the world? Could South Africa then resist the pressure to jettison apartheid?

Confronted with all these difficulties, dead-end roads, and a strong world opinion condemnatory of apartheid, South African whites must begin to doubt the wisdom of their racial policy and come to accept the idea of its modification.

In the parliamentary election held on April 22, 1970, the National party for the first time since it came to power in 1948 suffered a reversal. Its percentage of the total vote declined 5.53 percent from the peak of 1966, while that of the United party increased by 1.01 percent, and that of the Progressives rose from 2.74 to 3.43 percent. The National party lost nine seats while the United party gained eight and the Progressives retained their one seat and nearly won another. Prime Minister Vorster succeeded in destroying the extremist right-wing Reconstituted National party of Albert Hertzog, but he failed to attract English-speaking voters. In spite of its losses the National party is still in a position of overwhelming strength in Parliament, with 117 seats in the House to 47 for the United party. The results of the election do indicate a shift among Afrikaners toward middle-class attitudes and a more liberal approach to the racial question.

Prime Minister Vorster made only minor changes in his cabinet after the election, and there were no indications of a significant change in domestic policy. In pursuit of his outward-looking policy the prime minister made visits to Malawi, Rhodesia, and Portugal.

The victory of the Conservatives in the British parliamentary election in June 1970 raised hopes in South Africa for improvement in relations with Britain, more specifically, that the Edward Heath government would relax, if not withdraw, support for the United Nations embargo on arms to South Africa and would put life into the Simonstown naval base agreement. Because of British and West

European dependence on the transportation of oil from the Middle East in large tankers by way of the Cape and because of the alleged presence of Russian naval vessels in the Indian Ocean, the Vorster government seems to be convinced that the Cape has again become a matter of the highest strategic importance to the West. In the words of the Simonstown agreement, Britain and South Africa need each other "to ensure the safety, by the joint operations of their respective maritime forces, of the sea routes round southern Africa."

Bibliographical Note

Since the Union of South Africa only gradually moved toward an active and independent external policy, government publications in the field of foreign policy are scarce, especially in the early years. The best source is the parliamentary debates. The official reports of the proceedings of Parliament carry the titles *Debates of the House of Assembly (Hansard)* and *The Senate of South Africa, Debates* until May 31, 1961, after which date the latter became *The Senate of the Republic of South Africa, Debates*. These debates are printed by the Government Printer, Cape Town. No debates were published from 1916 to 1923 inclusive. The library of the South African Railways at Johannesburg has for these years practically verbatim reports of the proceedings of the two bodies, clipped from the Cape Town newspapers and assembled in book form for more convenient use.

A second source for the study of South African foreign relations is the official proceedings of the organs of the League of Nations and of the United Nations. Since World War II the South African government has put out white books on the work of its delegation in the General Assembly, but they contain little more than the relevant sections of the official proceedings of that body. A number of speeches by Foreign Minister Eric H. Louw before the General Assembly setting forth the position of South Africa were published in 1963 under the title *The Case for South Africa*, edited by H. H. H. Biermann (New York, 1963). Because of the long close relations of South Africa with Britain, British parliamentary debates and papers constitute an important source for certain periods and subjects.

GENERAL WORKS

For the historical background, *A History of Southern Africa* by Eric A. Walker, 3d edition (London, 1962), is indispensable. For a more interpretive history see *The Imperial Factor in South Africa* (Cambridge, Eng., 1937) and *A History of South Africa, Social and Economic* (London, 1941), both by Cornelis de Kiewit. A good brief history of the Union from its formation to 1948 is *The Age of the Generals* (Johannesburg, 1961) by D. W. Kruger. Other good brief surveys are *South Africa* by A. Keppel-Jones, 4th edition (London, 1963) and *The Making of South Africa* by M. S. Green (Cape Town, 1958). Several books on the domestic politics of South Africa have been published in recent years, the most comprehensive of which is *The Politics of Inequality* by Gwendolen M. Carter, rev. edition (New York, 1959). Briefer accounts are: *South Africa: A Political and Economic History* by Alex Hepple (London, 1966), and *Politics in the Republic of South Africa* by Leonard M. Thompson (Boston, 1966). See *From Union to Apartheid* by Margaret Ballinger (Cape Town, 1969) and *South Africa: The Struggle for a Birthright* by Margaret Ballinger (New York, 1969), for treatment of the political struggle from a point of view distinctly sympathetic with the Africans. Margaret Ballinger represented the Africans in Parliament from 1937 to 1960. There is a massive literature on South Africa's racial problems and policy. For an extensive bibliography of this literature see *White Laager* (Fortress) by William Henry Vatcher, Jr. (New York, 1965), pp. 193–241.

Few books on South Africa's external relations have yet appeared. Gert D. Scholtz, for many years assistant editor and editor of *Die Transvaler*, is the author of a suggestive but sketchy survey, *Suid-Afrika en die Wereld-politiek, 1652–1952* [South Africa and World Politics] (Johannesburg, 1954). In the preface he states that his purpose was to show that the history of South Africa cannot be isolated from great world events, that only in relation to them can South Africa's history be understood properly. In *Die Republiek van Suid-Afrika en die Nuwe Wereld* [The Republic of South Africa and the New World] (Johannesburg, 1962) he deals more specifically with the period after World War II. Scholtz writes from an Afrikaner, Nationalist point of view. Two brief books on South African foreign policy have appeared in England. *South Africa and World Opinion* by Peter Calvocoressi (London, 1961) deals with the situation as it was in 1960. *Republic under Pressure: A Study of South African Foreign Policy* by J. E. Spence (London, 1965) deals only with the current situation. In *South Africa 1906–1961: The Price of Magnanimity* Nicholas Mansergh reproachfully reconsiders "in the context of imperial and Commonwealth history the beginnings of the Union in the light of its ending."

In view of Smuts's long years of domination of his country's external policy, the monumental biography by Sir Keith Hancock, *Smuts*, Volume I, *The Sanguine Years, 1870–1919*, and Volume II, *The Fields of Force, 1919–1950* (Cambridge, Eng., 1962, 1968), is of basic importance for the student of South African foreign politics. Sir Keith had access to the very extensive Smuts papers. Scholars in the field of South African politics are indebted to Hancock and Jean van der Poel for editing the four volumes of *Selections from the Smuts Papers* (Cambridge, Eng., 1966) but these volumes contain documents only of the years up to 1919. Presumably the selections from the papers of the last thirty years of Smuts's life will soon be published. A critical, full-length biography of Hertzog has not yet been published. *Generaal J. B. M. Hertzog* by C. M. van den Heever (Afrikaans edition, Johannesburg, 1943, abridged English edition, 1946) is highly partisan. *James Barry Munnik Hertzog* by Oswald Pirow (London, 1958), a member of Hertzog's cabinet from 1929 to 1939, suffers from the same defect and in addition is bitterly anti-Smuts.

Very helpful to any student of South African affairs is the annual, *A Survey of Race Relations in South Africa*, put out by the South African Institute of Race Relations at Johannesburg. Each issue carries a section on foreign relations.

For the geographic background of southern Africa as it relates to political problems of the region, *A Geography of Subsaharan Africa* by Harm J. de Blij (Chicago, 1964) is recommended.

Insights into the forces which operate in the daily, practical politics of South Africa are to be found in the writings of Edwin S. Munger, who represented the American Universities Field Staff in southern Africa in the decade of the 1950s. His reports were published as *Letters and Reports from Africa* (New York). His *Notes on the Formation of South African Foreign Policy* (Pasadena, Calif., 1965) and *Afrikaner and African Nationalism* (London, 1967) present the observations and reflections of a scholar who knows the inner workings of white South

African politics. They contain shrewd observations. Professor Munger is concerned about being fair to South Africa to the point of giving the reader the impression of being uncritical.

SPECIALIZED WORKS

For a comprehensive introduction to South African questions before the United Nations, *Apartheid in the Republic of South Africa,* ed. A. G. Mezerik (International Review Service, Vol. 12, No. 92, New York, 1967), is helpful. The problem of applying United Nations sanctions against South Africa has received considerable attention. The following publications on this subject may be noted: *Apartheid and United Nations Collective Measures: An Analysis,* ed. Amelia C. Leiss, prepared under the auspices of The Carnegie Endowment for International Peace (New York, 1965); *South Africa: Crisis for the West* by Colin and Margaret Legum (London, 1964), and *Sanctions against South Africa,* ed. Ronald Segal (Penguin Special, Middlesex, Eng., 1964). The Legum book gives an excellent analysis of the South African racial and political background.

Much has been written on South West Africa in recent years. A very good general book is *South West Africa and Its Human Problems* by John H. Wellington (Oxford, 1967). The author is a geographer, but his work also gives a history of the mandate and examines the current situation. For a good examination of the current problem see *South West Africa and the United Nations* by Faye Carroll (Lexington, Ky., 1967). Other significant books on South West Africa are: *South West Africa* by Ruth First (Penguin, Middlesex, Eng., 1962); *Brutal Mandate: A Journey to South West Africa* by Allard K. Lowenstein (New York, 1962); *South West Africa: Travesty of Trust,* ed. Ronald Segal and Ruth First (London, 1967); *South West Africa: The Last Pioneer Country* by Thomas Molnar (New York, 1966). The last named is sympathetic with the policy of South Africa in the mandate.

In view of South Africa's outward-looking policy, relations between the Republic and the former High Commission Territories are important. An excellent book for the background of the present situation is *The Republic of South Africa and the High Commission Territories* by Lord Hailey (London, 1963). Other recent books on these new states are: *South Africa's Hostages* by Jack Halpern (Penguin, Middlesex,

Eng., 1965); *Bechuanaland: Pan African Outpost or Bantu Homeland* by Edwin S. Munger (London, 1965); *Lesotho: The Politics of Dependence* by J. E. Spence (London, 1968); and *Southern Africa in Transition,* ed. John A. Adams and James K. Baker (New York, 1966). The last book deals with all the political entities in the region.

Of utmost importance for South Africa are its relations with Britain and the United States. Relations between the first two are thoughtfully examined by Dennis Austin in *Britain and South Africa* (London, 1966). Four specialists on Africa—William A. Hance (editor), Leo Kuper, Vernon McKay, and Edwin S. Munger—examine United States relations with South Africa in *Southern Africa and the United States* (New York, 1968).

Index

Abyssinia, 155, 166; and League sanctions against Italy, 92–94. *See also* Ethiopia

African Charter, 148, 157, 160, 162, 164, 180

African Doctrine, 67

African National Congress, 260

Africans: and service in armed forces, 108, 108 n, 109–10. *See also* Bantu

Afrikaner, 61, 114

Amery, Leopold, S.: and Balfour Declaration, 76

Anglo-Boer War: First, 7; Second, 7, 58

Angola, 149, 257, 274, 275, 279, 285. *See also* Portugal

apartheid: policy of, 24–28, 228–32; term first applied to policy of segregation, 128; and 1948 election, 130; and United Nations, 231–54. *See also* Bantustans; native policy; racial policy; segregation; territorial separation

Ayub Khan, 184

Balfour Declaration, 74–81, 90

Ballinger, Mrs. Margaret, 161; on incorporation of Protectorates, 139; on native policy and relations with African countries, 157

Bantu: migration of, 56; and franchise, 60; and war in Abyssinia, 92–93. *See also* Africans; apartheid; Bantustans; native policy; racial policy; segregation; territorial separation

Bantustans, 255, 269, 272; Verwoerd inaugurates policy of, 26–28; and incorporation of Protectorates, 140–42

Basutoland, 59, 156. *See also* Lesotho

Bechuana, 58. *See also* Botswana

Bevin, Ernest, 138

Birkenhead, Lord: and Balfour Declaration, 76

"Black Manifesto," 65

"Black Peril" election, 67

Boer: term applied to descendants of early settlers, 4; complaints against British rule, 5–6

border territories, 56–69; race policy and, 57, 61, 66, 67, 68. *See also* Angola; Mozambique; Protectorates; Rhodesia; Southern Rhodesia; South West Africa; Swaziland

Botha, Louis: and movement for formation of Union, 8–9; politics of conciliation, 19–21; and campaign against Germans in South West Africa, 31–34; and World War I, 32, 35; and Paris Peace Conference, 41–42; on Protectorates and Southern Rhodesia, 59–62; on future of German East Africa, 65

Botswana, 58, 58 n, 274, 275, 276; area, population, social and economic